1001
FINANCIAL
WORDS
You Need to Know

1001 FINANCIAL WORDS

You Need to Know

DAVID BACH
Editor

ERIN McKEAN
Series Editor

OXFORD
UNIVERSITY PRESS
2003

Oxford   New York

Auckland   Bangkok   Buenos Aires   Cape Town   Chennai
Dar es Salaam   Delhi   Hong Kong   Istanbul   Karachi   Kolkata
Kuala Lumpur   Madrid   Melbourne   Mexico City   Mumbai   Nairobi
São Paulo   Shanghai   Singapore   Taipei   Tokyo   Toronto
and an associated company in Berlin

Published by Oxford University Press, Inc.
198 Madison Avenue, New York, New York 10016
www.oup.com

Oxford is a registered trademark of Oxford University Press

Library of Congress Cataloging-in-Publication Data

1001 financial words you need to know / David Bach, editor.
   p. cm.
   ISBN 0-19-517050-4 (hardcover : alk. paper)
   1. Finance--Dictionaries. 2. Finance, Personal--Dictionaries. I.
Title: One thousand and one financial words you need to know. II.
Title:
One thousand one financial words you need to know. III. Bach, David.
   HG151 .A15 2003
   332'.03--dc22

                                                  2003016993

                    3   5   7   9   8   6   4   2

                 Printed in the United States of America
                         on acid-free paper

EDITORIAL STAFF

Erin McKean, *Series Editor*
Constance Baboukis, *Managing Editor*
Bruce McDougall, *Sidebars Editor*
Christine Lindberg, Carol Braham, Deborah Posner, *Editors*
Marina Padakis, *Proofreader*
Ryan Sullivan, *Editorial Assistant*

CONTENTS

PREFACE

This book, *1001 Financial Words You Need to Know*, is part of a new Oxford University Press series of concise, helpful guides to the vocabularies of significant fields. We have distilled and enhanced general dictionary entries (taken from our groundbreaking *New Oxford American Dictionary*) to make useful, browsable books that present the most important words needed to understand a particular topic, selected and updated by recognized experts. By stripping away the words you don't immediately need, we bring these complicated topics into sharper focus.

In addition to these essential 1001 words, we've included explanatory essays about important (and often confusing) related concepts and a list of essential resources for further reading, making this work more than just a dictionary—it is a truly practical all-around guide and reference book.

Erin McKean
Senior Editor, U.S. Dictionaries,
Oxford University Press

INTRODUCTION

When it comes to money, knowing the right words can make you rich!

I'll never forget the first time I realized that I knew the words that could make me rich. I was twelve years old and enjoying dinner at my best friend Kevin's house. His father, a brain surgeon, and his mother, a respected interior designer, were discussing the investment they had just made in some CDs at the bank.

Dr. Martin was complaining to his wife about how low the CD interest rates were. He'd just bought one that paid 6 percent and he was not happy. Mrs. Martin started grilling Dr. Martin about how he had shopped for the CDs. Had he made sure he was getting a good deal by shopping around by going to more than one bank to ask about rates? After a lot of hemming and hawing, Dr. Martin admitted that he hadn't. He'd simply taken what the bank had offered him. A serious argument was about to start at the dinner table, and it wasn't going to be pretty.

Without thinking, I jumped into the situation. "You know, Dr. and Mrs. Martin," I blurted out, "you're arguing about the wrong issue. The question isn't what kind of rate you can get on a CD right now. It's why you would buy a CD at 6 percent when you could get a much better deal investing in triple-A rated municipal bonds."

Kevin and his parents gawked at me as if I had suddenly started speaking a foreign language. I kept on talking. "I happen to know for a fact that, right now, you can buy triple-A tax-free California munis at 5 percent. In your high tax bracket, earning 5 percent tax-free is the same as earning about 9 percent taxable. Hands down, you'd come out way ahead with tax-free munis over CDs."

You could have heard a pin drop....

The room went silent. You could have heard a pin drop. Dr. Martin stared at me with an expression that seemed to ask, "Who is this strange kid?"

Finally, Mrs. Martin broke the silence. "I'm sorry, David," she said, "what did you just say?"

I started over again—this time explaining the issue in layman's terms. "It's really pretty simple, Mrs. Martin. When you buy a tax-free bond, you don't have to pay taxes on the interest you earn. Not paying taxes is a good thing. It means you get more money *for* your money. You get rich faster."

Mrs. Martin looked back at Dr. Martin with a look that asked another question—namely, "Why does a twelve-year-old know more about investments than you do?"

Not very willing to concede this was the case, Dr. Martin went into attack mode. "Your muni bonds may sound good," he said, "but we don't want to take any risks. Bank CDs are safe. They are guaranteed!" He sat back in his chair, radiating confidence.

"Well," I said, "that's certainly a good point, but when you invest in a triple-A muni, you're getting insurance. That's why the bond is rated triple-A. It means the bond has been insured. The municipality that's issued it is guaranteeing that you're going to get your money back. There's virtually no risk."

Mr. Martin had heard enough. "Why don't you and Kevin excuse yourselves and go play?" he suggested through gritted teeth. Our discussion had ended.

The fastest way to become wealthy is to learn the language.

I really wasn't trying to be a twelve-year-old know-it-all. It's just that I knew the language of money, and the Martins didn't. I had learned the language early because my father was a financial advisor who taught a personal-finance class every week at a local college. Every few weeks, my sister and I would get dragged to the class with him so my mother could have an evening to herself.

What I realized that night at dinner with the Martins was that, because I had learned the language of money, I actually knew more about personal finance and investing than a brain surgeon did. Because I knew the language, I was on my way. Now you can learn it, too, and you can do it in just a few hours.

How this dictionary can help you:
From the first moment Oxford approached me to work on this dictionary, I was in love with the concept. Over the years, as a financial advisor, teacher, and author, I've seen firsthand that most people think they need some sort of special break to succeed in investing—a stock tip or an insider opportunity. It's not true. What you need is to know the words that are used to explain money. Money has its own language, and the sooner you learn the basic vocabulary, the better your chance to live and finish rich. So what better idea than to create a dictionary that would draw from the ***New Oxford American Dictionary,*** but focus on words and issues related to money?

If you've read any of my other books on money (*Smart Women Finish Rich, Smart Couples Finish Rich, The Finish Rich Workbook,* and *The Automatic Millionaire*), you know that I go out of my way to make learning about money easy to do, easy to understand, and easy to act upon. But despite all this, many readers still get confused by many of the new terms they are forced to learn.

What they need is a user-friendly dictionary that can help them learn the terminology of money. That's what this book is.

Don't be afraid to admit that you don't know what something means.
Most people don't like to admit it when they don't understand something. This is especially true when it comes to money. So what happens when, in order to look smart, you pretend to

understand something about money when you really don't? The answer, more often than not, is that you end up broke. Here's an example of what I mean.

You can't buy an IRA.

Is there a term more basic in today's financial vocabulary than "IRA"? The definition (on page 100) notes that IRA stands for Individual Retirement Account. It goes on to explain (on p. 95, under "individual retirement account") that this retirement account is a holding tank for funds that are meant to be invested for the long term, to be used for retirement sometime after you reach the age of 59-1/2 (the age at which the government lets you start withdrawing money from your IRA without incurring a penalty).

Now, you may already understand what IRA means, but after listening to thousands of participants each year at my Finish Rich Seminars, I've learned that many people don't. Many people think that you "buy an IRA." They think their IRA is an investment like a CD, not an account in which investments are held. They think they went to a bank and bought something that pays a certain rate of return.

The fact is, they didn't. What happened is they went to the bank and opened an IRA account. They then took the funds they used to open the account and invested them in some sort of interest-bearing financial instrument (most likely a certificate of deposit, or CD).

This may strike you as, well, dumb. How can people put their money in an IRA and not know how it works or what they actually own? It's simple, actually. No one taught them the language of money. It is probable that no one taught you, either.

I once explained this at a seminar I was giving. A participant named Glenda became furious. She said, "David Bach, you don't know what you are talking about. I've been buying IRAs at the local bank for ten years!"

As gently as I could, I explained to Glenda that what she

was saying simply wasn't possible. You can't "buy an IRA." But Glenda continued to insist that I was wrong, so I invited her to come to my office, where we could call the bank together to find out what she owned.

"Fine," Glenda said, "but I'm telling you I know you're wrong."

Needless to say, when Glenda and I called the bank, we learned that I wasn't wrong. What Glenda had done was open a new IRA account every year for the previous ten years. Because she hadn't specified otherwise, the bank put the money she used to open the accounts into the lowest yielding investment available—savings certificates earning just 2 percent a year. Glenda didn't know the language of money, and as a result she paid the price—literally.

When you know the words, you can ask better questions. This little dictionary is not just a resource for words. It's also a simple guide to personal finance. In other words, not only will it come in handy whenever you want to know the meaning of a particular money-related word, but it is also a great book to flip through. Read a page a day. Read the special sections we've created to explain common terms or answer basic questions about money. If you do this, in just a few months, you'll know the language of money—and you'll be unstoppable.

Knowing the terms creates confidence. When you're at home, channel surfing in front of the television, and you flip past one of those financial news shows, you'll understand what they are talking about. A business newspaper like *The Wall Street Journal* will stop being a mystery and become your friend. Most important, you'll find yourself wanting to listen and learn more about money because, now, you "get it."

Learning about money is fun once you realize that the only thing that made it complicated was a few words you didn't know but now understand completely.

And, who knows—maybe, in a few weeks, you'll be out with friends, and the subject of money will come up, and you'll find yourself sharing what you've learned to help them be smarter with their money. You'll be the one who makes the room go silent with your newfound knowledge.

As you continue on your journey through life, remember—it's the language of money that puts you on the road to living and finishing rich! And you are never too old—or too young—to learn it. Enjoy.

David L. Bach
New York
May, 2003

USING THIS DICTIONARY

The "entry map" below explains the different parts of an entry.

Syllabification

Pronunciation set off with slashes / /

cred•it /ˈkredit/ (abbr.: **cr**) ▸**n. 1** the ability of a customer to obtain goods or services before payment, based on the trust that payment will be made in the future: *I've got unlimited credit.*

■ the money lent or made available under such an arrangement: *the bank refused to extend their credit.* ──────── Examples in *italic*

2 an entry recording a sum received, listed on the right-hand side or column of an account. The opposite of DEBIT. ╲ Cross references in BOLD SMALL CAPITALS

Subsenses signalled by ■

■ a payment received: *you need to record debits or credits made to your account.* Grammar information in square brackets [ ]

▸**v.** (**cred•it•ed**, **cred•it•ing**) [trans.] (often **be credited**) add (an amount of money) to an account: *this deferred tax can be credited to the profit and loss account.*

Phrases section, phrases in **bold face**

PHRASES **on credit** with an arrangement to pay later.

Derivative section, derivatives in **bold face**

DERIVATIVES **cred•it•less** adj.

Etymology section

ORIGIN mid 16th cent. (originally in the senses 'belief,' 'credibility'): from French *crédit*, probably via Italian *credito* from Latin *creditum*, neuter past participle of *credere* 'believe, trust.'

| xv |

cred•it score /'kredit ,skôr/ ▶ **n.** a number assigned to a person that indicates to lenders their capacity to repay a loan.

USAGE: A **credit score** is based on factors such as a person's record for making timely payments, total debt, and credit history. It influences the person's ability to obtain a loan and the cost of the loan. This score is often called a **FICO score,** because most companies calculate the number using software from Fair Isaac Corporation. See note at **FICO** SCORE.

Usage notes provide extra information to help you understand the use or importance of the term.

Main entries and other boldface forms

Main entries appear in boldface type, as do inflected forms, idioms and phrases, and derivatives. The words PHRASES and DERIVATIVES introduce those elements. Main entries and derivatives of two or more syllables show syllabification with centered dots.

Parts of speech

Each new part of speech is introduced by a small right-facing arrow.

Senses and subsenses

The main sense of each word follows the part of speech and any grammatical information (e.g., [trans.] before a verb definition). If there are two or more main senses for a word, these are numbered in boldface. Closely related subsenses of each main sense are introduced by a solid black box. In the entry for **credit** above, the main sense of "the ability of a customer to obtain goods or services before payment, based on the trust that payment will be made in the future" is followed by a related sense, "the money lent or made available under such an arrangement."

Example sentences

Example sentences are shown in italic typeface; certain common expressions appear in bold italic typeface within examples, as in the entry for credit above: *this deferred tax can be credited to the profit and loss account.*

Cross references

Cross references to main entries appear in small capitals. For example, in the entry **credit** seen previously, a cross reference is given in bold small capitals to the entry for DEBIT.

PRONUNCIATION KEY

This dictionary uses a simple respelling system to show how entries are pronounced, using the following symbols:

æ	*as in* **hat** /hæt/, **fashion** /ˈfæsHən/, **carry** /ˈkærē/
ā	*as in* **day** /dā/, **rate** /rāt/, **maid** /mād/, **prey** /prā/
ä	*as in* **lot** /lät/, **father** /ˈfäTHər/, **barnyard** /ˈbärn,yärd/
b	*as in* **big** /big/
CH	*as in* **church** /CHərCH/, **picture** /ˈpikCHər/
d	*as in* **dog** /dôg/, **bed** /bed/
e	*as in* **men** /men/, **bet** /bet/, **ferry** /ˈferē/
ē	*as in* **feet** /fēt/, **receive** /riˈsēv/
er	*as in* **air** /er/, **care** /ker/
ə	*as in* **about** /əˈbowt/, **soda** /ˈsōdə/, **mother** /ˈməTHər/, **person** /ˈpərsən/
f	*as in* **free** /frē/, **graph** /græf/, **tough** /təf/
g	*as in* **get** /get/, **exist** /igˈzist/, **egg** /eg/
h	*as in* **her** /hər/, **behave** /biˈhāv/
i	*as in* **guild** /gild/, **women** /ˈwimin/
ī	*as in* **time** /tīm/, **fight** /fīt/, **guide** /gīd/, **hire** /hīr/
ir	*as in* **ear** /ir/, **beer** /bir/, **pierce** /pirs/
j	*as in* **judge** /jəj/, **carriage** /ˈkærij/
k	*as in* **kettle** /ˈketl/, **cut** /kət/
l	*as in* **lap** /læp/, **cellar** /ˈselər/, **cradle** /ˈkrādl/
m	*as in* **main** /mān/, **dam** /dæm/
n	*as in* **honor** /ˈänər/, **maiden** /ˈmādn/
NG	*as in* **sing** /siNG/, **anger** /ˈæNGgər/
ō	*as in* **go** /gō/, **promote** /prəˈmōt/
ô	*as in* **law** /lô/, **thought** /THôt/, **lore** / lôr/
oi	*as in* **boy** /boi/, **noisy** /ˈnoizē/
o͝o	*as in* **wood** /wo͝od/, **football** /ˈfo͝ot,bôl/, **sure** /SHo͝or/
o͞o	*as in* **food** /fo͞od/, **music** /ˈmyo͞ozik/
ow	*as in* **mouse** /mows/, **coward** /ˈkowərd/

| *xvii* |

p	*as in*	**put** /pŏŏt/, **cap** /kæp/
r	*as in*	**run** /rən/, **fur** /fər/, **spirit** /'spirit/
s	*as in*	**sit** /sit/, **lesson** /'lesən/
SH	*as in*	**shut** /SHət/, **social** /'sōSHəl/, **action** /'ækSHən/
t	*as in*	**top** /täp/, **seat** /sēt/
t̲	*as in*	**butter** /'bət̲ər/, **forty** /'fôrt̲ē/, **bottle** /'bät̲l̲/
TH	*as in*	**thin** /THin/, **truth** /trōoTH/
T̲H̲	*as in*	**then** /T̲H̲en/, **father** /'fäT̲H̲ər/
v	*as in*	**never** /'nevər/, **very** /'verē/
w	*as in*	**wait** /wāt/, **quick** /kwik/
(h)w	*as in*	**when** /(h)wen/, **which** /(h)wiCH/
y	*as in*	**yet** /yet/, **accuse** /ə'kyōoz/
z	*as in*	**zipper** /'zipər/, **musician** /myōo'ziSHən/
ZH	*as in*	**measure** /'meZHər/, **vision** /'viZHən/

Foreign Sounds

KH	*as in*	**Bach** /bäKH/
N	*as in*	**en route** /äN 'rōot/, **Rodin** /rō'dæN/
œ	*as in*	**hors d'oeuvre** /ôr 'dœvrə/, **Goethe** /'gœtə/
Y	*as in*	**Lully** /lY'lē/, **Utrecht** /'Y‚treKHt/

Stress marks

Stress marks are placed before the affected syllable. The primary stress mark is a short vertical line above the letters ['] and signifies greater pronunciation emphasis should be placed on that syllable. The secondary stress mark is a short vertical line below the letters [‚] and signifies a weaker pronunciation emphasis.

A

ABM ▶ **abbr.** Canadian automated banking machine.

ac•cept /æk'sept/ ▶ v. [trans.] agree to meet (a draft or bill of exchange) by signing it.

ORIGIN late Middle English: from Latin *acceptare*, frequentative of *accipere* 'take something to oneself,' from *ad-* 'to' + *capere* 'take.'

USAGE: **Accept**, which means 'to take that which is offered,' may be confused with the verb **except**, which means 'to exclude.' Thus: *I* **accept** *the terms of your offer, but I wish to* **except** *the clause calling for repayment of the deposit.*

ac•cept•ance /æk'septəns/ ▶ n. agreement to meet a draft or bill of exchange, effected by signing it.

■ a draft or bill so accepted.

ORIGIN mid 16th cent.: from Old French, from *accepter* (see **AC-CEPT**).

ac•cep•tor /æk'septər/ ▶ n. a person or bank that accepts a draft or bill of exchange.

ac•count /ə'kownt/ (abbr.: **acct.**) ▶ n. **1** a record or statement of financial expenditure or receipts relating to a particular period or purpose: *the ledger contains all the income and expense accounts | he submitted a quarterly account.*

■ the department of a company that deals with such records.

2 an arrangement by which a body holds funds on behalf of a client or supplies goods or services to the client on credit: *a bank account | charge it to my account | I began buying things* **on account**.

■ the balance of funds held under such an arrangement. *I wanted to get some money from the ATM and check my account.* ■ a client having such an arrangement with a supplier: *selling bibles to estab-lished accounts in the North.* ■ a contract to do work periodically for a client: *another agency was awarded the account.*

ORIGIN Middle English: from Old French *acont* (noun), *aconter* (verb), based on *conter* 'to count.'

ac•count•ant /ə'kownt(ə)nt/ (abbr.: **acct.**) ▸ n. a person whose job is to keep or inspect financial accounts.

ORIGIN Middle English: from legal French, present participle of Old French *aconter* (see ACCOUNT). The original use was as an adjective meaning 'liable to give an account,' hence denoting a person who must do so.

ac•count ex•ec•u•tive /ə'kownt ig,zekyətiv/ ▸ n. a business executive who manages the interests of a particular client, typically in advertising.

ac•count•ing /ə'kowntiNG/ ▸ n. the action or process of keeping financial accounts.

ac•counts pay•a•ble /ə'kownts 'pāəbəl/ ▸ plural n. money owed by a company to its creditors.

ac•counts re•ceiv•a•ble /ə'kownts ri'sēvəbəl/ ▸ plural n. money owed to a company by its debtors.

ac•crue /ə'krōō/ ▸ v. (**ac•crues, ac•crued, ac•cru•ing**) [intrans.] (of sums of money or benefits) be received by someone in regular or increasing amounts over time: *interest on your account will accrue at the rate of 2 percent.*
■ [trans.] accumulate or receive (such payments or benefits).
■ make provision for (a charge) at the end of a financial period for work that has been done but not yet invoiced.

DERIVATIVES **ac•cru•al n.**

ORIGIN late Middle English: from Old French *acreue*, past participle of *acreistre* 'increase,' from Latin *accrescere* 'become larger.'

acct. ▸ abbr. ■ accounting. ■ accountant.

ac•cu•mu•la•tion /ə,kyōōmyə'lāSHən/ ▸ n. the growth of a sum of money by the regular addition of interest.

ac•quire /ə'kwīr/ ▸ v. [trans.] buy or obtain (an asset or object) for oneself.

ORIGIN late Middle English *acquere*, from Old French *aquerre,* based on Latin *acquirere* 'get in addition,' from *ad-* 'to' + *quaerere* 'seek.' The English spelling was modified (*c.*1600) by association with the Latin word.

ac•qui•si•tion /ˌækwə'zɪsHən/ ▸ n. an act of purchase of one company by another: *expanding by growth or acquisition.*
■ buying or obtaining an asset or object.
ORIGIN late Middle English (in the sense 'act of acquiring something'): from Latin *acquisitio(n-)*, from the verb *acquirere* (see AC-QUIRE).

ac•qui•si•tion ac•count•ing /ækwə'zɪsHən ə,kowntɪNG/ ▸ n. a procedure in accounting in which the value of the assets of a company is changed after a takeover from book to fair market level.

ac•tive /'æktɪv/ ▸ adj. 1 (of a bank account) in continuous use.
2 denoting a style of investing in which the individual or mutual-fund manager actively makes investment decisions to buy and sell stocks or other securities in order to maximize returns. Compare with PASSIVE.
ORIGIN Middle English: from Latin *activus*, from *act-* 'done,' from the verb *agere* .

ac•tu•ar•y /'ækcHoo͞,erē/ ▸ n. (pl. **ac•tu•ar•ies**) a person who compiles and analyzes statistics and uses them to calculate insurance risks and premiums.
DERIVATIVES **ac•tu•ar•i•al adj.**
ORIGIN mid 16th cent. (originally denoting a clerk or registrar of a court): from Latin *actuarius* 'bookkeeper,' from *actus* (see ACTIVE). The current sense dates from the mid 19th cent.

ad•just•a•ble-rate mort•gage /ə'jəstəbəl 'rāt ,môrgij/ (abbr.: **ARM**) ▸ n. a mortgage agreement between a lender, usually a financial institution, and a purchaser of real estate, allowing for predetermined adjustments of the interest rate at specified intervals. Also called VARIABLE-RATE MORTGAGE.

ADR ▸ abbr. American depositary receipt.

ad va•lo•rem /ˌæd və'lôrəm/ ▸ adv. & adj. (of the levying of tax or customs duties) in proportion to the estimated value of the goods or transaction concerned.
ORIGIN late 17th cent.: Latin, literally 'according to the value.'

ad•vice /əd'vīs/ ▶ n. a formal notice of a financial transaction: *remittance advices.*

ORIGIN Middle English: from Old French *avis,* based on Latin *ad* 'to' + *visum,* past participle of *videre* 'to see.' The original sense was 'way of looking at something, judgment,' later 'an opinion given.'

af•fin•i•ty card /ə'finitē ˌkärd/ ▶ n. a credit card carrying the name of an organization to which a portion of the money spent using the card is paid.

af•ter•mar•ket /'æftərˌmärkit/ ▶ n. 1 the market for shares and bonds after their original issue.

2 the market for spare parts, accessories, and components, esp. for motor vehicles.

a•gainst /ə'genst/ ▶ prep. in relation to (an amount of money owed or due) so as to reduce or cancel it: *money was advanced against the value of the property.*

ORIGIN Middle English: from *again* + -*s* (adverbial genitive) + -*t* probably by association with superlatives (as in *amongst*).

al•ter•na•tive min•i•mum tax /ôl'tərnətiv 'minəməm 'tæks/ ▶ see AMT.

A•mer•i•can de•pos•i•tar•y re•ceipt /ə'merikən di'päziˌterē riˌsēt/ (also **American depositary share**) (abbr.: **ADR**) ▶ n. (in the US) a negotiable certificate of title to a number of shares in a non-US company that are deposited in an overseas bank.

USAGE: Instead of buying shares in foreign-based companies through an overseas market, Americans can use their domestic broker or discount brokerage to buy ADRs, denominated in US dollars, for hundreds of stocks from many countries. This avoids currency conversion, additional fees, unfamiliar tax conventions, and cumbersome or unreliable procedures.

Am•ex /'æmˌeks/ ▶ abbr. American Stock Exchange.

am•or•tize /'æmərˌtīz/ ▶ v. [trans.] reduce or extinguish (a debt) by money regularly put aside: *loan fees can be amortized over the life of the mortgage.*

■ gradually write off the initial cost of (an asset): *they want to amortize the tooling costs quickly.*

ORIGIN late Middle English: from Old French *amortiss-*, lengthened stem of *amortir*, based on Latin *ad-* 'to, at' + *mors, mort-* 'death.'

AMT ▶ abbr. alternative minimum tax, introduced to prevent companies and individuals from using deductions and credits to pay no tax.

an•nu•al•ized /'ænyōōə,līzd/ ▶ adj. (of a rate of interest, inflation, or return on an investment) recalculated as an annual rate: *an annualized yield of about 11.5%.*

An•nu•al Per•cent•age Rate /'ænyōōəl pər'sentij ,rāt/ (abbr.: **APR**) ▶ the annual rate of interest applied by a lender to a loan or other form of credit.

USAGE: Under the federal Truth in Lending Act, a lender must disclose the **Annual Percentage Rate** in large bold type on all consumer loan agreements. A lender must also disclose the total cost of a loan and any special terms associated with the loan. Also called the Consumer Credit Protection Act, this federal legislation was passed in 1968.

an•nu•i•tant /ə'n(y)ōōit̪(ə)nt/ ▶ n. formal a person who receives an annuity.

ORIGIN early 18th cent.: from ANNUITY, on the pattern of *accountant*.

an•nu•i•ty /ə'n(y)ōōit̪ē/ ▶ n. (pl. **an•nu•i•ties**) a fixed sum of money paid to someone each year, typically for the rest of their life: *he left her an annuity of $1,000 in his will.*

■ a form of insurance or investment entitling the investor to a series of annual sums: [as adj.] *an annuity plan.*

ORIGIN late Middle English: from French *annuité*, from medieval Latin *annuitas*, from Latin *annuus* 'yearly,' from *annus* 'year.'

an•swer•ing serv•ice /'ænsəriNG ,sərvis/ ▶ n. a business that receives and answers telephone calls for its clients.

an•ti•trust /,æntē'trəst; ,æntī-/ ▶ adj. of or relating to legislation preventing or controlling trusts or other monopolies, with the intention of promoting competition in business.

APEC /'ā,pek/ ▶ abbr. Asia Pacific Economic Cooperation, a regional economic forum established in 1989, including the US, Japan, China, Australia, Indonesia, Hong Kong, and Thailand.

APR ▸ **abbr.** annual or annualized percentage rate, typically of interest on loans or credit.

ar•bi•trage /ˈärbiˌträzʜ/ ▸ **n.** the simultaneous buying and selling of securities, currency, or commodities in different markets or in derivative forms in order to take advantage of differing prices for the same asset.

▸ **v.** [intrans.] buy and sell assets in such a way.

ORIGIN late Middle English: from French, from *arbitrer* 'give judgment,' from Latin *arbitrari* 'to judge,' from *arbiter* 'judge, supreme ruler.' The current sense dates from the late 19th cent.

ar•bi•tra•geur /ˌärbiträˈzʜər/ (also **ar•bi•trag•er** /ˈärbiˌträzʜər/) ▸ **n.** a person who engages in arbitrage.

ARM /ärm/ ▸ **abbr.** adjustable-rate mortgage.

ASEAN ▸ **abbr.** Association of Southeast Asian Nations.

ask /æsk/ ▸ **v.** [trans.] request (a specified amount) as a price for selling something: *he was asking $250 for the guitar.*

▸ **n.** [in sing.] the price at which an item, esp. a financial security, is offered for sale: [as adj.] *ask prices for bonds.*

ORIGIN Old English *āscian*, *āhsian*, *āxian*, of West Germanic origin.

ask•ing price /ˈæskiNG ˌprīs/ ▸ **n.** the price at which something is offered for sale.

as•sess /əˈses/ ▸ **v.** [trans.] (usu. **be assessed**) calculate or estimate the price or value of: *the damage was assessed at $5 billion.*

■ (often **be assessed**) set the value of a tax, fine, etc., for (a person or property) at a specified level: *all empty properties will be assessed at 50 percent.*

DERIVATIVES **as•sess•ment n.**

ORIGIN late Middle English: from Old French *assesser*, based on Latin *assidere* 'sit by' (in medieval Latin 'levy tax'), from *ad-* 'to, at' + *sedere* 'sit.'

as•ses•sor /əˈsesər/ ▸ **n.** a person who calculates or estimates the value of something or an amount to be paid, chiefly for tax or insurance purposes.

as•set /ˈæset/ ▸ **n.** (usu. **assets**) property owned by a person or company, regarded as having value and available to meet debts, commitments, or legacies: *growth in net assets.*

ORIGIN mid 16th cent. (in the plural in the sense 'sufficient estate to allow discharge of a will'): from an Anglo-Norman French legal term, from Old French *asez* 'enough,' based on Latin *ad* 'to' + *satis* 'enough.'

as•set al•lo•ca•tion /'æset ˌælō'kāsHən/ ▸ n. the distribution of investment funds by an investor among different categories of assets, such as cash and cash equivalents, stocks, fixed-income securities, and real estate.

USAGE: The term also describes the distribution of investment funds among different subcategories of assets, such as government and municipal bonds, domestic and foreign stocks, and stocks distinguished by industry or capitalization (for example, small-cap or large-cap). A central concept in personal financial planning, **asset allocation** influences the risk and return of an investor's portfolio.

as•set-backed /'æset ˌbækt/ ▸ adj. denoting securities having as collateral the return on a series of mortgages, credit agreements, or other forms of lending.

as•set-strip•ping /'æset 'stripiNG/ ▸ n. the practice of taking over a company in financial difficulties and selling each of its assets separately at a profit without regard for the company's future.
DERIVATIVES **as•set-strip•per** n.

As•so•ci•a•tion of South•east A•sian Na•tions /əˌsōsē'āsHən əv 'sowTHˌēst 'āzHən 'nāsHənz/ (abbr.: **ASEAN**) a regional organization intended to promote economic cooperation and now comprising the countries of Indonesia, Malaysia, the Philippines, Singapore, Thailand, Brunei, Vietnam, Laos, Myanmar, and Cambodia.

ATM ▸ abbr. automated (or automatic) teller machine, a machine that automatically provides cash and performs other banking services on insertion of a special card by the account holder.

au•dit /'ôdit/ ▸ n. an official inspection of an individual's or organization's accounts, typically by an independent body.
▸ v. (**aud•it•ed, aud•it•ing**) [trans.] conduct an official financial examination of (an individual's or organization's accounts): *companies must have their accounts audited.*
ORIGIN late Middle English: from Latin *auditus* 'hearing,' from

audire 'hear,' in medieval Latin *auditus (compoti)* 'audit (of an account),' an audit originally being presented orally.

au•di•tor /'ôdiṯər/ ▶ n. a person who conducts an audit.
ORIGIN Middle English: from Old French *auditeur*, from Latin *auditor*, from *audire* 'to hear.'

aus•ter•i•ty /ô'steriṯē/ ▶ n. difficult economic conditions created by government measures to reduce a budget deficit, esp. by reducing public expenditure: *a prolonged period of austerity* [as adj.] *austerity measures.*
ORIGIN late Middle English: from French *austérité*, from Latin *austeritas*, from *austerus*, from Greek *austēros,* 'severe.'

av•er•age /'æv(ə)rij/ ▶ n. the apportionment of financial liability resulting from loss of or damage to a ship or its cargo.

■ reduction in the amount payable under an insurance policy, e.g., in respect to partial loss.
ORIGIN late 15th cent.: from French *avarie* 'damage to ship or cargo,' earlier 'customs duty,' from Italian *avaria*, from Arabic *'awār* 'damage to goods'; the suffix *-age* is on the pattern of *damage.*

USAGE: Originally denoting a charge or customs duty payable by the owner of goods to be shipped, the term later denoted the financial liability from goods lost or damaged at sea, and specifically the equitable apportionment of this between the owners of the vessel and the cargo (late 16th cent.); this gave rise to the general sense of the equalizing out of gains and losses by calculating the mean (mid 18th cent.).

B

ba•by bo•nus /ˈbābē ˌbōnəs/ ▸ n. Canadian family allowance or child tax benefit.

back-end /ˈbæk ˈend/ ▸ adj. relating to the end or outcome of a project, process, or investment: *many annuities have back-end surrender charges.*

back•load /ˈbækˌlōd/ ▸ v. [trans.] (usu. **be backloaded**) place more charges at the later stages of (a financial agreement) than at the earlier stages.

bad debt /ˈbæd ˈdet/ ▸ n. a debt that cannot be recovered.

bail•out /ˈbālˌowt/ ▸ n. informal an act of giving financial assistance to a failing business or economy to save it from collapse.

bait-and-switch /ˈbāt ən(d) ˈswiCH / ▸ n. the action (generally illegal) of advertising goods that are an apparent bargain, with the intention of substituting inferior or more expensive goods: [as adj.] *a bait-and-switch scheme.*

bal•ance /ˈbæləns/ ▸ n. a figure representing the difference between credits and debits in an account; the amount of money held in an account: *he accumulated a healthy balance with the savings bank.*
■ the difference between an amount due and an amount paid: *unpaid credit-card balances.*
▸ v. [trans.] compare debits and credits in (an account), typically to ensure that they are equal: *the law requires the council to **balance its books** each year.*
■ [intrans.] (of an account) have credits and debits equal.
PHRASES **balance of payments** the difference in total value between payments into and out of a country over a period. **balance of trade** the difference in value between a country's imports and exports.

ORIGIN Middle English: from Old French *balance* (noun), *balancer* (verb), referring to a scale with two weighing pans, based on late Latin *(libra) bilanx* '(balance) having two scalepans,' from *bi-* 'twice, having two' + *lanx* 'scalepan.'

bal•ance sheet /ˈbæləns ˌSHēt/ (abbr.: **BS**) ▶ n. a statement of the assets, liabilities, and capital of a business or other organization at a particular point in time, detailing the balance of income and expenditure over the preceding period.

bal•loon pay•ment /bəˈlo͞on ˌpāmənt/ ▶ n. a repayment of the outstanding principal sum made at the end of a loan period, interest only having been paid hitherto.

USAGE: Even though the terms may seem easier to meet, the borrower may not have the money required to make the large final payment.

bank draft /ˈbæNGk ˌdræft/ ▶ n. a check drawn by a bank on its own funds in another bank.

bank•note /ˈbæNGkˌnōt/ (also **bank note**) ▶ n. a piece of paper money, constituting a central bank's promissory note to pay a stated sum to the bearer on demand: *is the $1 bill the only banknote with George Washington's picture on it?*

bank•rupt /ˈbæNGkˌrəpt/ ▶ adj. (of a person or organization) declared in law unable to pay outstanding debts: *the company was declared bankrupt | he committed suicide after **going bankrupt**.*
▶ n. a person judged by a court to be insolvent, whose property is taken and disposed of for the benefit of creditors.
▶ v. [trans.] reduce (a person or organization) to bankruptcy: *the strike nearly bankrupted the union.*
DERIVATIVES **bank•rupt•cy** n.
ORIGIN mid 16th cent.: from Italian *banca rotta* 'broken bench,' from Medieval Latin *banca, bancus* 'bench, moneychanger's table' (ultimately of Germanic origin) and *rompere* 'to break.' The change in the ending was due to association with Latin *rupt-* 'broken.'

ba•sis point /ˈbāsis ˌpoint/ (abbr.: **bp**) ▶ n. one hundredth of one percent, used chiefly in expressing differences in interest rates.

bas•ket /ˈbæskit/ ▶ n. a group or range of currencies or investments.

ORIGIN Middle English: from Old French *basket*, of unknown ultimate origin.

Bay Street /ˈbā ˌstrēt/ ▸ **n.** Canadian a street in Toronto where the headquarters of many financial institutions are located.■ the moneyed interests of Toronto, especially as opposed to other regions of Canada : *Bay Street is nervous about the election*).

BDC ▸ **abbr.** Canadian Business Development Bank of Canada.

bean count•er /ˈbēn ˌkowntər/ ▸ **n.** informal, derogatory a person, typically an accountant or bureaucrat, perceived as placing excessive emphasis on controlling expenditure and budgets.

bear /be(ə)r/ ▸ **n.** a person who forecasts that prices of stocks or commodities will fall, esp. a person who sells shares hoping to buy them back later at a lower price.

ORIGIN Old English *bera*, of West Germanic origin; related to Dutch *beer* and German *Bär* .

bear•er /ˈbe(ə)rər/ ▸ **n.** a person who presents a check or other order to pay money: *promissory notes payable to the bearer.*
■ [as adj.] payable to the possessor: *bearer bonds.*
ORIGIN Middle English *berere* from Old English *beran* 'to carry, bear.'

bear•ish /ˈb(ə)riSH/ ▸ **adj.** characterized by falling share prices.
■ (of a dealer) inclined to sell because of an anticipated fall in prices.

bear mar•ket /ˈbe(ə)r ˌmärkit/ ▸ **n.** a market in which prices are falling, encouraging selling.

be•ta /ˈbātə/ (also **be•ta co•ef•fi•cient** /ˈbātə ˌkōə,fiSHənt/) ▸ **n.** a measure of a stock's volatility.

USAGE: The Standard & Poor's 500 stock index has a **beta** of 1. A stock with a higher **beta** is more volatile than the market; a stock with a lower **beta** is less volatile, that is, it will rise and fall in value more slowly than the market. The higher a stock's **beta**, the higher the risk but the higher the potential reward.

bid price /ˈbid ˌprīs/ ▸ **n.** the price that a dealer or other prospective buyer is prepared to pay for securities or other assets.

Big Board /ˈbig ˈbôrd/ **n.** informal term for the New York Stock Exchange.

bill•ing /'biliNG/ ▶ **n.** the process of making out or sending invoices: *faster, more accurate order fulfillment and billing.*

■ the total amount of business conducted in a given time, esp. that of an advertising agency: *the account was worth about $2 million a year in billings.*

bill of ex•change /'bil əv iks'cHānj/ ▶ **n.** a written order to a person requiring the person to make a specified payment to the signatory or to a named payee; a promissory note.

bill of goods /'il əv 'gŏŏdz/ ▶ **n.** a consignment of merchandise.

bill of sale /'bil əv 'sāl/ ▶ **n.** a certificate of transfer of personal property.

black mon•ey /'blæk 'mənē/ ▶ **n.** income illegally obtained or not declared for tax purposes.

blank check /'blæNGk 'cHek/ ▶ **n.** a bank check with the amount left for the payee to fill in.

block /bläk/ ▶ **v.** [trans.] restrict the use or conversion of (currency or any other asset).

ORIGIN Middle English (denoting a log or tree stump): from Old French *bloc* (noun), *bloquer* (verb), from Middle Dutch *blok*, of unknown ultimate origin.

blue-chip /'blŏŏ 'cHip/ ▶ **adj.** denoting companies or their shares considered to be a reliable investment, though less secure than gilt-edged stock.

ORIGIN early 20th cent. (originally US): from the *blue chip* used in gambling games, which usually has a high value.

Board of Trade /'bôrd əv 'trād/ ▶ **n. 1** another term for CHAMBER OF COMMERCE.

2 (also **Chicago Board of Trade**) the Chicago futures exchange.

boil•er room /'boilər ˌrŏŏm; ˌrŏŏm/ ▶ **n.** a room used for intensive telephone selling: [as adj.] *boiler-room stock salesmen.*

bond /bänd/ ▶ **n. 1** a certificate issued by a government or a public company promising to repay borrowed money at a fixed rate of interest at a specified time.

2 (**in bond**) (of dutiable goods) a state of storage in a bonded warehouse until the importer pays the duty owing.

3 an insurance policy held by a company, which protects against losses resulting from circumstances such as bankruptcy or misconduct by employees.

ORIGIN Middle English: variant of Old English *band,* 'restraint, shackle,' from Old Norse, reinforced in Middle English by Old French *bande,* of Germanic origin.

bond•ed /'bändid/ ▶ adj. 1 (of a person or company) bound by a legal agreement.

■ (of a debt) secured by bonds.

2 (of dutiable goods) placed in bond.

bond•ed ware•house /'bändid 'we(ə)r₁hows/ ▶ n. a customs-controlled warehouse for the retention of imported goods until the duty owed is paid.

bo•nus•ing /'bōnəsiNG/ ▶ n. Canadian an act of subsidizing something, especially as an inducement for development etc.

bo•nus is•sue /'bōnəs ₁iSHŌŌ/ ▶ n. an issue of additional shares to shareholders instead of a dividend, in proportion to the shares already held.

book•keep•ing /'book₁kēpiNG/ ▶ n. the activity or occupation of keeping records of the financial affairs of a business.

DERIVATIVES **book•keep•er n.**

book val•ue /'book ₁vælyōō/ ▶ n. the value of a security or asset as entered in a company's books.

bounce /bowns/ informal ▶ v. [intrans.] (of a check) be returned by a bank when there are insufficient funds to meet it: *my rent check bounced.*

■ [trans.] write (a check) on insufficient funds: *I've never bounced a check.*

▶ n. a sudden rise in the level of something: *economists agree there could be a bounce in prices next year.*

ORIGIN Middle English *bunsen* 'beat, thump,' perhaps imitative, or from Low German *bunsen* 'beat,' Dutch *bons* 'a thump.'

bourse /boors/ ▶ n. a stock market in a non-English-speaking country, esp. France.

■ (**Bourse**) the Paris stock exchange.

ORIGIN mid 16th cent. (as *burse,* the usual form until the mid 19th cent.): from French, literally 'purse,' via medieval Latin from Greek *bursa* 'leather.'

bp ▶ **abbr.** ■ basis point(s).

BPR ▶ **abbr.** business process reengineering.

brand a•ware•ness /'brænd ə,we(ə)rnis/ ▶ n. the extent to which consumers are familiar with the distinctive qualities or image of a particular brand of goods or services.

brand ex•ten•sion /'brænd ik,stensHən/ ▶ n. an instance of using an established brand name or trademark on new products, so as to increase sales.

brand im•age /'brænd ,imij/ ▶ n. the impression of a product held by real or potential consumers.

brand lead•er /'brænd ,lēdər/ ▶ n. the best-selling or most highly regarded product or brand of its type.

brand loy•al•ty /'brænd ,loiəltē/ ▶ n. the tendency of some consumers to continue buying the same brand of goods despite the availability of competing brands.

brand man•age•ment /'brænd ,mænijmənt/ ▶ n. the activity of supervising the promotion of a particular brand of goods.

brand name /'brænd 'nām/ ▶ n. a name given by the maker to a product or range of products, esp. a trademark.

Brand X /'brænd 'eks/ ▶ n. a name used for an unidentified brand contrasted unfavorably with a product of the same type being promoted.

break /brāk/ ▶ v. (past **broke**; past part. **bro•ken**) [trans.] (of prices on the stock exchange) fall sharply.
  ▶ **break even** reach a point in a business venture when the profits are equal to the costs.
  ORIGIN Old English *brecan* (verb), of Germanic origin; related to Dutch *breken* and German *brechen*, from an Indo-European root shared by Latin *frangere* 'to break.'

break-e•ven /'brāk ,ēvən/ ▶ n. the point or state at which a person or company breaks even.

bridge loan /'brij ,lōn/ ▶ n. a sum of money lent by a bank to cover an interval between two transactions, typically the buying of one house and the selling of another.

bro•ker /'brōkər/ ▶ n. a person who buys and sells goods or assets for others.

▶v. [trans.] arrange or negotiate (a settlement, deal, or plan): *who brokered the sale of your apartment?*
ORIGIN Middle English (denoting a retailer or peddler): from Anglo-Norman French *brocour*, of unknown ultimate origin.
bro•ker•age /'brōkərij/ ▶n. the business or service of acting as a broker.
■ a fee or commission charged by a broker: *a revenue of $1,400 less a sales brokerage of $12.50.* ■ a company that buys or sells goods or assets for clients.
bro•ker-deal•er /'brōkər 'dēlər/ ▶n. a brokerage firm that buys and sells securities on its own account as a principal before selling the securities to customers.
BS ▶abbr. balance sheet.
bub•ble e•con•o•my /'bəbəl i,känəmē/ ▶n. an unstable expanding economy; in particular, a period of heightened prosperity and increased commercial activity in Japan in the late 1980s brought about by artificially adjusted interest rates.
buck•et shop /'bəkit ,SHäp/ ▶n. informal, derogatory an unauthorized office for speculating in stocks or currency using the funds of unwitting investors.

USAGE: Like the characters in the David Mamet play *Glengarry Glen Ross,* **bucket-shop** employees usually call people at home, around dinnertime, with a deal that is too good to be true.

budg•et /'bəjit/ ▶n. an estimate of income and expenditure for a set period of time.
■ an annual or other regular estimate of national revenue and expenditure put forward by the government, often including details of changes in taxation. ■ the amount of money needed or available for a purpose: *they have a limited budget.*
ORIGIN late Middle English: from Old French *bougette*, diminutive of *bouge* 'leather bag,' from Latin *bulga* 'leather bag, knapsack,' of Gaulish origin.

USAGE: This word originally meant a pouch or wallet, and later its contents. In the mid 18th cent., the Chancellor of the Exchequer in the UK, in presenting his annual statement, was said "to open the budget." In the late 19th cent. the use of the term was extended from governmental to private or commercial finances.

bulk buy•ing /'bəlk 'biɪNG/ ▸ **n.** the purchase of goods in large amounts, typically at a discount.

DERIVATIVES **bulk-buy v.**

bull /boŏl/ ▸ **n.** a person who buys shares hoping to sell them at a higher price later.

ORIGIN late Old English *bula* (recorded in place names), from Old Norse *boli* .

bull•ish /'boŏlisH/ ▸ **adj.** characterized by rising share prices: *the market was bullish.*

■ (of a dealer) inclined to buy because of an anticipated rise in prices.

bull mar•ket /'boŏl ˌmärkit/ ▸ **n.** a market in which share prices are rising, encouraging buying.

buoy•an•cy /'boiənsē; 'boŏyənsē/ ▸ **n.** a high level of activity in an economy or stock market: *there is renewed buoyancy in the demand for steel.*

busi•ness cy•cle /'biznis ˌsīkəl/ ▸ **n.** a cycle or series of cycles of economic expansion and contraction.

busi•ness proc•ess re•en•gi•neer•ing /'biznis ˌpräses ˌrēenjə 'ni(ə)riNG/ (abbr.: **BPR**) ▸ **n.** the process or activity of restructuring a company's organization and methods, esp. to exploit the capabilities of computers.

busi•ness stud•ies /'biznis ˌstədēz/ ▸ **plural n.** [treated as sing.] the study of economics and management, esp. as an educational topic.

buy-back /'bī ˌbæk/ ▸ **n.** the buying back of goods by the original seller.

■ the buying back by a company of its own shares. ■ a form of borrowing in which shares or bonds are sold with an agreement to repurchase them at a later date: [as adj.] *a share buy-back.*

USAGE: Companies often buy back their shares when they think the shares' value has fallen too low. This can sometimes signal a buying opportunity for investors.

buy•er /'bīər/ ▸ n. a person who makes a purchase.

■ a person employed to select and purchase stock or materials for a large retail or manufacturing business, etc.

PHRASES **a buyer's market** an economic situation in which goods or shares are plentiful and buyers can keep prices down.

buy-in /'bī ˌin/ ▸ n. a purchase of shares by a broker after a seller has failed to deliver similar shares, the original seller being charged any difference in cost.

buy•out /'bīˌowt/ ▸ n. the purchase of a controlling share in a company, esp. by its own managers.

HOW TO DETERMINE IF YOU HAVE A CREDIT CARD PROBLEM

There are many different rules of thumb that determine if you have a credit card problem. Some experts insist that, if you're making only the minimum payments on your credit card bills, you definitely have a problem! Other experts maintain that you're in credit card trouble if more than 20 percent of your monthly take-home pay is being spent to pay off credit card debt. The truth is that when it comes to debt, there's often more than just simple rules and formulas, there's the issue of how you feel about your debt.

So how do you feel?

The following simple exercise will help you figure this out. To begin, get out all your credit cards and all your credit card statements and put them on the dining room table. (If you're married or have a partner, get him or her to do the same with his or her cards and statements.) Now determine:

- how many cards you have;

- how many cards your spouse or partner has;

- how many cards your children or other dependents living with you have; and

- how many cards your whole family, together, has.

Now, list each credit card account and its current outstanding balance, starting with the largest debt and working down to the smallest. How much is it? What's your grand total?

Next, calculate the total amount that you owe and the total monthly minimum payments due. What will it cost you monthly just to pay the minimums?

Finally, having looked at these numbers, let's look inside. How do you feel about your credit card situation, now that you see it in black and white? Do you have too many cards, carry too much debt, feel comfortable with the number of cards you have and the amount of debt you're carrying, or still feel uncertain? Tell yourself the truth. How do you really feel? Is enough, enough? Are you tired of worrying about bills each month and wondering how you will pay them? Isn't it time to go on a credit-card diet?

Lower your interest rate

Now that you've identified your debt situation, the next step is to lower the interest rate on your credit card debt.

The average U.S. credit card charges an annualized interest rate of just under 20 percent. But you can easily get new credit cards with rates of 10 to 15 percent, and many companies offer rates below 10 percent. (To find out current rates being offered nationwide, go to *www.bankrate.com* or look in *USA Today* or *The Wall Street Journal.*)

Here's how to get your credit card company to lower your interest rate: First, call the company and ask them to tell you your current effective annual rate. Don't be confused if they quote a rate over prime—as in, "Your rate is 9 percent over prime." This doesn't mean your rate is 9 percent; it means your rate is 9 percent plus whatever the prime lending rate happens to be. If the prime rate were 5 percent, for example, your effective annual rate would be 14 percent.

Once you know your interest rate, ask to speak with a supervisor. Do not—I repeat, do not—ever try to negotiate a lower rate with the first person who answers the phone. Explain to the supervisor that you just received a new credit card application from a competing company that is offering a much lower interest rate and that, unless she can match or beat the competitor's interest rate, you intend to transfer your balance today. The credit card business has become so competitive that, in most cases, the supervisor will agree to lower your rate on the spot. If you're paying around 20 percent now, you should have no trouble getting your rate lowered to less than 14 percent.

Another way to get your credit card company to lower your interest rate is to offer to consolidate all your credit card debt with them. Consolidating your debt at one company is generally a good idea. If nothing else, it means less paperwork for you, since now you have only one credit card company to deal with (and write checks to), making it that much easier to focus on getting debt-free. Just call your credit card company, ask to speak to a supervisor, tell the supervisor that you've received an offer from a competitor to consolidate all your credit card debt on the competitor's card at a lower rate, but that you'll stay with your current credit card company if they'll match the offer.

Even after you've paid off your credit card balances, you shouldn't assume your credit rating is intact. Rating agencies and the people who provide them with information about your credit history can make mistakes. There's nothing worse than finding out that you have credit problems when you're about to make a major purchase—say, when you're ready to buy your first home.

Even if you think your credit rating is fine, you should get a copy of your credit reports. It's actually quite simple. There are three main credit-reporting companies—Equifax, Experian, and TransUnion—and, on request, they will each provide you with a copy of your personal credit report for a charge of no more than $8.50. (In certain states and in some special cases, the reports are free.)

Here's how to contact the companies:

Equifax
P.O. Box 740241
Atlanta, GA 30374
(800) 685-1111, (770) 612-3200
(800) 548-4548 (residents of Georgia, Vermont, and
Massachusetts)
(800) 233-7654 (residents of Maryland)
www.equifax.com

Experian
P.O. Box 2002
Allen, TX 75013
(888) 567-8688
www.experian.com

TransUnion Corporation
Consumer Disclosure Center
P.O. Box 390
Chester, PA 19022
(800) 916-8800
(800) 888-4213 (if you have been denied credit)
www.transunion.com

If you discover any inaccuracies or mistakes in any of your credit reports, get them fixed immediately. The procedures for doing so are relatively simple, and the individual companies will tell you exactly what's required.

If you still have trouble dealing with your debts, it may be time to seek outside help through a reputable agency such as Consumer Credit Counseling Services, reachable online at *www.cccsintl.org* or toll-free at (800) 388-2227, or Myvesta (formerly known as Debt Counselors of America), reachable online at *www.myvesta.org* or toll-free at (800) 680-3328.

C

CAD ▶ **abbr.** Canadian Canadian dollars.

ca•das•tral /kə'dæstrəl/ ▶ **adj.** (of a map or survey) showing the extent, value, and ownership of land, esp. for taxation.

ORIGIN mid 19th cent.: from French, from *cadastre* 'register of property,' from Provençal *cadastro*, from Italian *catastro* (earlier *catastico*), from late Greek *katastikhon* 'list, register,' from *kata stikhon* 'line by line.'

ca•das•tre /kə'dæstər/ ▶ **n.** a register of property showing the extent, value, and ownership of land for taxation.

CAF ▶ **abbr.** cost and freight.

caisse po•pu•laire /'kes ˌpōpo͞o'le(ə)r/ ▶ **n.** Canadian (in Quebec and other francophone communities) a cooperative financial institution similar to a credit union.

ORIGIN French.

call /kôl/ ▶ **n.** a demand for payment of lent or unpaid capital.
■ short for CALL OPTION.

ORIGIN late Old English *ceallian*, from Old Norse *kalla* 'summon loudly.'

call mon•ey /'kôl ˌmənē/ ▶ **n.** money lent by a bank or other institutions that is repayable on demand.

call op•tion /'kôl ˌäpSHən/ ▶ **n.** an option to buy stocks or commodities at an agreed price on or before a particular date.

Can•a•da Sav•ings Bond /'kænədə 'sāviNGz ˌbänd/ ▶ **n.** Canadian a savings bond issued by the Canadian federal government.

cap /kæp/ ▶ **n.** ■ an upper limit imposed on spending or other activities.

▶ **v.** (**capped, cap•ping**) [trans.] (often **be capped**) place a limit or restriction on (prices, expenditure, or other activity): *council budgets will be capped.*

ORIGIN Old English *cæppe* 'hood,' from late Latin *cappa*, perhaps from Latin *caput* 'head.'

cap•i•tal /'kæpiṯl/ ▸ n. wealth in the form of money or other assets owned by a person or organization or available or contributed for a particular purpose such as starting a company or investing: *the senior partner would provide the initial capital* | *rates of return on invested capital were high.*

■ the excess of a company's assets over its liabilities.

ORIGIN Middle English: via Old French from Latin *capitalis*, from *caput* 'head.'

cap•i•tal ad•e•qua•cy /'kæpiṯl 'ædikwəsē/ ▸ n. the statutory minimum reserves of capital that a bank or other financial institution must have available.

cap•i•tal gain /'kæpiṯl 'gān/ ▸ n. (often **capital gains**) a profit from the sale of property or of an investment.

cap•i•tal gains tax /'kæpiṯl 'gānz ‚tæks/ (abbr.: **CGT**) ▸ n. a tax levied on profit from the sale of property or of an investment.

cap•i•tal goods /'kæpiṯl 'goödz/ ▸ plural n. goods that are used in producing other goods, rather than being bought by consumers.

cap•i•tal-in•ten•sive /'kæpiṯl in'tensiv/ ▸ adj. (of a business or industrial process) requiring the investment of large sums of money.

cap•i•tal•ize /'kæpiṯl‚īz/ ▸ v. [trans.] **1** provide (a company or industry) with capital.

2 realize (the present value of an income); convert into capital.

■ reckon (the value of an asset) by setting future benefits against the cost of maintenance: *a trader will want to capitalize repairs expenditure.*

DERIVATIVES **cap•i•tal•i•za•tion** n.

cap•i•tal mar•ket /'kæpiṯl 'märkit/ ▸ n. the part of a financial system concerned with raising capital by dealing in shares, bonds, and other long-term investments.

cap•i•tal sum /'kæpiṯl 'səm/ ▸ n. a lump sum of money payable to an insured person or paid as an initial fee or investment.

cap•i•ta•tion /‚kæpi'tāsHən/ ▸ n. the payment of a fee or grant to a

doctor, school, or other person or body providing services to a number of people, such that the amount paid is determined by the number of patients, pupils, or customers: *the increased capitation enabled schools to offer pupils an enhanced curriculum.*
ORIGIN early 17th cent.: from late Latin *capitatio* 'poll tax,' from *caput* 'head.'

cap•tive /'kæptiv/ ▸ adj. (of a facility or service) controlled by, and typically for the sole use of, an establishment or company: *a captive power plant.*
ORIGIN late Middle English: from Latin *captivus*, from *capere* 'seize, take.'

car•bon tax /'kärbən ˌtaks/ ▸ n. a tax on fossil fuels, esp. those used by motor vehicles, intended to reduce the emission of carbon dioxide.

card•hold•er /'kärdˌhōldər/ ▸ n. a person who has a credit card or debit card.

car•ry /'kærē/ ▸ n. (pl. **car•ries**) [usu. in sing.] the maintenance of an investment position in a securities market, esp. with regard to the costs or profits accruing.
ORIGIN late Middle English: from Anglo-Norman French and Old Northern French *carier*, based on Latin *carrus* 'wheeled vehicle.'
USAGE: If you hire a broker to administer your portfolio, the fee that you pay the broker is part of your cost of **carry**.

car•ry•ing charge /'kærēiNG ˌtæks/ ▸ n. 1 an expense or effective cost arising from unproductive assets such as stored goods or unoccupied premises.
2 a sum payable for the conveying of goods.

car•tel /kär'tel/ ▸ n. an association of manufacturers or suppliers with the purpose of maintaining prices at a high level and restricting competition: *the Colombian drug cartels.*
ORIGIN late 19th cent.: from German *Kartell*, from French *cartel*, from Italian *cartello*, diminutive of *carta*, from Latin *carta* .
USAGE: **Cartel** was originally used to refer to the coalition of the Conservatives and National Liberal parties in Germany (1887), and hence any political combination. By the early 20th cent. it was used to denote a trade agreement.

car•tel•ize /kär'tel͵īz; 'kärt̬l-/ ▸ v. [trans.] (of manufacturers or suppliers) form a cartel in (an industry or trade).

cash and car•ry /'kæsн ən(d) 'kærē/ ▸ n. a system of wholesale trading whereby goods are paid for in full at the time of purchase and taken away by the purchaser.

■ a wholesale store operating this system.

cash cow /'kæsн ͵kow/ ▸ n. informal a business, investment, or product that provides a steady income or profit: *traditional cash cows like cars and VCRs.*

cash flow /'kæsн ͵flō/ ▸ n. the total amount of money being transferred into and out of a business, esp. as affecting liquidity.

usage: During the technology stock boom in the late 1990s, many dot-coms with soaring stock prices had no **cash flow** to support their stocks' valuations. When the stock bubble burst, they had no underlying **cash flow** to support them.

cash•ier /kæ'sнi(ə)r/ ▸ n. a person handling payments and receipts in a store, bank, or other business.

origin late 16th cent.: from Dutch *cassier* or French *caissier,* from *caisse* 'cash.'

cash nex•us /'kæsн ͵neksəs/ ▸ n. the relationship constituted by monetary transactions.

cash on de•liv•er•y /'kæsн än di'liv(ə)rē; ôn/ (abbr.: **COD**) ▸ n. the system of paying for goods when they are delivered.

cash reg•is•ter /'kæsн ͵rejistər/ ▸ n. a machine used in places of business for regulating money transactions with customers. It typically has a compartmental drawer for cash, and it totals, displays, and records the amount of each sale.

CCRA ▸ abbr. Canadian Canada Customs and Revenue Agency.

CD ▸ abbr. certificate of deposit.

CDIC ▸ abbr. Canadian Canada Deposit Insurance Corporation.

cen•tral bank /'sentrəl 'bæNGk/ ▸ n. a national bank that provides financial and banking services for its country's government and commercial banking system and implements the government's monetary policy and issuing currency.

cer•tif•i•cate of de•pos•it /sər'tifikit əv di'pozit/ (abbr.: **CD**) ▸ n. a certificate issued by a bank to a person depositing money for a specified length of time.

cer•ti•fied check /'sərtə,fīd 'CHek/ ▸ n. a check that is guaranteed by a bank.

cer•ti•fied pub•lic ac•count•ant /'sərtə,fīd 'pəblik ə'kownt(ə)nt/ (abbr.: **CPA**) ▸ n. a member of an officially accredited professional body of accountants.

c.f. ▸ abbr. carried forward (used to refer to figures transferred to a new page or account).

CGT ▸ abbr. capital gains tax.

c.h. (or **C.H.**) abbr. ▸ clearinghouse.

chae•bol /'kī,bäl; -,bôl/ ▸ n. (pl. same or **chae•bols**) (in South Korea) a large business conglomerate, typically a family-owned one. ORIGIN 1980s: Korean, literally 'money clan.'

cham•ber of com•merce /'CHāmbər əv 'kämərs/ ▸ n. a local association to promote and protect the interests of the business community in a particular place. Also called **BOARD OF TRADE.**

change man•age•ment /'CHānj ,mænijmənt/ ▸ n. the management of change and development within a business or similar organization, esp. the personal management of those having to adapt to new conditions.

Chap•ter 11 /'CHæptər i'levən/ ▸ n. protection from creditors given to a company in financial difficulties for a limited period to allow it to reorganize. ORIGIN with allusion to chapter 11 of the US bankruptcy code.

charge /CHärj/ ▸ v. [trans.] demand (an amount) as a price from someone for a service rendered or goods supplied: *the restaurant charged $15 for dinner.* ■ **(charge something to)** record the cost of something as an amount payable by (someone) or on (an account): *they* **charge** *the calls* **to** *their credit-card accounts.*
▸ n. a price asked for goods or services: *an admission charge.*
■ a financial liability or commitment: *an asset of $550,000 should have been taken as* ***a charge on*** *earnings.*
ORIGIN Middle English: from Old French *charger* (verb), *charge* (noun), from late Latin *carricare, carcare* 'to load,' from Latin *carrus* 'wheeled vehicle.'

charge ac•count /'CHärj ə͵kownt/ ▸ n. an account to which goods and services may be charged on credit.

charge card /'CHärj ͵kärd/ ▸ n. a credit card for use with an account that must be paid when a statement is issued.

USAGE: Although Diners Club developed the first credit card, the original and best-known corporate **charge card** was the American Express card.

char•tered bank /'CHärtərd 'bæNGk/ ▸ n. Canadian a large, privately-owned bank chartered by Parliament and operating under the provisions of the Bank Act.

char•tist /'CHärṭist/ ▸ n. a person who uses charts of financial data to predict future trends and to guide investment strategies.

child ben•e•fit /'CHīld ͵benəfit/ ▸ n. 1 Canadian see **child tax benefit**. 2 Brit., Canadian a State monetary allowance for each child in a family.

child tax ben•e•fit /'CHīld 'tæks ͵benəfit/ ▸ n. Canadian a federal government program providing tax-free monthly payments to low- and moderate-income families with children under 18 years of age.

churn /CHərn/ ▸ v. [trans.] (of a broker) encourage frequent turnover of (investments) in order to generate commission. ORIGIN Old English *cyrin*, of Germanic origin; related to Middle Low German *kerne* and Old Norse *kirna* .

cir•cu•la•tion /͵sərkyə'lāSHən/ (abbr.: **cir.** or **circ.**) ▸ n. the movement, exchange, or availability of money in a country: *the new coins go into circulation today.* ORIGIN late Middle English: from Latin *circulatio(n-)*, from the verb *circulare* (see CIRCULATE).

claim /klām/ ▸ v. [trans.] make a demand for (money) under the terms of an insurance policy: *she could have claimed the cost through her insurance.* ▸ n. 1 an application for compensation under the terms of an insurance policy. 2 a right or title to something: *they have first claim on the assets of the trust.* ORIGIN Middle English: from Old French *claime* (noun), *clamer* (verb), from Latin *clamare* 'call out.'

clear /'kli(ə)r/ ▸ **adj.** (of a sum of money) net: *a clear profit of $1,100.*

▸ **v. 1** [trans.] pass (a check) through a clearinghouse so that the money goes into the payee's account: *the check could not be cleared until Monday.*

■ [intrans.] (of a check) pass through a clearinghouse in such a way. **2** [trans.] earn or gain (an amount of money) as a net profit: *I would hope to clear $50,000 profit.*

ORIGIN Middle English: from Old French *cler*, from Latin *clarus* .

clear•ing•house /'kli(ə)riNG,hows/ (also **clear•ing house**) (abbr.: **c.h.** or **C.H.**) ▸ **n.** a bankers' establishment where checks and bills from member banks are exchanged, so that only the balances need be paid in cash.

CLI ▸ **abbr.** cost-of-living index.

closed-end /'klōzd 'end/ ▸ **adj.** denoting an investment trust or company that issues a fixed number of shares.

closed shop /'klōzd 'sHäp/ ▸ **n.** a place of work where membership in a union is a condition for being hired and for continued employment.

■ a system whereby such an arrangement applies: *the outlawing of the closed shop.*

clos•ing price /'klōziNG ,prīs/ ▸ **n.** the price of a security at the end of the day's business in a financial market.

Co. ▸ **abbr.** company: *the Consett Iron Co.*

PHRASES **and Co.** used as part of the titles of commercial businesses to designate the partner or partners not named.

co•de•ter•mi•na•tion /,kōdi,tərmə'nāsHən/ ▸ **n.** cooperation between management and workers in decision making, esp. by the representation of workers on management boards.

ORIGIN 1950s: from *co-* 'together' + *determination* (translating German *Mitbestimmung*).

COLA ▸ **abbr.** cost-of-living adjustment, an increase made to wages or Social Security benefits to keep them in line with inflation.

col•lat•er•al /kə'læt(ə)rəl/ ▸ **n.** something pledged as security for a loan, to be forfeited in the event of a default.

ORIGIN late Middle English: from medieval Latin *collateralis*, from *col-* 'together with' + *lateralis* (from *latus, later-* 'side'). This meaning (originally US) is from the phrase *collateral security*, denoting something pledged in addition to the main obligation of a contract.

col•lat•er•al•ize /kə'læt(ə)rə,līz/ ▸ v. [trans.] provide something as collateral for (a loan): *these loans are collateralized by property.*

col•lec•tive a•gree•ment /kə'lektiv ə'grēmənt/ ▸ n. an agreement about pay and working conditions reached collectively by management and the workforce.

col•lec•tive own•er•ship /kə'lektiv 'ōnər,SHip/ ▸ n. ownership of something, typically land or industrial assets, by all members of a group for the mutual benefit of all.

com•mand e•con•o•my /kə'mænd i,känəmē/ ▸ n. an economy in which production, investment, prices, and incomes are determined centrally by a government.

com•mer•cial bank /kə'mərsHəl 'bæNGk/ ▸ n. a bank that offers services to the general public and to companies.

com•mer•cial pa•per /kə'mərsHəl 'pāpər/ (abbr.: **CP**) ▸ n. short-term unsecured promissory notes issued by companies.

com•mod•i•ty /kə'mädi̱tē/ ▸ n. (pl. **com•mod•i•ties**) a raw material or primary agricultural product that can be bought and sold, such as copper or coffee.

ORIGIN late Middle English: from Old French *commodite* or Latin *commoditas*, from *commodus* 'convenient.'

com•mon car•ri•er /'kämən 'kærēər/ ▸ n. a person or company that transports goods or passengers on regular routes at rates made available to the public.

■ a company providing public telecommunications facilities.

com•mon mar•ket /'kämən 'märkit/ ▸ n. a group of countries imposing few or no duties on trade with one another and a common tariff on trade with other countries.

■ (the **Common Market**) a name for the European Economic Community or European Union, used esp. in the 1960s and 1970s.

com•mon stock /'kämən 'stäk/ ▸ plural n. (also **com•mon stocks**) shares entitling their holder to dividends that vary in amount and may even be missed, depending on the fortunes of the company: *the company announced a public offering of 3.5 million shares of common stock.*

com•mu•ta•tion /ˌkämyəˈtāsHən/ ▸ n. the conversion of a legal obligation or entitlement into another form, e.g., the replacement of an annuity or series of payments by a single payment.
ORIGIN late Middle English: from Latin *commutatio(n-)*, from *commutare* 'exchange, interchange' (see COMMUTE).
com•mute /kəˈmyo͞ot/ ▸ v. [trans.] (**commute something for/into**) change one kind of payment or obligation for (another).
■ replace (an annuity or other series of payments) with a single payment: *if he had commuted some of his pension, he would have received $330,000.*
ORIGIN late Middle English: from Latin *commutare*, from *com-* 'altogether' + *mutare* 'to change.'
com•pound /kämˌpownd; ˈkämˌpownd/ ▸ adj. (of interest) payable on both capital and the accumulated interest: *compound interest.*
▸ v. [trans.] calculate (interest) on previously accumulated interest: *the yield at which the interest is compounded.*
■ [intrans.] (of a sum of money invested) increase by compound interest: *let your money compound for five years.*
ORIGIN late Middle English *compoune* (verb), from Old French *compoun-*, present tense stem of *compondre*, from Latin *componere* 'put together.' The final *-d* was added in the 16th cent. on the pattern of *expound* and *propound.*
comp•trol•ler /kənˈtrōlər; ˌkäm(p)ˈtrōlər/ ▸ n. a controller (used in the title of some financial officers).
ORIGIN late 15th cent.: spelling variant of CONTROLLER, by erroneous association with French *compte* 'calculation' or its source, late Latin *computus* .
con•ces•sion /kənˈsesHən/ ▸ n. the right to use land or other property for a specified purpose, granted by a government, company, or other controlling body: *new logging concessions.*
■ a commercial operation within the premises of a larger concern, typically selling refreshments: *operates the concessions at the stadium.*
ORIGIN late Middle English: from Latin *concessio(n-)*, from the verb *concedere*, from *con-* 'completely' and *cedere* 'yield.'
con•ces•sion•aire /kənˌsesHəˈne(ə)r/ (also **con•ces•sion•er** /kən

'seSHǝnǝr/) ▶ n. the holder of a concession or grant, esp. for the use of land or commercial premises.

ORIGIN mid 19th cent.: from French *concessionnaire*, from Latin *concessio* (see **CONCESSION**).

con•glom•er•ate ▶ n. /kǝn'glämǝrit/ a large corporation formed by the merging of separate and diverse firms: *a media conglomerate.*

▶adj. /kǝn'glämǝ‚rit/ of or relating to a conglomerate, esp. a large corporation: *conglomerate businesses.*

▶v. /kǝn'glämǝ‚rāt/ [intrans.] form a conglomerate by merging diverse businesses.

ORIGIN late Middle English: from Latin *conglomeratus*, past participle of *conglomerare*, from *con-* 'together' + *glomus, glomer-* 'ball.'

con•sign•ment /kǝn'sīnmǝnt/ ▶ n. a batch of goods destined for or delivered to someone: *a consignment of beef.*

■ agreement to pay a supplier of goods after the goods are sold: *new and used children's clothing on consignment.*

con•sol•i•date /kǝn'säli‚dāt/ ▶ v. [trans.] combine (a number of financial accounts or funds) into a single overall account or set of accounts.

DERIVATIVES **con•sol•i•da•tion** n.

ORIGIN early 16th cent.: from Latin *consolidare*, from *con-* 'together' + *solidare* 'make firm' (from *solidus* 'solid').

con•sor•ti•um /kǝn'sôrsH(ē)ǝm; -'sôrt̩ēǝm/ ▶ n. (pl. **con•sor•tia** or **con•sor•ti•ums**) an association, typically of several business companies.

ORIGIN early 19th cent. (in the sense 'partnership'): from Latin, from *consors* 'sharing, partner.'

con•sum•er /kǝn'so͞omǝr/ ▶ n. a person who purchases goods and services for personal use.

con•sum•er dur•a•ble /kǝn'so͞omǝr ‚d(y)o͞orǝbǝl/ ▶ n. (usu. **consumer durables**) a manufactured item, typically a car or household appliance, that is expected to have a relatively long useful life after purchase.

con•sum•er goods /kǝn'so͞omǝr ‚go͞odz/ ▶ plural n. goods bought and used by consumers, rather than by manufacturers for producing other goods.

con•sum•er•ism /kən'sōōmə,rizəm/ ▸ n. 1 the protection or promotion of the interests of consumers.
2 often derogatory the preoccupation of society with the acquisition of consumer goods.

con•sum•er price in•dex /kən'sōōmər 'prīs ,indeks/ (abbr.: **CPI**) ▸ n. an index of the variation in prices paid by typical consumers for retail goods and other items.

con•sum•er re•search /kən'sōōmər 're,sərCH/ ▸ n. the investigation of the needs and opinions of consumers, esp. with regard to a particular product or service.

con•sum•er so•ci•e•ty /kən'sōōmər sə'sīitē/ ▸ n. chiefly derogatory a society in which the buying and selling of goods and services is the most important social and economic activity.

con•sum•er sov•er•eign•ty /kən'sōōmər 'säv(ə)rintē/ ▸ n. the situation in an economy where the desires and needs of consumers control the output of producers.

con•sump•tion /kən'səm(p)sHən/ ▸ n. the purchase and use of goods and services by the public: *an article for mass consumption.*
ORIGIN late Middle English: from Latin *consumptio(n-)*, from the verb *consumere*, from *con-* 'altogether' + *sumere* 'to take up.'

con•tin•gen•cy fund /kən'tinjənsē ,fənd/ ▸ n. a reserve of money set aside to cover possible unforeseen future expenses.

USAGE: It is often recommended that people set aside enough money to cover six to eight months of living expenses.

con•tin•gent /kən'tinjənt/ ▸ adj. (of losses, liabilities, etc.) that can be anticipated to arise if a particular event occurs: *businesses need to be aware of their liabilities, both actual and contingent.*
ORIGIN late Middle English (in the sense 'of uncertain occurrence'): from Latin *contingere* 'befall,' from *con-* 'together with' + *tangere* 'to touch.'

con•trar•i•an /kən'tre(ə)rēən/ ▸ n. a person who opposes or rejects popular opinion, esp. in stock exchange dealing.

USAGE: A person who invests when the market is crashing and sells when the market is peaking is regarded as a **contrarian.**

con•trib•u•to•ry /kən'tribyə,tôrē/ ▸ adj. (of or relating to a pension or insurance plan) operated by means of a fund into which people pay: *contributory benefits.*

ORIGIN late Middle English (in the sense 'contributing to a fund'): from medieval Latin *contributorius*, from Latin *contribut-* 'added,' from *contribuere* 'bring together, add.'

con•trol ac•count /kən'trōl ə,kownt/ ▶ n. an account used to record the balances on a number of subsidiary accounts and to provide a cross-check on them.

con•trol•ler /kən'trōlər/ ▶ n. a person in charge of an organization's finances.

ORIGIN Middle English: from Anglo-Norman *contrerollour*, from *contreroller* 'keep a copy of a roll of accounts,' from medieval Latin *contrarotulare*, from *contrarotulus* 'copy of a roll,' from *contra* 'against' + *rotulus* 'a roll.' Compare with COMPTROLLER.

con•trol•ling in•ter•est /kən'trōliNG 'int(ə)rist/ ▶ n. the holding by one person or group of a majority of the stock of a business, giving the holder a means of exercising control: *the purchase of a controlling interest in a company in California.*

con•ver•sion fac•tor /kən'vərzHən ,fæktər/ ▶ n. the manufacturing cost of a product relative to the cost of raw materials.

con•vert /kən'vərt/ ▶ v. [trans.] change (money, stocks, or units in which a quantity is expressed) into others of a different kind.

DERIVATIVES **con•ver•sion n.**

ORIGIN Middle English: from Old French *convertir*, based on Latin *convertere* 'turn around,' from *con-* 'altogether' + *vertere* 'turn.'

con•vert•i•ble /kən'vərtəbəl/ ▶ adj. (of currency) able to be converted into other forms, esp. into gold or US dollars.

■ (of a bond or stock) able to be converted into ordinary or preference shares.

▶ n. (usu. **convertibles**) a convertible security.

ORIGIN late Middle English: from Old French, from Latin *convertibilis*, from *convertere* 'turn around' (see CONVERT).

co-op /'kō,äp/ ▶ n. informal a cooperative society, business, or enterprise.

ORIGIN mid 19th cent.: abbreviation of COOPERATIVE.

co•op•er•a•tion /kō,äpə'rāsʜən/ (also **co-op•er•a•tion**) ▶ n. the formation and operation of cooperatives.
ORIGIN late Middle English: from Latin *cooperatio(n-)*, from the verb *cooperari,* from *co-* 'together' + *operari* 'to work'; later reinforced by French *coopération* .

co•op•er•a•tive /kō'äp(ə)rəṯiv/ (also **co-op•er•a•tive**) ▶ adj. (of a farm, business, etc.) owned and run jointly by its members, with profits or benefits shared among them.
▶ n. a farm, business, or other organization that is owned and run jointly by its members, who share the profits or benefits.
ORIGIN early 17th cent.: from late Latin *cooperativus,* from Latin *cooperat-* 'worked together,' from the verb *cooperari* (see **COOPER-ATION**).

cor•ner /'kôrnər/ ▶ n. a position in which one dominates the supply of a particular commodity.
▶ v. [trans.] control (a market) by dominating the supply of a particular commodity: *whether they will **corner the market** in graphics software remains to be seen.*
■ establish a corner in (a commodity): *you cornered vanadium and made a killing.*
ORIGIN Middle English: from Anglo-Norman French, based on Latin *cornu* 'horn, tip, corner.'

Corp. ▶ abbr. ■ corporation: *IBM Corp.*

cor•po•rate /'kôrp(ə)rit/ ▶ adj. of or relating to a corporation, esp. a large company or group: *airlines are very keen on their corporate identity.*
■ (of a company or group of people) authorized to act as a single entity and recognized as such in law.
▶ n. a corporate company or group.
ORIGIN late 15th cent.: from Latin *corporatus,* past participle of *corporare* 'form into a body,' from *corpus, corpor-* 'body.'

cor•po•rate raid•er /'kôrp(ə)rit 'rādər/ ▶ n. a financier who makes a practice of making hostile takeover bids for companies, either to control their policies or to resell them for a profit.

cor•po•rate wel•fare bum /'kôrp(ə)rit 'welfe(ə)r ,bəm/ ▶ n. Canadian derogatory slang a business perceived to be exploiting tax loopholes, capital gains concessions, etc. or to be benefiting unduly from government subsidies or tax breaks. ■ a person who directs such a business.

ORIGIN coined by David Lewis.

cor•po•ra•tion /ˌkôrpəˈrāsHən/ (abbr.: **corp.** or **Corp.**) ▶ n. a company or group of people authorized to act as a single entity (legally a person) and recognized as such in law.

ORIGIN late Middle English: from late Latin *corporatio(n-)*, from Latin *corporare* 'combine in one body' (see CORPORATE).

cor•po•ra•tize /ˈkôrp(ə)rəˌtīz/ ▶ v. [trans.] convert (a state organization) into an independent commercial company.

cor•rec•tion /kəˈreksHən/ ▶ n. a temporary reversal in an overall trend of stock market prices, esp. a brief fall during an overall increase: *they're still looking for the market to go up and believe we are just going through a correction.*

ORIGIN Middle English: via Old French from Latin *correctio(n-)*, from *corrigere* 'make straight, bring into order,' from *cor-* 'together' + *regere* 'guide.'

cost ac•count•ing /ˈkôst əˌkowntiNG/ ▶ n. the recording of all the costs incurred in a business in a way that can be used to improve its management.

DERIVATIVES **cost ac•count•ant** n.

cost-ben•e•fit /ˈkôst ˌbenəfit/ ▶ adj. relating to or denoting a process that assesses the relation between the cost of an undertaking and the value of the resulting benefits: *a cost-benefit analysis.*

cost-ef•fec•tive /ˈkôst iˌfektiv/ ▶ adj. effective or productive in relation to its cost: *the most cost-effective way to invest in the stock market.*

cost of liv•ing /ˈkôst əv ˈliviNG/ ▶ n. the level of prices relating to a range of everyday items.

cost-of-liv•ing in•dex /ˈkôst əv ˈliviNG ˌindeks/ (abbr.: **CLI**) ▶ n. former term for CONSUMER PRICE INDEX.

cost-plus /ˈkôst ˈpləs/ ▶ adj. relating to or denoting a method of pricing a service or product in which a fixed profit factor is added to the costs.

cot•tage in•dus•try /ˈkätij ˌindəstrē/ ▶ n. a business or manufacturing activity carried on in a person's home.

coun•ter•of•fer /ˈkowntər͵ôfər; -͵äfər/ ▸ n. an offer made in response to another.

coun•ter•trade /ˈkowntər͵trād/ ▸ n. international trade by exchange of goods rather than by currency purchase.

coun•ter•vail•ing du•ty /ˈkowntər͵vāliNG ˈd(y)o͞otē/ ▸ n. an import tax imposed on certain goods in order to prevent dumping or counter export subsidies.

cou•pon /ˈk(y)o͞o͵pän/ ▸ n. a voucher entitling the holder to a discount off a particular product.

■ a detachable portion of a bond that is given up in return for a payment of interest.

ORIGIN early 19th cent. (denoting a detachable portion of a bond to be given up in return for payment of interest): from French, literally 'piece cut off,' from *couper* 'cut,' from Old French *colper* .

cou•pon bond /ˈk(y)o͞opän ͵bänd/ ▸ n. an investment bond on which interest is paid by coupons.

cov•er•age /ˈkəv(ə)rij/ ▸ n. the amount of protection given by an insurance policy.

CP ▸ abbr. commercial paper.

CPA ▸ abbr. certified public accountant.

CPI ▸ abbr. consumer price index.

CPP ▸ abbr. Canadian Canada Pension Plan.

cr ▸ abbr. ■ credit. ■ creditor.

cre•a•tive ac•count•an•cy /krēˈātiv əˈkownt(ə)nsē/ (also **cre•a•tive ac•count•ing**) ▸ n. informal the exploitation of loopholes in financial regulation in order to gain advantage or present figures in a misleadingly favorable light.

cred•it /ˈkredit/ (abbr.: **cr**) ▸ n. 1 the ability of a customer to obtain goods or services before payment, based on the trust that payment will be made in the future: *I've got unlimited credit.*

■ the money lent or made available under such an arrangement: *the bank refused to extend their credit.*

2 an entry recording a sum received, listed on the right-hand side or column of an account. The opposite of DEBIT.

■ a payment received: *you need to record debits or credits made to your account.*

▸v. (**cred•it•ed, cred•it•ing**) [trans.] (often **be credited**) add (an amount of money) to an account: *this deferred tax can be credited to the profit and loss account.*

PHRASES **on credit** with an arrangement to pay later.
DERIVATIVES **cred•it•less adj.**
ORIGIN mid 16th cent. (originally in the senses 'belief,' 'credibility'): from French *crédit*, probably via Italian *credito* from Latin *creditum*, neuter past participle of *credere* 'believe, trust.'

cred•it an•a•lyst /'kredit ˌænl-ist/ ▸n. a person employed to assess the credit rating of people or companies.

cred•it bu•reau /'kredit ˌbyo͞orō/ ▸n. a company that collects information relating to the credit ratings of individuals and makes it available to credit card companies, financial institutions, etc.

cred•it card /'kredit ˌkärd/ ▸n. a small plastic card issued by a bank, business, etc., allowing the holder to purchase goods or services on credit.

cred•i•tor /'kreditər/ ▸n. a person or company to whom money is owed.

cred•it rat•ing /'kredit ˌrātiNG/ ▸n. an estimate of the ability of a person or organization to fulfill their financial commitments, based on previous dealings.
■ the process of assessing this.

cred•it score /'kredit ˌskôr/ ▸n. a number assigned to a person that indicates to lenders their capacity to repay a loan.

USAGE: A **credit score** is based on factors such as a person's record for making timely payments, total debt, and credit history. It influences the person's ability to obtain a loan and the cost of the loan. This score is often called a **FICO score,** because most companies calculate the number using software from Fair Isaac Corporation. See note at **FICO SCORE.**

cred•it un•ion /'kredit ˌyo͞onyən/ ▸n. a nonprofit-making money cooperative whose members can borrow from pooled deposits at low interest rates.

cred•it•worth•y /'kredit₁wərT͟Hē/ ▸adj. (of a person or company) considered suitable to receive credit, esp. because of having been reliable in paying money back in the past.

cross own•er•ship /'krôs ˌōnərˌSHip/ ▶ n. the ownership by one corporation of different companies with related interests or commercial aims.

cross-rate /'krôs ˌrāt/ ▶ n. an exchange rate between two currencies computed by reference to a third currency, usually the US dollar.

cross-sell /'krôs 'sel/ ▶ v. (past and past part. **cross-sold**) [trans.] sell (a different product or service) to an existing customer: *their database is used to cross-sell financial services.*

cross-sub•si•dize /'krôs 'səbsiˌdīz/ ▶ v. [trans.] subsidize (a business or activity) out of the profits of another business or activity.

Crown cor•po•ra•tion /'krown kôrpəˌrāSHən/ ▶ n. Canadian a corporation owned by the federal or provincial governments, such as the Canadian Broadcasting Corporation, Canada Post, etc.

crunch /krənCH/ ▶ n. a severe shortage of money or credit: *the Fed would do what it could to ease America's credit crunch.*
ORIGIN early 19th cent.: variant of 17th-cent. *cranch* (probably imitative), by association with *crush* and *munch.*

CSB ▶ abbr. Canadian Canada Savings Bond.

ct. ▶ abbr. cent.

cum div•i•dend /'ko͞om 'diviˌdend; 'kəm/ ▶ adv. (of share purchases) with a dividend about to be paid.

cu•mu•la•tive pre•ferred stock /'kyo͞omyələtiv pri'fərd 'stäk/ ▶ n. a preferred stock whose annual fixed-rate dividend, if it cannot be paid in any year, accrues until it can and is paid before common dividends.

curb mar•ket /'kərb ˌmärkit/ ▶ n. a market for selling shares not dealt with on the normal stock exchange.

cur•rent as•sets /'kərənt 'æsits/ ▶ plural n. cash and other assets that are expected to be converted to cash within a year.

cur•rent cost ac•count•ing /'kərənt 'kôst əˌkowntiNG/ ▶ n. a method of accounting in which assets are valued on the basis of their current replacement cost, and increases in their value as a result of inflation are excluded from calculations of profit.

cur•rent li•a•bil•i•ties /'kərənt ˌlīə'bilitēz/ ▶ plural n. amounts due to be paid to creditors within a year.

cut•back /ˈkətˌbæk/ ▸ n. an act or instance of reducing something, typically expenditures: *cutbacks in defense spending.*

cut•o•ver /ˈkətˌōvər/ ▸ n. a rapid transition from one phase of a business enterprise or project to another.

c.w.o. ▸ abbr. cash with order.

D

day•book /ˈdāˌbo͝ok/ ▶ n. an account book in which a day's transactions are entered for later transfer to a ledger.

day shift /ˈdā ˌSHift/ ▶ n. a period of time worked during the daylight hours in a hospital, factory, etc., as opposed to the night shift.

■ [treated as sing. or pl.] the employees who work during this period.

day•work /ˈdāˌwərk/ ▶ n. casual work paid for on a daily basis.

dead /ded/ ▶ adj. (of money) not financially productive.

ORIGIN Old English *dēad*, of Germanic origin: related to Dutch *dood* and German *tot* .

dead cat bounce /ˈded ˈkæt ˌbowns/ ▶ n. informal a temporary recovery in share prices after a substantial fall, caused by speculators buying in order to cover their positions.

dead weight /ˈded ˈwāt/ (also **dead•weight**) ▶ n. losses incurred because of the inefficient allocation of resources, esp. through taxation or restriction.

deal•er /ˈdēlər/ ▶ n. a person or business that buys and sells goods: *a car dealer.*

■ a person who buys and sells shares, securities, or other financial assets as a principal (rather than as a broker or agent).

dear /dir/ ▶ adj. (**dear•er, dear•est**) (of money) available as a loan only at a high rate of interest.

ORIGIN Old English *dēore*, of Germanic origin; related to Dutch *dier* 'beloved,' also to Dutch *duur* and German *teuer* 'expensive.'

death tax /ˈdeTH ˌtæks/ ▶ n. 1 another term for ESTATE TAX.

2 another term for INHERITANCE TAX.

de•ben•ture /diˈbenCHər/ ▶ n. (also **de•ben•ture bond**) an unsecured loan certificate issued by a company, backed by general credit rather than by speciifed assets.

ORIGIN late Middle English (denoting a voucher issued by a royal household, giving the right to claim payment for goods or services): from Latin *debentur* 'are owing' (from *debere* 'owe'), used as the first word of a certificate recording a debt. The current sense dates from the mid 19th cent.

deb•it /'debit/ (abbr.: **dr.**) ▸ n. an entry recording an amount owed, listed on the left-hand side or column of an account. The opposite of CREDIT.

■ a payment made or owed.

▸v. (**deb•it•ed, deb•it•ing**) [trans.] (usu. **be debited**) (of a bank or other financial organization) remove (an amount of money) from a customer's account, typically as payment for services or goods: *$10,000 was debited from their account.*

■ remove an amount of money from (a bank account): *the tag on the rear window automatically activates the pump and debits any major credit card.*

ORIGIN late Middle English (in the sense 'debt'): from French *débit*, from Latin *debitum* 'something owed' (see DEBT). The verb sense dates from the 17th cent.; the current noun sense from the late 18th cent.

deb•it card /'debit ˌkärd/ ▸ n. a card issued by a bank allowing the holder to transfer money electronically to another bank account when making a purchase.

debt /det/ ▸ n. something, typically money, that is owed or due: *I paid off my debts* | *a way to reduce Third World debt.*

■ the state of owing money: *the firm is heavily in debt.*

ORIGIN Middle English *dette*: from Old French, based on Latin *debitum* 'something owed,' past participle of *debere* 'owe.' The spelling change in English was by association with the Latin word.

debt coun•se•lor /'det ˌkowns(ə)lər/ ▸ n. a person who offers professional advice on methods of debt repayment.

debt•or /'detər/ ▸ n. a person or institution that owes a sum of money.

debt se•cu•ri•ty /'det siˌkyo͞orité/ ▸ n. a negotiable or tradable liability or loan.

debt swap /'det ˌswäp/ (also **debt-for-na•ture swap**) ▸ n. a transaction in which a foreign exchange debt owed by a developing country is transferred to another organization on the condition that the country use local currency for a designated purpose, usually environmental protection.

dec•i•mal•ize /'desəməˌlīz/ ▸ v. [trans.] convert (a system of coinage) to a decimal system.

dec•la•ra•tion /ˌdeklə'rāsHən/ ▸ n. a listing of goods, property, income, etc., subject to duty or tax.

ORIGIN late Middle English: from Latin *declaratio(n-)*, from *declarare* 'make quite clear,' from *de-* 'thoroughly' + *clarare* 'make clear' (from *clarus* 'clear').

de•con•trol /ˌdēkən'trōl/ ▸ v. (**de•con•trolled, de•con•trol•ling**) [trans.] release (a commodity, market, etc.) from controls or restrictions: *whether gas prices should be totally decontrolled.*

de•duct•i•ble /di'dəktəbəl/ ▸ adj. able to be deducted, esp. from taxable income or tax to be paid: *child-care vouchers will be deductible expenses for employers.*

▸ n. (in an insurance policy) a specified amount of money that the insured must pay before an insurance company will pay a claim: *a traditional insurance policy with a low deductible.*

de•duc•tion /di'dəksHən/ ▸ n. the action of deducting or subtracting something: *the dividend will be paid without deduction of tax.*

■ an amount that is or may be deducted from something, esp. from taxable income or tax to be paid: *tax deductions.*

ORIGIN late Middle English: from Latin *deductio(n-)*, from the verb *deducere*, from *de* 'down' + *ducere* 'lead.'

deep-dis•count /'dēp 'disˌkownt/ ▸ adj. denoting financial securities carrying a low rate of interest relative to prevailing market rates and issued at a discount to their redemption value, thus mainly providing capital gain rather than income.

■ heavily discounted; greatly reduced in price: *deep-discount pricing has kept airfares affordable.*

de•ferred an•nu•i•ty /di'fərd ə'n(y)o͞oitē/ ▸ n. an annuity that commences only after a lapse of a specified time after the final purchase premium has been paid.

de•fi•cien•cy pay•ment /di'fisHənsē ˌpāmənt/ ▶ n. a payment made, typically by a government body, to cover a financial deficit incurred in the course of an activity such as farming or education.

def•i•cit /'defəsit/ ▶ n. the amount by which something, esp. a sum of money, is too small.

■ an excess of expenditure or liabilities over income or assets in a given period: *an annual operating deficit | the budget will remain in deficit.*

ORIGIN late 18th cent.: via French from Latin *deficit* 'it is lacking,' from the verb *deficere* 'desert' or 'fail,' from *de-* (expressing reversal) + *facere* 'do.'

def•i•cit fi•nanc•ing /'defəsit ˌfīnænsiNG/ ▶ n. government funding of spending by borrowing.

def•i•cit spend•ing /'defəsit ˌspendiNG/ ▶ n. government spending, in excess of revenue, of funds raised by borrowing rather than from taxation.

de•flate /di'flāt/ ▶ v. bring about a general reduction of price levels in (an economy).

ORIGIN late 19th cent.: from *de-* (expressing reversal) + *-flate* (as in *inflate*).

de•fla•tion /di'flāsHən/ ▶ n. reduction of the general level of prices in an economy.

ORIGIN late 19th cent. (in the sense 'release of air from something inflated'): from DEFLATE.

de•fla•tion•ar•y /di'flāsHəˌnerē/ ▶ adj. of, characterized by, or tending to cause economic deflation.

de•gres•sive /di'gresiv/ ▶ adj. (of taxation) at successively lower rates on lower amounts.

ORIGIN early 20th cent.: from Latin *degress-* 'descended' (from the verb *degredi*, from *de-* 'down' + *gradi* 'walk') + *-ive* .

de-in•dex /dē 'in,deks/ ▶ v. [trans.] end the indexation to inflation of (pensions or other benefits).

de•in•dus•tri•al•i•za•tion /ˌdē-in,dəstrēəli'zāsHən/ ▶ n. decline in industrial activity in a region or economy: *severe deindustrialization with substantial job losses.*

de•lin•quen•cy /di'liNGkwənsē/ ▸ **n.** (pl. **de•lin•quen•cies**) a failure to pay an outstanding debt.

ORIGIN mid 17th cent.: from ecclesiastical Latin *delinquentia*, from Latin *delinquent-* 'offending' (see DELINQUENT).

de•lin•quent /di'liNGkwənt/ ▸ **adj.** in arrears: *delinquent accounts*.

ORIGIN late 15th cent.: from Latin *delinquent-* 'offending,' from the verb *delinquere*, from *de-* 'away' + *linquere* 'to leave.'

de•list /dē'list/ ▸ **v.** [trans.] remove (a security) from the official register of a stock exchange: *the stock collapsed and was delisted.*

■ remove (a product) from the list of those sold by a particular retailer.

USAGE: The New York Stock Exchange will **delist** a company if it fails to meet any of several criteria, for example, if the company's average monthly trading volume falls below 100,000 shares or if its average global market capitalization and stockholders' equity fall below $50 million. The NASDAQ will **delist** a company for a number of reasons, for example, if stockholders' equity falls below $10 million or if the minimum bid price of the company's shares falls below $1.

de•liv•er•a•ble /di'livərəbəl/ ▸ **n.** (usu. **deliverables**) a thing able to be provided, esp. as a product of a development process.

de•mand /di'mænd/ ▸ **n.** the desire of purchasers, consumers, clients, employers, etc., for a particular commodity, service, or other item: *a recent slump in demand | a demand for specialists.*

ORIGIN Middle English: from Old French *demande* (noun), *demander* (verb), from Latin *demandare* 'hand over, entrust' (in medieval Latin 'demand'), from *de-* 'formally' + *mandare* 'to order.'

de•mand curve /di'mænd ˌkərv/ ▸ **n.** a graph showing how the demand for a commodity or service varies with changes in its price.

de•mand de•pos•it /di'mænd di,päzit/ ▸ **n.** a deposit of money that can be withdrawn without prior notice.

de•mand draft /di'mænd ˌdræft/ ▸ **n.** a financial draft payable on demand. Also called DEMAND NOTE.

de•mand-led /di'mænd ˌled/ (also **de•mand-driv•en**) ▸ **adj.** caused or determined by demand from consumers or clients.

de•mand note /di'mænd ‚nōt/ ▸ n. 1 a formal request for payment.
2 another term for DEMAND DRAFT.

de•mand pull /di'mænd ‚pool/ ▸ adj. relating to or denoting inflation caused by an excess of demand over supply.

de•ma•te•ri•al•ize /‚dēmə'ti(ə)rēə‚līz/ ▸ v. [trans.] [usu. as adj.] (**dematerialized**) replace (physical records or certificates) with a paperless computerized system: *a dematerialized stock lending service.*

dem•o•graph•ics /‚demə'græfiks/ ▸ plural n. statistical data relating to the population and particular groups within it: *the demographics of book buyers.*
DERIVATIVES **dem•o•graph•ic adj.**

USAGE: Some experts believe they can predict the direction of the stock market using demographic trends. Harry Dent (*www.harrydent.com*), for example, believes that **demographics** are the key to long-term market forecasting.

de•mon•e•tize /dē'mäni‚tīz; -'mən-/ ▸ v. [trans.] (usu. **be demonetized**) deprive (a coin or precious metal) of its status as money.
ORIGIN mid 19th cent.: from French *démonétiser*, from *dé-* (expressing reversal) + Latin *moneta* 'money.'

de•mo•nop•o•lize /‚dēmə'näpə‚līz/ ▸ v. [trans.] introduce competition into (a market or economy) by privatizing previously nationalized assets.

de•mu•tu•al•ize /dē'myōoCHōoə‚līz/ ▸ v. [trans.] change (a mutual organization such as a savings and loan association) to one of a different kind.
DERIVATIVES **de•mu•tu•al•i•za•tion n.**

de•nom•i•nate /di'nämə‚nāt/ ▸ v. [trans.] (**be denominated**) (of sums of money) be expressed in a specified monetary unit: *the borrowings were denominated in US dollars.*
ORIGIN late Middle English: from Latin *denominat-* 'named,' from the verb *denominare*, from *de-* 'away, formally' + *nominare* 'to name' (from *nomen, nomin-* 'name').

de•nom•i•na•tion /di‚nämə'nāsHən/ ▸ n. the face value of a banknote, a coin, or a postage stamp: *a hundred dollars or so, in small denominations.*

ORIGIN late Middle English: from Latin *denominatio(n-)*, from the verb *denominare* (see DENOMINATE).

de•ple•tion al•low•ance /di'plēsHən ə͵lowəns/ ▸ n. a tax concession allowable to a company whose normal business activities (in particular oil extraction) reduce the value of its own assets.

de•pos•it /di'päzit/ ▸ n. **1** a sum of money placed or kept in a bank account, usually to gain interest.

■ an act of placing money in a bank account: *I'd like to make a deposit.*

2 a sum payable as a first installment on the purchase of something or as a pledge for a contract, the balance being payable later: *we've saved enough for a deposit on a house.*

■ a returnable sum payable on the rental of something, to cover any possible loss or damage.

▸ v. (**de•pos•it•ed, de•pos•it•ing**) [trans.] pay (a sum of money) into a bank account: *the money is deposited with a bank.*

■ pay (a sum) as a first installment or as a pledge for a contract: *I had to deposit 10% of the price of the house.*

ORIGIN late 16th cent.: from Latin *depositum* (noun), medieval Latin *depositare* (verb), both from Latin *deposit-* 'laid aside,' from the verb *deponere* .

de•pos•i•tar•y /di'päzi͵terē/ (also **de•pos•i•to•ry** /di'päsi͵tôrē/) ▸ adj. (of a share or receipt) representing a share in a foreign company.

ORIGIN early 17th cent.: from late Latin *depositarius*, from the verb *deponere* 'put away.'

USAGE: The **depositary** share or receipt is traded on the stock exchange of the investor's country rather than the actual share, which is deposited in a foreign bank. It entitles the holder to all dividends and capital gains on the actual share, but relieves the purchaser of the sometimes onerous task of buying the stock on a foreign exchange.

de•pos•i•tor /di'päzitər/ ▸ n. a person who keeps money in a bank account.

de•pre•ci•ate /di'prēsHē͵āt/ ▸ v. [intrans.] diminish in value over a period of time: *the pound is expected to depreciate against the dollar.*

■ [trans.] reduce the recorded value in a company's books of (an asset) each year over a predetermined period: *the computers would be depreciated at 50 percent per annum.*

ORIGIN late Middle English: from late Latin *depreciat-* 'lowered in price, undervalued,' from the verb *depreciare*, from Latin *de-* 'down' + *pretium* 'price.'

de•pre•ci•a•tion /di͵prēsHēˈāsHən/ ▶ n. a reduction in the value of an asset with the passage of time, due in particular to wear and tear.

■ decrease in the value of a currency relative to other currencies: *depreciation leads to losses for nondollar-based investors | a currency depreciation.*

de•press /diˈpres/ ▶ v. [trans.] reduce the level or strength of activity in (an economic system or sector): *fear of inflation in America depressed bond markets.*

ORIGIN late Middle English: from Old French *depresser*, from late Latin *depressare*, frequentative of *deprimere* 'press down.'

de•pres•sant /diˈpresənt/ ▶ n. an influence that depresses economic activity: *higher taxation is a depressant.*

de•pres•sion /diˈpresHən/ ▶ n. a long and severe recession in an economy or market: *the depression in the housing market.* ■ **(the Depression** or **the Great Depression)** the financial and industrial slump of 1929 and subsequent years.

ORIGIN late Middle English: from Latin *depressio(n-)*, from *deprimere* 'press down' (see **DEPRESS**).

de•riv•a•tive /diˈrivətiv/ ▶ adj. (of a financial product) having a value deriving from an underlying variable asset: *equity-based derivative products.*

▶ n. (often **derivatives**) an arrangement or instrument (such as a futures contract, an option, or a warrant) whose value derives from and is dependent on the value of an underlying asset.

ORIGIN late Middle English (in the adjective sense 'having the power to draw off'): from French *dérivatif, -ive*, from Latin *derivativus*, from *derivare*, from *de-* 'down, away' + *rivus* 'brook, stream.'

de•rived de•mand /diˈrīvd diˈmænd/ ▶ n. a demand for a commodity, service, etc., that is a consequence of the demand for something else.

de•skill /dēˈskil/ ▸ v. [trans.] reduce the level of skill required to carry out (a job): *advances in technology had deskilled numerous working-class jobs.*
■ make the skills of (a worker) obsolete.

de•val•ue /dēˈvælyo͞o/ ▸ v. (**de•val•ues, de•val•ued, de•val•u•ing**) [trans.] (often **be devalued**) reduce the official value of (a currency) in relation to other currencies: *the dinar was devalued by 20 percent.*
DERIVATIVES **de•val•u•a•tion** n.

de•vel•op•ing coun•try /diˈveləpiNG ˈkəntrē/ ▸ n. a poor agricultural country that is seeking to become more advanced economically and socially.

dig•it•al cash /ˈdijitl ˈkæSH/ (also **dig•i•tal mon•ey**) ▸ n. money that may be transferred electronically from one party to another during a transaction. Also called E-CASH.

di•lute /diˈlo͞ot; dī-/ ▸ v. [trans.] (often **be diluted**) reduce the value of (a shareholding) by issuing more shares in a company without increasing the values of its assets.
ORIGIN mid 16th cent.: from Latin *dilut-* ‘washed away, dissolved,’ from the verb *diluere* .

di•lu•tion /diˈlo͞oSHən; dī-/ ▸ n. a reduction in the value of a shareholding due to the issue of additional shares in a company without an increase in assets.

dir. ▸ abbr. director.

di•rect la•bor /dəˈrekt ˈlābər; dī-/ ▸ n. **1** labor involved in production rather than administration, maintenance, and other support services. **2** labor employed by the authority commissioning the work, not by a contractor.

di•rect mail /dəˈrekt ˈmāl; dī-/ ▸ n. unsolicited advertising sent to prospective customers through the mail.
DERIVATIVES **di•rect mail•ing** n.

USAGE: **Direct mail** accounted for more than 20% of the volume of mail delivered by the US Postal Service in 2002, up from 15% in 1972.

di•rect mar•ket•ing /də'rekt 'märki̯tiNG; dī-/ ▶ n. the business of selling products or services directly to the public, e.g., by mail order or telephone selling, rather than through retailers.

di•rec•tor /də'rektər; dī-/ (abbr.: **dir.**) ▶ n. a member of the board of people that manages or oversees the affairs of a business.

ORIGIN late Middle English: from Anglo-Norman French *directour*, from late Latin *director* 'governor,' from *dirigere* 'to guide.'

di•rec•to•rate /də'rektərit; dī-/ ▶ n. the board of directors of a company.

di•rect tax /də'rekt 'tæks; dī-/ ▶ n. a tax, such as income tax, that is levied on the income or profits of the person who pays it, rather than on goods or services.

dirt•y mon•ey /'dərtē 'mənē/ ▶ n. money obtained unlawfully or immorally: *the bank was found to have been laundering dirty money.*

dis•count /'dis͵kownt/ ▶ n. a deduction from the usual cost of something, typically given for prompt or advance payment or to a special category of buyers: *many stores will offer a discount on bulk purchases.*

■ a percentage deducted from the face value of a bill of exchange or promissory note when it changes hands before the due date.

▶ v. [trans.] deduct an amount from (the usual price of something).

■ reduce (a product or service) in price: *merchandise that was deeply discounted, up to 50 percent.* [as adj.] (**discounted**) *discounted books.* ■ buy or sell (a bill of exchange) before its due date at less than its maturity value.

▶ adj. (of a store or business) offering goods for sale at discounted prices: *a discount drugstore chain.*

■ at a price lower than the usual one: *a discount flight.*

PHRASES **at a discount** below the nominal or usual price: *a plan that allows tenants to buy their homes at a discount.*

ORIGIN early 17th cent. (denoting a reduction in the amount or value of something): from obsolete French *descompte* (noun), *descompter* (verb), or (in commercial contexts) from Italian *(di)scontare*, both from medieval Latin *discomputare*, from Latin *dis-* (expressing reversal) + *computare* (from *com-* 'together' + *putare* 'to settle [an account]').

dis•count•ed cash flow /'dis₁kowntid 'kæsʜ ₁flō/ ▶ n. a method of assessing investments taking into account the expected accumulation of interest.

dis•count house /'dis₁kownt ₁hows/ ▶ n. another term for DISCOUNT STORE.

dis•count rate /'dis₁kownt ₁rāt/ ▶ n. 1 the minimum interest rate set by the Federal Reserve for lending to other banks. 2 a rate used for discounting bills of exchange.

dis•count store /'dis₁kownt ₁stôr/ ▶ n. a store that sells goods at less than the normal retail price. Also called DISCOUNT HOUSE.

dis•cre•tion•ar•y /dis'kresʜə₁nerē/ ▶ adj. denoting or relating to investment funds placed with a broker or manager who has discretion to invest them on the client's behalf: *discretionary portfolios.*

dis•cre•tion•ar•y in•come /dis'kresʜə₁nerē 'inkəm/ ▶ n. income remaining after deduction of taxes, other mandatory charges, and expenditure on living expenses.

dis•e•con•o•my /₁disi'känəmē/ ▶ n. (pl. **dis•e•con•o•mies**) an economic disadvantage such as an increase in cost arising from an increase in the size of an organization: *in an ideal world, these diseconomies of scale would be minimized.*

dis•e•qui•lib•ri•um /dis₁ēkwə'librēəm/ ▶ n. a loss or lack of equilibrium in relation to supply, demand, and prices.

dis•hon•or /dis'änər/ ▶ v. [trans.] refuse to accept or pay (a check or a promissory note).
ORIGIN Middle English: from Old French *deshonor* (noun), *deshonorer* (verb), based on Latin *honor* 'honor.'

dis•in•cor•po•rate /₁disin'kôrpə₁rāt/ ▶ v. [trans.] dissolve (a corporate body).
■ [intrans.] undergo this process.

dis•in•fla•tion /₁disin'flāsʜən/ ▶ n. reduction in the rate of inflation.
DERIVATIVES **dis•in•fla•tion•ar•y** adj.

dis•in•ter•me•di•a•tion /₁disintər₁mēdē'āsʜən/ ▶ n. reduction in the use of banks and savings institutions as intermediaries in the borrowing and investment of money, in favor of direct involvement in the securities market.

dis•in•vest /ˌdisin'vest/ ▸ v. [intrans.] withdraw or reduce an investment: *the oil industry began to disinvest, and oil share prices have fallen.*
DERIVATIVES **dis•in•vest•ment n.**

dis•pos•a•ble /dis'pōzəbəl/ ▸ adj. (chiefly of financial assets) readily available for the owner's use as required: *he made a mental inventory of his disposable assets.*

dis•pos•a•ble in•come /dis'pōzəbəl 'in‚kəm/ ▸ n. income remaining after deduction of taxes and other mandatory charges, available to be spent or saved as one wishes.

dis•sav•ing /di(s)'sāviNG/ ▸ n. the action of spending more than one has earned in a given period.
■ (**dissavings**) the excess amount spent.

dis•tressed /dis'trest/ ▸ adj. (of property) for sale, esp. below market value, due to mortgage foreclosure or because it is part of an insolvent estate.■ (of goods) for sale at unusually low prices or at a loss because of damage or previous use.

dis•tri•bu•tion /ˌdistrə'byooSHən/ ▸ n. the action or process of supplying goods to stores and other businesses that sell to consumers: *a manager has the choice of four types of distribution.*
ORIGIN late Middle English: from Latin *distributio(n-)*, from the verb *distribuere,* from *dis-* 'apart' + *tribuere* 'assign.'

dis•tri•bu•tive /dis'tribyəṯiv/ ▸ adj. concerned with the supply of goods to stores and other businesses that sell to consumers: *transportation and distributive industries.*
ORIGIN late Middle English: from Old French *distributif, -ive* or late Latin *distributivus,* from Latin *distribut-* 'divided up,' from the verb *distribuere* (see DISTRIBUTION).

dis•trib•u•tor /dis'tribyəṯər/ (abbr.: **distr.**) ▸ n. an agent who supplies goods to stores and other businesses that sell to consumers: *a wholesale liquor distributor | the movie's distributor booked the film into theaters.*

dis•u•til•i•ty /ˌdisyoo'tiliṯē/ ▸ n. (pl. **dis•u•til•i•ties**) the adverse or harmful effects associated with a particular economic activity or process, esp. when carried out over a long period.

di•ver•si•fy /di'vərsəˌfī; dī-/ ▸ v. (**di•ver•si•fies, di•ver•si•fied**) [intrans.] (of a company) enlarge or vary its range of products or field of operation: *the company expanded rapidly and* ***diversified into*** *computers.*

■ [as adj.] (**diversified**) enlarge or vary the range of products or the field of operation of (a company): *the rise of the diversified corporation.* ■ [trans.] spread (investment) over several enterprises, asset categories, industries, or geographical regions in order to reduce the risk of loss: *prudent investors should diversify their portfolios.*

DERIVATIVES **di•ver•si•fi•ca•tion n.**

ORIGIN late Middle English (in the sense 'show diversity'): via Old French from medieval Latin *diversificare* 'make dissimilar,' from Latin *diversus*, past participle of *divertere,* from *di-* 'aside' + *vertere* 'turn.'

di•vest /di'vest; dī-/ ▸ **v.** [intrans.] rid oneself of something that one no longer wants or requires, such as a business interest or investment: *it appears easier to carry on in the business than to divest* | *the government's policy of* ***divesting itself of*** *state holdings.*

ORIGIN early 17th cent.: alteration of *devest*, from Old French *desvestir*, from *des-* (expressing removal) + Latin *vestire* (from *vestis* 'garment').

di•vest•i•ture /di'vesti,CHər; -,CHo͝or; dī-/ (also **di•ves•ture** /di'vesCHər; -CHo͝or; dī-/, **di•vest•ment** /di'vestmənt; dī-/) ▸ **n.** the action or process of selling off subsidiary business interests or investments: *the divestiture of state-owned assets.*

ORIGIN early 17th cent.: from medieval Latin *divestit-* 'divested' (from the verb *divestire*) + *-ure* .

div•i•dend /'divi,dend/ ▸ **n.** a sum of money paid regularly (typically quarterly) by a company to its shareholders out of its profits (or reserves).

■ a payment divided among a number of people, e.g., members of a cooperative or creditors of an insolvent estate. ■ an individual's share of a dividend.

ORIGIN late 15th cent. (in the general sense 'portion, share'): from Anglo-Norman French *dividende*, from Latin *dividendum* 'something to be divided,' from the verb *dividere,* 'force apart, remove.'

div•i•dend cov•er•age /'divi,dend ,kəv(ə)rij/ ▸ **n.** the ratio of a company's dividends to its net income.

div•i•dend yield /'divi͵dend ͵yēld/ ▸ n. a dividend expressed as a percentage of a current share price.

di•vi•sion•al•ize /di'viZHǝnl͵īz/ ▸ v. [trans.] subdivide (a company or other organization) into a number of separate divisions: *a large divisionalized Western corporation.*

■ [intrans.] undergo this process.

DJIA ▸ abbr. Dow Jones Industrial Average.

dock•et /'däkit/ ▸ n. a document or label listing the contents of a package or delivery.

▸ v. (**dock•et•ed, dock•et•ing**) [trans.] (usu. **be docketed**) mark (goods or a package) with a document or label listing the contents. ORIGIN late 15th cent.: origin unclear.

dol•lar ar•e•a /'dälǝr ͵e(ǝ)rēǝ/ ▸ n. the area of the world in which currency is linked to the US dollar.

dol•lar gap /'dälǝr ͵gæp/ ▸ n. the amount by which a country's import trade with the dollar area exceeds the corresponding export trade.

dol•lar•i•za•tion /͵dälǝrǝ'zāSHǝn/ (also **dol•lar•i•sa•tion**) ▸ n. **1** the process of aligning a country's currency with the US dollar.

2 the dominating effect of the US on the economy of a country.

dom•i•cile /'dämǝ͵sīl; -sil; 'dō-/ (also **dom•i•cil** /'dämǝsil; 'dō-/) ▸ n. the place at which a company or other body is registered, esp. for tax purposes.

ORIGIN late Middle English: via Old French from Latin *domicilium* 'dwelling,' from *domus* 'home.'

dou•ble-en•try /'dǝbǝl 'entrē/ ▸ adj. denoting a system of bookkeeping in which each transaction is entered as a debit in one account and a credit in another.

dou•ble in•dem•ni•ty /'dǝbǝl in'demnit̬ē/ ▸ n. provision for payment of double the face amount of an insurance policy under certain conditions, e.g., when death occurs as a result of an accident.

dou•ble time /'dǝbǝl 'tīm/ ▸ n. a rate of pay equal to double the standard rate, sometimes paid for working on holidays or outside normal working hours.

Dow /dow/ short for **DOW JONES INDUSTRIAL AVERAGE**: *the Dow fell sharply that summer.*

Dow Jones In•dus•tri•al Av•er•age /'dow 'jōnz in'dǝstrēǝl ͵æv(ǝ)rij/

(also **Dow Jones Av•er•age**) (abbr. **DJIA**) an index of figures indicating the relative price of shares on the New York Stock Exchange, based on the average price of selected stocks.

ORIGIN from the name of *Dow Jones & Co, Inc.*, a financial news agency founded by Charles H. *Dow* (1851–1902) and Edward D. *Jones* (*c*.1855–1920), American economists whose company compiled the first average of US stock prices in 1884.

down•mar•ket /downmarket/ (also **down-market**) ▶ adj. & adv. toward or relating to the cheaper or less prestigious sector of the market; downscale: [as adj.] *an interview for the downmarket tabloids* | [as adv.] *competition threatens to drive broadcasters further downmarket.*

down pay•ment /'down 'pāmənt/ ▶ n. an initial payment made when something is bought on credit.

down•side /'down͵sīd/ ▶ n. a downward movement of share prices: [often as adj.] *each fund aims to reduce the downside risk by using futures and options.*

down•turn /'down͵tərn/ (also **down•swing**) ▶ n. a decline in economic, business, or other activity: *a downturn in the housing market.*

dr. ▶ abbr. debit (formerly representing 'debtor').

draft /dræft/ ▶ n. a written order to pay a specified sum; a check.

ORIGIN mid 16th cent.: phonetic spelling of *draught* .

draw•down /'drô͵down/ ▶ n. a withdrawal of oil or other commodity from stocks.

draw•ee /͵drô'ē/ ▶ n. the person or organization, typically a bank, who must pay a draft or bill.

draw•er /'drô(ə)r/ ▶ n. a person who writes a check.

due date /'d(y)o͞o ͵dāt/ ▶ n. the date on which something falls due, esp. the payment of a bill.

dump /dəmp/ ▶ v. [trans.] send (goods unsalable in the home market) to a foreign market for sale at a low price: *other countries dump steel in the US at below-market prices.*

■ informal sell off (assets) rapidly: *investors dumped shares in scores of other consumer-goods firms.*

ORIGIN Middle English: perhaps from Old Norse; related to

Danish *dumpe* and Norwegian *dumpa* 'fall suddenly' (the original sense in English); in later use partly imitative; compare with THUMP.

du•op•o•ly /d(y)o͞o'äpəlē/ ▸ n. (pl. **du•op•o•lies**) a situation in which two suppliers dominate the market for a commodity or service.
ORIGIN 1920s: from *duo*, on the pattern of *monopoly*.

Dutch auc•tion /'dəCH 'ôksHən/ ▸ n. a method of selling in which the price is reduced until a buyer is found.

du•ti•a•ble /'d(y)o͞ot̬ēəbəl/ ▸ adj. liable to customs or other duties: *dutiable goods.*

du•ty /'d(y)o͞ot̬ē/ ▸ n. (pl. **du•ties**) a payment due and enforced by law or custom, in particular:
■ a payment levied on the import, export, manufacture, or sale of goods: *a 6 percent **duty on** imports | goods subject to excise duty.*
ORIGIN late Middle English: from Anglo-Norman French *duete*, from Old French *deu* 'owed,' based on Latin *debitus,* from *debere* 'owe.'

FIND YOUR
LATTE FACTOR™ AND
LEARN HOW COMPOUND
INTEREST WORKS
FOR YOU

Most of us don't really think about how we spend our money. If we do, we focus solely on the big items, while ignoring the small but steady expenses that drain away our cash. We don't think about what it costs us to earn our money, and we don't realize how much wealth we could have if, instead of wasting our income, we invested it.

By understanding the Latte Factor, you can change all that. The Latte Factor helps you to understand how small amounts of money, spent daily, can add up to a fortune spent over your lifetime, and how you can live a life of abundance by saving just a little money at a time from each paycheck, no matter how small your paycheck may be.

The Latte Factor is a concept that represents the amount that people spend every day on items such as a double nonfat latte, cigarettes, soft drinks, and candy bars, which they could instead save and invest for their future. If you purchased a $3.50 latte every day for a year, for example, you'd spend $1,260; over a decade, $12,600. If you invested that money at 10 percent over 10 years, you would wind up with $21,870.

You may wonder what good it will do to put aside a small fraction of your income, especially if your income isn't very large to begin with. But even if you earn what seems to you a modest salary, the amount of money that will pass through your hands during your lifetime is truly phenomenal. If you earn only $1,000 a month, for example, you will have made a total of $360,000 over the course of 30 years. If you earn $4,000 a month, you'll make more than $1.4 million over 30 years.

So, even though you may not receive much in each paycheck, you'll accumulate a substantial amount over time. And the sooner you start saving some of it, the less you'll need to put away. That's because of the magic of compound interest.

Albert Einstein called compound interest "the greatest mathematical discovery of all time." That's because compound interest helps you earn money not only on your own hard-earned savings, but also on the interest that your savings accumulate. In the first year, for example, you earn interest on your initial investment. The next year, you earn interest not only on your investment, but also on the interest that you've already earned.

Compound interest has all sorts of implications for saving money. For one thing, it favors people who start saving at an early age. If you start at the age of 25 to save $100 a month, and it earns interest at a rate of 4 percent, you'll accumulate $118,590 by the time you turn 65. If you wait till you're 40, you'll accumulate only $51,584.

Or let's say you invest $2,000 a year at the age of 14, at a 10 percent annual rate of return, and you set aside the same amount at the same return for the next four years. In other words, you put aside a total of $10,000 over five years, beginning when you're 14 and stopping when you're 18. If you don't invest another penny and your money keeps growing at the same rate of interest, you'll have almost $1.2 million by the time you're 65. By comparison, if you wait till you're 27 years old to start investing $2,000 a year, and you invest that amount every year at a 10 percent annual return for the next 38 years, when you turn 65, you'll have only $883,000. So start saving money as soon as you can.

Think about what you bought today that you could do

without tomorrow and start saving a few dollars. It might be something that you're in the habit of buying every day, like two double nonfat lattes and a couple of nonfat muffins. If you cut these out of your daily spending tomorrow, how much money would you save a day? How much would it save you a month? This is your personal Latte Factor, and it can quickly add up to a lot of money.

Even if you're older and you weren't fortunate enough to start saving when you were in your 20s or 30s, don't worry. The miracle of compound interest does not depend on how old you are. The only thing that matters is how long your money has been invested and at what rate it is growing.

Remember—the combined power of the Latte Factor and the miracle of compound interest is truly amazing. The only thing that can short-circuit it is the all-too-human tendency to procrastinate. Too many people put off doing what they know they should, and as a result, these two powerful tools never get the chance to work for them. Don't make this mistake.

E

---

ear•ly re•tire•ment /'ərlē ri'tīrmənt/ ▸ n. the practice of leaving employment before the statutory age, esp. on favorable financial terms.

earn /ərn/ ▸ v. [trans.] (of a person) obtain (money) in return for labor or services: *they earn $35 per hour* | *he now earns his living as a truck driver.*

■ (of capital invested) gain (money) as interest or profit.

ORIGIN Old English *earnian*, of West Germanic origin, from a base shared by Old English *esne* 'laborer.'

earned in•come /'ərnd 'in‚kəm/ ▸ n. money derived from paid work.

earnings per share /'ərniNGz pər 'sHe(ə)r/ ▸ a company's after-tax profit, minus payments to preferred shareholders and bondholders, divided by the total number of outstanding shares.

ease /ēz/ ▸ v. [intrans.] (of share prices, interest rates, etc.) decrease in value or amount: *these shares should be bought and tucked away for when interest rates ease.*

ORIGIN Middle English: from Old French *aise*, based on Latin *adjacens* 'lying close by,' present participle of *adjacere*. The verb is originally from Old French *aisier*, from the phrase *a aise* 'at ease'; in later use from the noun.

eas•y mon•ey /'ēzē 'mənē/ ▸ n. money available at relatively low interest.

EC ▸ abbr. European Community.

e-cash /'ē ‚kæsH/ ▸ n. electronic cash; money that may be transferred electronically from one party to another during a transaction. Also called DIGITAL CASH.

e•con•o•met•rics /i‚känə'metriks/ ▸ plural n. [treated as sing.] the branch of economics concerned with the use of mathematical methods (esp. statistics) in describing economic systems.

DERIVATIVES e•con•o•met•ric adj.; e•con•o•me•tri•cian n.; e•con•o•met•rist n.

ORIGIN 1930s: from ECONOMY, on the pattern of words such as *biometrics* and *cliometrics*.

ec•o•nom•ic /ˌekə'nämik; ˌēkə-/ ▶ adj. of or relating to economics or the economy: *the government's economic policy | pest species of great economic importance.*

■ justified in terms of profitability: *many organizations must become larger if they are to remain economic.* ■ requiring fewer resources or costing less money: *solar power may provide a more economic solution.* ■ (of a subject) considered in relation to trade, industry, and the creation of wealth: *economic history.*

ORIGIN late Middle English: via Old French and Latin from Greek *oikonomikos*, from *oikonomia* (see ECONOMY). Originally a noun, the word denoted household management or a person skilled in this, hence the early sense of the adjective (late 16th cent.) 'relating to household management.' Modern senses date from the mid 19th cent.

USAGE: **Economic** means 'concerning economics': *he's rebuilding a solid economic base for the country's future.* **Economical** is commonly used to mean 'thrifty, avoiding waste': *small cars should be inexpensive to buy and economical to run.*

ec•o•nom•i•cal /ˌekə'nämikəl; ˌēkə-/ ▶ adj. giving good value or service in relation to the amount of money, time, or effort spent: *a small, economical car.* ■ (of a person or lifestyle) careful not to waste money or resources. ■ using no more of something than is necessary.

USAGE: See usage at ECONOMIC.

ec•o•nom•i•cal•ly /ˌekə'nämik(ə)lē; ˌēkə-/ ▶ adv. 1 in a way that relates to economics or finance: *the region is important economically.* 2 in a way that involves careful use of money or resources: *the new building was erected as economically as possible.*

ec•o•nom•ic good /'ekə,nämik 'good; 'ēkə,nämik/ ▶ n. a product or service that can command a price when sold: *water is an economic good and should be treated as such.*

ec•o•nom•ics /ˌekəˈnämiks; ˌēkə-/ ▶ **plural n.** [often treated as sing.] the branch of knowledge concerned with the production, consumption, and transfer of wealth.

■ the condition of a region or group as regards material prosperity: *he is responsible for the island's modest economics.*

ORIGIN late 16th cent. (denoting the science of household management): from ECONOMIC + the plural suffix -*s*, originally on the pattern of Greek *ta oikonomika* (plural), the name of a treatise by Aristotle. Current senses date from the late 18th cent.

e•con•o•mist /iˈkänəmist/ ▶ n. an expert in economics.

ORIGIN late 16th cent. (originally in the Greek sense): from Greek *oikonomos* 'household manager' (see ECONOMY) + -*ist* . The current sense dates from the early 19th cent.

e•con•o•my /iˈkänəmē/ ▶ n. (pl. **e•con•o•mies**) the wealth and resources of a country or region, esp. in terms of the production and consumption of goods and services.

■ a particular system or stage of an economy: *a free-market economy* | *the less-developed economies.*

▶ **adj.** (of a product) offering the best value for the money: [in comb.] *an economy pack.*

■ designed to be economical to use: *an economy car.*

PHRASES **economy of scale** a proportionate saving in costs gained by an increased level of production. **economy of scope** a proportionate saving gained by producing two or more distinct goods, when the cost of doing so is less than that of producing each separately.

ORIGIN late 15th cent. (in the sense 'management of material resources'): from French *économie*, or via Latin from Greek *oikonomia* 'household management,' based on *oikos* 'house' + *nemein* 'manage.'

EDC ▶ **abbr.** Canadian Export Development Corporation.

EEC ▶ **abbr.** European Economic Community.

ef•fec•tive /iˈfektiv/ ▶ **adj.** assessed according to actual rather than face value: *an effective price of $176 million.*

ORIGIN late Middle English: from Latin *effectivus*, from *efficere* 'work out, accomplish,' from *ex-* 'out, thoroughly' + *facere* 'do, make.'

ef•fec•tive de•mand /i'fektiv di'mænd/ ▸ n. the level of demand that represents a real intention to purchase by people with the means to pay.

EFTPOS ▸ abbr. electronic funds transfer at point of sale (used to describe retail outlets that record information electronically).

EI ▸ abbr. Canadian employment insurance.

e•las•tic /i'læstik/ ▸ adj. (of demand or supply) sensitive to changes in price or income: *the labor supply is very elastic*.
ORIGIN mid 17th cent. (originally describing a gas in the sense 'expanding spontaneously to fill the available space'): from modern Latin *elasticus*, from Greek *elastikos* 'propulsive,' from *elaunein* 'to drive.'

em•bar•go /em'bärgō/ ▸ n. (pl. **em•bar•goes**) an official ban on trade or other commercial activity with a particular country: *an embargo on grain sales* | *the oil embargo of 1973*.
▸ v. (**em•bar•goes, em•bar•goed**) [trans.] (usu. **be embargoed**) impose an official ban on (trade or a country or commodity): *the country has been virtually embargoed by most of the noncommunist world.*
ORIGIN early 17th cent.: from Spanish, from *embargar* 'arrest,' based on Latin *in-* 'in, within' + *barra* 'a bar.'

e•mol•u•ment /i'mälyəmənt/ ▸ n. (usu. **emoluments**) formal a salary, fee, or profit from employment or office: *the directors' emoluments*.
ORIGIN late Middle English: from Latin *emolumentum*, originally probably 'payment to a miller for grinding grain,' from *emolere* 'grind up,' from *e-* (variant of *ex-*) 'out, thoroughly' + *molere* 'grind.'

em•ploy•ment in•sur•ance /em'ploimənt in,sHŏŏrəns/ (abbr.: **EI**) ▸ n. Canadian a federal government program providing payments to eligible unemployed people, funded by tax revenues and contributions by employers and workers.

USAGE: **Employment insurance** was formerly called unemployment insurance.

EMU ▶ abbr. European Monetary Union.

en•dorse /en'dôrs/ ▶ v. [trans.] sign (a check or bill of exchange) on the back to make it payable to someone other than the stated payee or to accept responsibility for paying it.

DERIVATIVES **en•dors•er** n.

ORIGIN late 15th cent. (in the sense 'write on the back of'; formerly also as *indorse*): from medieval Latin *indorsare*, from Latin *in-* 'in, on' + *dorsum* 'back.'

en•dorse•ment /en'dôrsmənt/ ▶ n. **1** a clause in an insurance policy detailing an exemption from or change in coverage. **2** the action of endorsing a check or bill of exchange.

en•dow•ment /en'dowmənt/ ▶ n. an income or form of property given or bequeathed to someone. ■ [usu. as adj.] a form of life insurance involving payment of a fixed sum to the insured person on a specified date, or to their estate should they die before this date: *an endowment policy.*

end us•er /'end ˌyo͞ozər/ (also **end-us•er**) ▶ n. the person who actually uses a particular product.

en•ter•prise zone /'entər,prīz ˌzōn/ ▶ n. an impoverished area in which incentives such as tax concessions are offered to encourage business investment and provide jobs for the residents.

en•tre•pre•neur /ˌäntrəprə'no͞or; -'nər/ ▶ n. a person who starts, organizes, and operates a business or businesses, taking on greater than normal financial risks in order to do so.

ORIGIN early 19th cent. (denoting the director of a musical institution): from French, from *entreprendre* 'undertake,' based on Latin *prendere, prehendere* 'to take.'

en•try-lev•el /'entrē ˌlevəl/ ▶ adj. at the lowest level in an employment hierarchy: *he was hired as an entry-level research assistant.*

EPOS ▶ abbr. electronic point of sale (used to describe retail outlets that record information electronically).

eps ▶ abbr. short for EARNINGS PER SHARE.

e•qui•lib•ri•um /ˌēkwə'librēəm; ˌekwə-/ ▶ n. a situation in which supply and demand are matched and prices stable: *certain consumer goods remain* **in equilibrium.**

ORIGIN early 17th cent. (in the sense 'well-balanced state of mind'): from Latin *aequilibrium*, from *aequi-* 'equal'+ *libra* 'balance.'

eq•ui•ty /'ekwitē/ ▶ n. (pl. **eq•ui•ties**) **1** the value of the shares issued by a company: *he owns 62 percent of the group's equity.*
■ **(equities)** stocks and shares that carry no fixed interest.
2 the value of a mortgaged property after deduction of charges against it.
ORIGIN Middle English: from Old French *equité*, from Latin *aequitas*, from *aequus* 'equal.'

es•ca•la•tor clause /'eskə‚lātər ‚klôz/ ▶ n. a clause in a contract that allows for an increase or a decrease in wages or prices under certain conditions.

es•crow /'eskrō/ ▶ n. a bond, deed, or other document kept in the custody of a third party, taking effect only when a specified condition has been fulfilled.
■ [usu. as adj.] a deposit or fund held in trust or as a security: *an escrow account.* ■ the state of being kept in custody or trust in this way: *the board holds funds in escrow.*
▶v. [trans.] place in custody or trust in this way.
ORIGIN late 16th cent.: from Old French *escroe* 'scrap, scroll,' from medieval Latin *scroda*, of Germanic origin; related to *shred* .

es•tate tax /i'stāt ‚tæks/ ▶ n. a tax levied on the net value of the estate of a deceased person before distribution to the heirs.

EU ▶ abbr. European Union.

eu•ro /'yo͞orō; 'yərō/ ▶ n. (also **Eu•ro**) the single European currency introduced into some of the European Union countries in 1999 as an alternative currency in noncash transactions, replacing national currencies in 2002.
ORIGIN independent usage of *euro-*.

Eu•ro•bond /'yo͞orə‚bänd; 'yər-/ ▶ n. an international bond issued in Europe or elsewhere outside the country in whose currency its value is stated (usually the US or Japan).

Eu•ro•cheque /'yo͞orō‚CHek; 'yər-/ ▶ n. a check issued under an arrangement between European banks that enables account holders from one country to use their checks in another.

Eu•ro•cur•ren•cy /'yo͞orō‚kərənsē; 'yər-/ ▶ n. (pl. **Eu•ro•cur•ren•**

cies) **1** a form of money held or traded outside the country in whose currency its value is stated (originally US dollars held in Europe). **2** [in sing.] a single currency for use by the member states of the European Union.

Eu•ro•dol•lar /'yo͞orō₁dälər; 'yər-/ ▶ n. a US dollar deposit held in Europe or elsewhere outside the US.

Eu•ro•mar•ket /'yo͞orō₁märkit; 'yər-/ ▶ n. **1** a financial market that deals with Eurocurrencies.
2 the European Union regarded as a single commercial or financial market.

Eu•ro•pe•an Com•mu•ni•ty /₁yo͞orə'pēən kə'myo͞oni̱tē; ₁yər-/ (abbr.: **EC**) ▶ n. an economic and political association of certain European countries, incorporated since 1993 in the European Union.

Eu•ro•pe•an Ec•o•nom•ic Com•mu•ni•ty /₁yo͞orə'pēən ₁ekə'nämik kə'myo͞oni̱tē; ₁ēkə'nämik; ₁yərə'pēən/ (abbr.: **EEC**) ▶ n. an institution of the European Union, an economic association of western European countries set up by the Treaty of Rome (1957). The original members were France, West Germany, Italy, Belgium, the Netherlands, and Luxembourg.

Eu•ro•pe•an Un•ion /'yo͞orə₁pēən 'yo͞onyən; 'yər-/ (abbr.: **EU**) ▶ n. an economic and political association of certain European countries as a unit with internal free trade and common external tariffs.

USAGE: The European Union was created on November 1, 1993, with the coming into force of the Maastricht Treaty. It encompasses the old European Community (EC) together with two intergovernmental 'pillars' for dealing with foreign affairs and with immigration and justice.

ex /eks/ ▶ prep. **1** (of goods) sold direct from: *carpet tiles offered at a special price, ex stock.*
2 without; excluding: *the discount and market price are ex dividend.*
ORIGIN mid 19th cent.: from Latin, 'out of.'

ex an•te /'eks 'æntē/ ▶ adj. & adv. based on forecasts rather than actual results: *this is an ex ante estimate of the variance.*
ORIGIN modern Latin, from Latin *ex* 'from, out of' + *ante* 'before.'

ex•change /iks'CHānj/ ▸ n. 1 the giving of money for its equivalent in the money of another country.

■ the fee or percentage charged for converting the currency of one country into that of another. ■ a system or market in which commercial transactions involving currency, shares, commodities, etc., can be carried out within or between countries.

2 a building or institution used for the trading of a particular commodity or commodities: *the New York Stock Exchange.*

ORIGIN late Middle English: from Old French *eschange* (noun), *eschangier* (verb), based on *changer* 'to change,' based on late Latin *cambiare,* from Latin *cambire* 'barter,' prob. of Celtic origin. The spelling was influenced by Latin *ex-* 'out, utterly.'

ex•change con•trol /iks'CHānj kən‚trōl/ ▸ n. a governmental restriction on the movement of currency between countries.

ex•change rate /iks'CHānj ‚rāt/ (also **rate of ex•change**) ▸ n. the value of one currency for the purpose of conversion to another.

ex•cise /'ek‚sīz/ ▸ n. [usu. as adj.] a tax levied on certain goods and commodities produced or sold within a country and on licenses granted for certain activities: *excise taxes on cigarettes.*

ORIGIN late 15th cent. (in the general sense 'a tax or toll'): from Middle Dutch *excijs, accijs,* perhaps based on Latin *accensare* 'to tax,' from *ad-* 'to' + *census* 'tax,' from *censere* 'assess.'

ex•clu•sive ec•o•nom•ic zone /ik'sklo͞osiv ‚ekə'nämik ‚zōn; ‚ēkə 'nämik/ ▸ n. an area of coastal water and seabed within a certain distance of a country's coastline, to which the country claims exclusive rights for fishing, drilling, and other economic activities.

ex div. ▸ abbr. ex dividend.

ex div•i•dend /‚eks 'divi‚dend/ (abbr.: **ex div., xd**) ▸ adj. & adv. (of stocks or shares) not including the next dividend.

ex•ec /eg'zek/ ▸ n. informal an executive: *top execs.*

ORIGIN late 19th cent.: abbreviation for **EXECUTIVE**.

ex•ec•u•tive /ig'zekyətiv; eg-/ ▸ n. a person with senior managerial responsibility in a business organization.

■ an executive committee or other body within an organization: *the union executive.*

ORIGIN late Middle English (as an adjective): from medieval Latin *executivus*, from *exsequi* 'carry out, punish, follow up,' from *ex-* 'out' + *sequi* 'follow.'

ex•emp•tion /ig'zem(p)sHən/ (also **per•son•al ex•emp•tion**) ▶ n. a direct reduction from gross income, set by the Internal Revenue Service.

ORIGIN late Middle English: from Old French, or from Latin *exemptio(n-)*, from *eximere* 'take out, free.'

ex•er•cise price /'eksər‚sīz ‚prīs/ ▶ n. the price per share at which the owner of a traded option is entitled to buy or sell the underlying security.

ex•pense /ik'spens/ ▶ n. the cost required for something; the money spent on something: *we had ordered suits* ***at great expense*** | *the committee does not expect members to be* ***put to*** *any* ***expense***.
■ (**expenses**) the costs incurred in the performance of one's job or a specific task, esp. one undertaken for another person: *his hotel and travel expenses.*
▶ v. (usu. **be expensed**) offset (an item of expenditure) as an expense against taxable income.

ORIGIN late Middle English: from Anglo-Norman French, alteration of Old French *espense*, from late Latin *expensa (pecunia)* '(money) spent,' from Latin *expendere* 'pay out,' from *ex-* 'out' + *pendere* 'weigh, pay.'

ex•pense ac•count /ik'spens ə‚kownt/ ▶ n. an arrangement under which sums of money spent in the course of business by an employee are later reimbursed by their employer.

ex•pi•ra•tion /‚ekspə'rāsHən/ ▶ n. the ending of the fixed period for which a contract is valid: *the expiration of the lease.*

ORIGIN late Middle English (denoting a vapor or exhalation): from Latin *exspiratio(n-)*, from the verb *exspirare* 'breathe out,' from *ex-* 'out' and *spirare* 'breathe.'

ex•port ▶ v. /ik'spôrt; 'ekspôrt/ [trans.] send (goods or services) to another country for sale: *we exported $16 million worth of mussels to Japan.*
▶ n. /'ekspôrt/ (usu. **exports**) a commodity, article, or service sold abroad: *wool and mohair were the principal exports.*
■ (**exports**) sales of goods or services to other countries, or the

revenue from such sales: *meat exports.* ■ the selling and sending out of goods or services to other countries: *the export of Western technology.* ■ [as adj.] of a high standard suitable for export: *high-grade export coal.*

ORIGIN late 15th cent.: from Latin *exportare,* from *ex-* 'out' + *portare* 'carry.'

ex•port sur•plus /'ekspôrt ˌsərpləs/ ▶ n. the amount by which the value of a country's exports exceeds that of its imports.

ex post /ˌeks 'pōst/ ▶ adj. & adv. based on actual results rather than forecasts: [as adj.] *the ex post trade balance.* | [as adv.] *the real-wage rate has fallen ex post.*

ORIGIN modern Latin, from *ex* 'from' and *post* 'after.'

ex•po•sure /ik'spōzʜər/ ▶ n. the action of placing oneself at risk of financial losses, e.g., through making loans, granting credit, or underwriting insurance.

ORIGIN early 17th cent.: from *expose,* on the pattern of words such as *enclosure.*

ex•ter•nal•i•ty /ˌekstər'nælitē/ ▶ n. (pl. **ex•ter•nal•i•ties**) a side effect or consequence of an industrial or commercial activity that affects other parties without this being reflected in the cost of the goods or services involved, such as the pollination of surrounding crops by bees kept for honey.

ex•tinc•tion /ik'stiNG(k)sʜən/ ▶ n. the wiping out of a debt.

ORIGIN late Middle English: from Latin *exstinctio(n-),* from *exstinguere* 'quench' (see EXTINGUISH).

ex•tin•guish /ik'stiNGgwisʜ/ ▶ v. [trans.] (often **be extinguished**) cancel (a debt) by full payment: *the debt was absolutely extinguished.*

ORIGIN mid 16th cent.: from Latin *exstinguere,* from *ex-* 'out' + *stinguere* 'quench.'

ex•traor•di•nar•y /ik'strôrdnˌerē; ˌekstrə'ôrdn-/ ▶ n. (pl. **ex traor•di• nar•ies**) (usu. **extraordinaries**) an item in a company's accounts not arising from its normal activities.

ORIGIN late Middle English: from Latin *extraordinarius,* from *extra ordinem* 'outside the normal course of events.'

F

---

face val•ue /'fās ‚vælyo͞o/ ▶ n. the value printed or depicted on a coin, banknote, postage stamp, ticket, etc., esp. when less than the actual or intrinsic value.

fac•tor /'fæktər/ ▶ n. a business agent; a merchant buying and selling on commission.

■ a company that buys a manufacturer's invoices at a discount and takes responsibility for collecting the payments due on them.

▶ v. [trans.] sell (one's receivable debts) to a factor.

ORIGIN late Middle English (meaning 'doer, perpetrator,' also in the Scots sense 'agent'): from French *facteur* or Latin *factor*, from *fact-* 'done,' from the verb *facere* .

fac•tor•age /'fæktərij/ ▶ n. the commission or charges payable to a factor.

fac•tor cost /'fæktər ‚kôst/ ▶ n. the cost of an item or a service in terms of the various factors that have played a part in its production or availability, and exclusive of tax costs.

Fair I•saac Cor•po•ra•tion /'fe(ə)r 'īzək kôrpə‚rāsHən/ (abbr.: **FICO**) ▶ n. the largest and best known of several companies that provide software for calculating a person's credit score.

fair-mar•ket val•ue /'fe(ə)r 'märkit ‚vælyo͞o/ ▶ n. a selling price for an item to which a buyer and seller can agree.

Fan•nie Mae /'fænē 'mā/ ▶ n. informal the Federal National Mortgage Association, a corporation (now privately owned) that trades in mortgages.

ORIGIN 1940s: elaboration of the acronym FNMA, suggested by the given names *Fanny* and *Mae*.

USAGE: Fannie Mae helps low- and middle-income families to buy homes by providing low-cost capital to mortgage lenders throughout the country. It is the country's second largest corporation in terms of assets and the largest provider of funds for home mortgages.

FCC ▸ abbr. Canadian (in Canada) Farm Credit Corporation.

FDIC ▸ abbr. Federal Deposit Insurance Corporation, a body that underwrites most private bank deposits.

feath•er•bed /'feᴛʜər,bed/ ▸ v. [trans.] (also **feath•er-bed**) provide (someone) with advantageous economic or working conditions: *apart from the fees he earns, a practicing lawyer is not featherbedded in any way.*

■ [usu. as n.] (**featherbedding**) deliberately limit production or retain excess staff in (a business) in order to create jobs or prevent unemployment, typically as a result of a union contract.

Fed /fed/ ▸ n. informal (usu. **the Fed**) short for FEDERAL RESERVE.
ORIGIN early 20th cent.: abbreviation of FEDERAL. The abbreviation *fed* had previously been used in the late 18th cent. to denote a member of the Federalist party, who advocated a union of American colonies after the American Revolution.

Fed•er•al Re•serve /'fed(ə)rəl ri'zərv/ the federal banking authority in the US that performs the functions of a central bank and is used to implement the country's monetary policy and provide a national system of reserve cash available to banks.

USAGE: Created in 1913, the Federal Reserve System consists of twelve Federal Reserve Districts, each having a Federal Reserve Bank. These are controlled from Washington, DC by the Federal Reserve Board consisting of governors appointed by the US president with Senate approval.

Fed•er•al Trade Com•mis•sion /'fed(ə)rəl 'trād kə'misʜən/ ▸ n. a federal agency, established in 1914, that administers antitrust and consumer protection legislation in pursuit of free and fair competition in the marketplace.

fi•at mon•ey /'fēət 'mənē/ ▸ n. inconvertible paper money made legal tender by a government decree.

FICO score /ˈfīkō ˌskôr/ ▸ n. a person's credit score calculated with software from Fair Isaac Corporation (FICO).

USAGE: The **FICO score** is a number between 300 and 850, which indicates a person's capacity to repay a loan. The higher the number, the lower the risk that the borrower will default. Information about one's credit score and how to improve it is at *www.myfico.com.*

fi•du•ci•ar•y /fəˈdo͞oSHēˌerē; -SHərē/ ▸ adj. involving trust, esp. with regard to the relationship between a trustee and a beneficiary: *the company has a fiduciary duty to shareholders.*
▸ n. (pl. **fi•du•ci•ar•ies**) a trustee.
ORIGIN late 16th cent. (in the sense 'something inspiring trust; credentials'): from Latin *fiduciarius,* from *fiducia* 'trust,' from *fidere* 'to trust.'
FIFO /ˈfīˌfō/ ▸ abbr. first in, first out (chiefly with reference to methods of stock valuation and data storage).
fi•nance /ˈfīnæns; fəˈnæns/ ▸ n. the management of large amounts of money, esp. by governments or large companies.
■ monetary support for an enterprise: *housing finance.*
■ (**finances**) the monetary resources and affairs of a country, organization, or person: *the finances of the school were causing serious concern.*
▸ v. [trans.] provide funding for (a person or enterprise): *the city and county originally financed the project.*
ORIGIN late Middle English: from Old French, from *finer* 'make an end, settle a debt,' from *fin* 'end,' from Latin *finis.*
fi•nance com•pa•ny /ˈfīnæns ˌkəmpənē/ ▸ n. a company concerned primarily with providing money, e.g., for short-term loans.
fi•nan•cial /fəˈnænCHəl; fī-/ ▸ adj. of or relating to finance: *an independent financial adviser.*
Fi•nan•cial Times in•dex /fəˈnænCHəl ˈtīmz ˌindeks; fī-/ another term for FTSE INDEX.
fin•an•cier /ˌfinənˈsi(ə)r; ˌfī-/ ▸ n. a person concerned with the management of large amounts of money on behalf of governments or other large organizations.
ORIGIN early 17th cent.: from French, from *finance* (see FINANCE).

firm[1] /fərm/ ▸ **adj.** (of a currency, a commodity, or shares) having a steady value or price that is more likely to rise than fall: *the dollar was firm against the yen.*
▸ **v.** [intrans.] (of a price) rise slightly to reach a level considered secure: *he believed house prices would firm by the end of the year.*
ORIGIN Middle English: from Old French *ferme*, from Latin *firmus* .

firm[2] /fərm/ ▸ **n.** a business concern, esp. one involving a partnership of two or more people: *a law firm.*
ORIGIN late 16th cent.: from Spanish and Italian *firma*, from medieval Latin, from Latin *firmare* 'fix, settle' (in late Latin 'confirm by signature'), from *firmus* 'firm.'

USAGE: **Firm** originally denoted one's autograph or signature; later (mid 18th cent.) the name under which the business of a firm was transacted, hence the firm itself (late 18th cent.).

fis•cal /'fiskəl/ ▸ **adj.** of or relating to government revenue, esp. taxes: *monetary and fiscal policy.*
■ of or relating to financial matters: *the domestic fiscal crisis.*
■ used to denote a fiscal year: *the budget deficit for fiscal 1996.*
ORIGIN mid 16th cent.: from French, or from Latin *fiscalis*, from *fiscus* 'purse, treasury.'

fis•cal year /'fiskəl 'yi(ə)r/ (abbr.: **FY**) ▸ **n.** a year as reckoned for taxing or accounting purposes: *the firm is expected to turn a profit for its fiscal year ending April 30.*

fixed as•sets /'fikst 'æsits/ ▸ **plural n.** assets that are purchased for long-term use and are not likely to be converted quickly into cash, such as land, buildings, and equipment.

fixed cap•i•tal /'fikst 'kæpitl/ ▸ **n.** capital invested in fixed assets.

fixed charge /'fikst 'cHärj/ ▸ **n.** a liability to a creditor that relates to specific assets of a company.

fixed costs /'fikst 'kôsts/ ▸ **plural n.** business costs, such as rent, that are constant whatever the amount of goods produced.

flat /flæt/ ▸ **adj.** (**flat•ter, flat•test**) **1** (of a market, prices, etc.) not showing much activity; sluggish: *cash flow was flat at $214 million* | *flat sales in the drinks industry.*

2 (of a fee, wage, or price) the same in all cases, not varying with changed conditions or in particular cases: *a $30 flat fare.*
ORIGIN Middle English: from Old Norse *flatr* .

fli•er /'flīər/ (also **fly•er**) ▶ n. **1** a small handbill advertising an event or product.
2 a speculative investment.

flight cap•i•tal /'flīt ˌkæpiṯl/ ▶ n. money transferred abroad to avoid taxes or inflation, achieve better investment returns, or to provide for possible emigration.

float /flōt/ ▶ v. **1** [trans.] offer the shares of (a company) for sale on the stock market for the first time.
2 [intrans.] (of a currency) fluctuate freely in value in accordance with supply and demand in the financial markets: *a policy of letting the pound float.*
■ [trans.] allow (a currency) to fluctuate in such a way.
3 [intrans.] (of a mortgage) to fluctuate in terms of the interest rate payable until the borrower decides to lock in the rate at a specified level.
ORIGIN Old English *flotian* (verb), of Germanic origin, reinforced in Middle English by Old French *floter*, also from Germanic.

float•er /'flōṯər/ ▶ n. **1** a worker who is required to do a variety of tasks as the need for each arises.
2 an insurance policy covering loss of articles without specifying a location.

float•ing debt /'flōṯiNG 'det/ ▶ n. a debt that is repayable in the short term.

floor /flôr/ ▶ n. **1** the minimum level of prices or wages: *the dollar's floor against the yen.*
2 (of the stock exchange) the large central hall where trading takes place.
ORIGIN Old English *flōr*, of Germanic origin; related to Dutch *vloer* and German *Flur* .

flo•ta•tion /flō'tāSHən/ (also **float•a•tion**) ▶ n. the process of offering a company's shares for sale on the stock market for the first time.
ORIGIN early 19th cent.: alteration of *floatation* (from FLOAT) on

the pattern of French *flottaison* . The spelling *flot-* was influenced by *flotilla* .

f.o.b. ▶ abbr. free on board.

f.o.r. ▶ abbr. free on rail.

fore•clo•sure /fôr'klōzHər/ ▶ n. the process of taking possession of a mortgaged property as a result of someone's failure to keep up mortgage payments.

for•eign ex•change /'fôrən iks'CHānj; 'färən/ ▶ n. the currency of other countries.

■ an institution or system for dealing in such currency.

fran•chise /'fræn‚CHīz/ ▶ n. an authorization granted by a government or company to an individual or group enabling them to carry out specified commercial activities, e.g., providing a broadcasting service or acting as an agent for a company's products.

■ a business or service given such authorization to operate. ■ an authorization given by a league to own a sports team.

▶ v. [trans.] grant a franchise to (an individual or group).

■ grant a franchise for the sale of (goods) or the operation of (a service): *all the catering was franchised out.*

D E R I VAT I V E S **fran•chi•see** n.; **fran•chis•er, fran•chi•sor** n.

O R I G I N Middle English (denoting a grant of legal immunity): from Old French, based on *franc, franche* 'free.' These senses date from the 20th cent.

USAGE: As the popularity of **franchising** has increased, a number of public and private organizations at the local, regional, state, and national levels have been formed to provide information and support to individuals interested in acquiring a business franchise. One of the more helpful organizations is the International Franchise Association (*www.franchise.org*), based in Washington, DC.

Fred•die Mac /'fredē 'mæk/ ▶ informal the Federal Home Loan Mortgage Corporation, a corporation that buys mortgages from lenders such as commercial banks, mortgage bankers, savings institutions, and credit unions.

USAGE: **Freddie Mac** packages the mortgages into securities and sells the securities to investors. The money that it pays for these mortgages then enables lenders to make more mortgage funds available. Even though it is practically invisible to most consumers, the process reduces the cost of mortgages to borrowers and gives them better access to financing.

free en•ter•prise /'frē 'entər,prīz/ ▸ n. an economic system in which private business operates in competition and largely free of state control.

free mar•ket /'frē 'märkit/ ▸ n. an economic system in which prices are determined by unrestricted competition between privately owned businesses.

free on board /'frē än 'bôrd; ôn/ (abbr.: **f.o.b.**) ▸ including or assuming delivery without charge to the buyer's named destination.

free trade /'frē 'trād/ ▸ n. international trade left to its natural course without tariffs, quotas, or other restrictions.

freeze /frēz/ ▸ v. (past **froze**; past part. **fro•zen**) [trans.] hold (something) at a fixed level or in a fixed state for a period of time: *new spending on defense was to be frozen.*

■ prevent (assets) from being used for a period of time: *the charity's bank account has been frozen.*

▸ n. an act of holding or being held at a fixed level or in a fixed state: *workers faced a pay freeze.*

ORIGIN Old English *frēosan* (in the phrase *hit frēoseth* 'it is freezing, it is so cold that water turns to ice'), of Germanic origin.

fric•tion•al un•em•ploy•ment /'friksHənl ,ənim'ploimənt/ ▸ n. the unemployment that exists in any economy due to people being in the process of moving from one job to another.

fringe ben•e•fit /'frinj ,benəfit/ ▸ n. an extra benefit supplementing an employee's salary, for example, a company car, subsidized meals, health insurance, etc.

front-end /'frənt 'end/ ▸ adj. informal (of money) paid or charged at the beginning of a transaction: *a front-end fee.*

front-end load /'frənt 'end ,lōd/ ▸ n. the deduction of commission fees and expenses from mutual fund shares at the time of purchase.

front-run•ning /'frənt ,rəniNG/ ▸ n. the practice by market makers of dealing on advance information provided by their brokers and investment analysts, before their clients have been given the information.

FRS ▸ **abbr.** ■ Federal Reserve System.

FTA ▸ **abbr.** Free Trade Agreement, used to refer to that signed in 1988 between the US and Canada.

FTC ▸ **abbr.** Federal Trade Commission.

FT in•dex /'ef 'tē ˌindeks/ ▸ another term for **FTSE INDEX**.

FTSE in•dex /'ef 'tē ˌes 'ē ˌindeks; 'fʊʊtsē/ a figure (published by the *Financial Times*) indicating the relative prices of shares on the London Stock Exchange, esp. (also **FTSE 100 in•dex**) one calculated on the basis of Britain's one hundred largest public companies.

ORIGIN *FTSE*, abbreviation of *Financial Times Stock Exchange*.

fund /fənd/ ▸ **n.** a sum of money saved or made available for a particular purpose: *he had set up a fund to coordinate economic investment.*

■ (**funds**) financial resources: *the misuse of public funds.* ■ an organization set up for the administration and management of a monetary fund.

▸ **v.** [trans.] provide with money for a particular purpose: *the World Bank refused to fund the project.*

ORIGIN mid 17th cent.: from Latin *fundus* 'bottom, piece of landed property.'

USAGE: The earliest sense of the word **fund** was 'the bottom or lowest part,' later 'foundation or basis'; the association with money has perhaps arisen from the idea of landed property being a source of wealth.

fund•ed debt /'fəndid 'det/ ▸ **n.** debt in the form of securities with long-term or indefinite redemption.

fund man•ag•er /'fənd ˌmænijər/ ▸ **n.** an employee of a large institution (such as a pension fund or an insurance company) who manages the investment of money on its behalf.

fun•gi•ble /'fənjəbəl/ ▸ **adj.** (of goods contracted for without an individual specimen being specified) able to replace or be replaced by another identical item; mutually interchangeable: *money is fungi-*

ble—money that is raised for one purpose can easily be used for another.

DERIVATIVES **fun•gi•bil•i•ty** n.

ORIGIN late 17th cent.: from medieval Latin *fungibilis*, from *fungi* 'perform, enjoy,' with the same sense as *fungi vice* 'serve in place of.'

fu•tures con•tract /ˈfyo͞oCHərz ˌkäntrækt/ (also **fu•tures**) ▶ n. [treated as sing or pl.] an agreement traded on an organized exchange to buy or sell assets, esp. commodities or shares, at a fixed price but to be delivered and paid for later.

FY ▶ abbr. fiscal year.

HOW THE FEDERAL
RESERVE WORKS

You hear about the U.S. Federal Reserve almost every day. Most of us know something about it—that it has something to do with controlling inflation, for example, and that it plays a big role in the economy, not just of the United States, but of the world.

But few of us know that the "Fed" was created in 1913 to smooth out the boom-and-bust business cycles that the country had experienced in the past. And not many of us know that the Fed administers the U.S. payment system and provides services to banks, as well as conducting monetary policy.

There are actually 12 regional Federal Reserve Banks in the U.S. Each of them monitors economic activity in its region. The Fed has a board of governors appointed by the President, and the Chairman—currently Alan Greenspan—is its most important and visible member.

The Fed tries to maintain the country's long-term economic health, creating conditions that keep employment and production high while keeping prices stable and inflation low. It does all this by setting monetary policy for the country. And it has two basic ways to do this: changing interest rates and raising or lowering the supply of money available for us to spend.

Economic theory says that, when the economy is strong, inflation goes up. When the economy is strong, and everybody has a good job and makes lots of money, we want to buy things. But things are usually in limited supply. Like the *Mona Lisa* or a painting by Van Gogh, if enough people want something, its price will increase. When prices go up, so does inflation. The same thing happens, in reverse, when the economy weakens. Demand falls, and prices go down. The Fed tries to influence these ups and downs so that we don't lose our jobs six months after we get them and so that the dollar that buys a loaf of bread today still buys it in six months. It does this in a couple of ways.

When the economy is strong and inflation is going up, the Fed can increase interest rates. That makes it more expensive to borrow money, so individuals and businesses think twice about borrowing to buy things. When we stop buying things, demand goes down and the economy chills out. If the Fed wants to get things moving again, during an economic slowdown, it can lower interest rates. This makes it cheaper to borrow money, which we can use to buy things. As the demand for things goes up, so do production and employment, and the economy grows.

The other tool that the Fed uses to influence the economy is controlling the supply of money. Money is used to pay salaries, make purchases, lend to borrowers, etc. When the Fed puts more money in the system, by purchasing securities, for example, or lending money to banks, it gives the economy a boost. When it takes money out of the system, there's less to go around, and the economy slows down.

You can find out more about the Federal Reserve at its Web site, *www.federalreserve.gov.*

G

GATT /gæt/ General Agreement on Tariffs and Trade, an international treaty (1948–94) to promote trade and economic development by reducing tariffs and other restrictions. It was superseded by the establishment of the World Trade Organization in 1995.

GDP ▶ abbr. gross domestic product.

GIC ▶ abbr. Canadian see **guaranteed investment certificate**.

gilt-edged /'gilt ˌejd/ ▶ adj. relating to or denoting stocks or bonds that are regarded as extremely reliable investments.

GIS ▶ abbr. Canadian see **Guaranteed Income Supplement**.

GNP ▶ abbr. gross national product.

gold card /'gōld ˌkärd/ ▶ n. a charge card or credit card issued to people with a high credit rating and giving benefits not available with the standard card.

USAGE: So many millions of people now carry a **gold card** that the companies that issue them have created yet another category, the **platinum card,** to distinguish and reward low-risk, high-spending individuals.

gold•en par•a•chute /'gōldən 'pærəˌSHo͞ot/ ▶ n. informal a large payment or other financial compensation guaranteed to a company executive should the executive be dismissed as a result of a merger or takeover.

gold re•serve /'gōld riˌzərv/ ▶ n. a quantity of gold held by a central bank to support the issue of currency.

good•will /'go͝od'wil/ (also **good will**) ▶ n. the established reputation of a business regarded as a quantifiable asset, e.g., as represented by the excess of the price paid at a takeover for a company over its fair-market value.

gov•ern•ment se•cu•ri•ties /ˈgəvər(n)mənt siˌkyŏŏritēz/ ▸ **plural n.** bonds or other promissory certificates issued by the government.

gray mar•ket /ˈgrā ˈmärkit/ ▸ **n.** an unofficial market or trade in something, esp. unissued shares or controlled or scarce goods: *the discounting of bonds in the gray market.* [as adj.] *a gray market price.*

green•mail /ˈgrēnˌmāl/ ▸ **n.** the practice of buying enough shares in a company to threaten a takeover, forcing the owners to buy them back at a higher price in order to retain control.
DERIVATIVES **green•mail•er n.**
ORIGIN 1980s: blend of *green* and *blackmail* .

Gresh•am's law /ˈgreSHəmz ˈlô/ **n.** the tendency for money of lower intrinsic value to circulate more freely than money of higher intrinsic and equal nominal value (often expressed as "Bad money drives out good").

USAGE: Thomas Gresham formulated his law when he was trying to persuade Queen Elizabeth I to get rid of debased currency in England. He argued that people would hoard the good coins and spend the bad (or melt down the good coins for the worth of the metal) and that eventually only bad coins would be left in circulation.

gross /grōs/ ▸ **adj.** (of income, profit, or interest) without deduction of tax or other contributions; total: *the gross amount of the gift was $1,000 | the current rate of interest is about 6.1 percent gross.* Often contrasted with NET.
▸**adv.** without tax or other contributions having been deducted.
▸**v.** [trans.] produce or earn (an amount of money) as gross profit or income: *the film went on to gross $8 million in the US.*
▸**n.** a gross profit or income.
ORIGIN Middle English (in the sense 'thick, massive, bulky'): from Old French *gros, grosse* 'large,' from late Latin *grossus* .

gross do•mes•tic prod•uct /ˈgrōs dəˈmestik ˈprädəkt/ (abbr.: **GDP**) ▸ **n.** the total value of goods produced and services provided in a country during one year.

gross na•tion•al prod•uct /ˈgrōs ˈnæSH(ə)nl ˈprädəkt/ (abbr.: **GNP**) ▸ **n.** the total value of goods produced and services provided by a country during one year, equal to the gross domestic product plus the net income from foreign investments.

group /groōp/ ▶ **n.** a commercial organization consisting of several companies under common ownership.

ORIGIN late 17th cent.: from French *groupe*, from Italian *gruppo*, of Germanic origin; related to *crop* .

growth in•dus•try /ˈgrōTH ˌindəstrē/ ▶ **n.** an industry that is developing particularly rapidly.

growth stock /ˈgrōTH ˌstäk/ ▶ **n.** shares of a company whose profits promise to grow more quickly than those of its peers, thus generating a substantial captial gain. Compare with VALUE STOCK.

guar•an•tee /ˌgærənˈtē; ˌge(ə)r-/ ▶ **v.** [trans.] provide financial security for; underwrite: *a demand that $100,000 be deposited to guarantee their costs.*

Guar•an•teed In•come Sup•ple•ment /ˌgærənˈtēd ˈinˌkəm ˌsəpləmənt; ˌge(ə)rənˈtēd/ (abbr.: **GIS**) ▶ **n.** Canadian a federally-supported supplement to the monthly pension payments of those with little income other than that derived from Old Age Security.

guar•an•teed in•vest•ment cer•tif•i•cate /ˌgærənˈtēd inˈvestmənt sərˌtifikit; ˌge(ə)rənˈtēd/ (abbr.: **GIC**) ▶ **n.** Canadian a certificate guaranteeing a fixed interest rate on a sum of money deposited with a financial institution for a fixed term, usually between one and seven years, which may not be withdrawn before term.

guar•an•tee fund /ˌgærənˈtē ˌfənd/ ▶ **n.** a sum of money pledged as a contingent indemnity for loss.

guar•an•ty /ˈgærənˌtē/ (also **guar•an•tee**) ▶ **n.** (pl. **guar•an•ties**) a formal pledge to pay another person's debt or to perform another person's obligation in the case of default.

■ a thing serving as security for such a pledge.

ORIGIN early 16th cent.: from Old French *garantie*, from *garantir*; related to WARRANT.

H

Hang Seng in•dex /ˈhæNG ˈsENG ˌindeks/ a figure indicating the relative price of shares on the Hong Kong Stock Exchange.

ORIGIN named after the *Hang Seng Bank* in Hong Kong, where it was devised.

hard /härd/ ▶ adj. (of prices of stock, commodities, etc.) stable or firm in value.

ORIGIN Old English *hard*, *heard*, of Germanic origin; related to Dutch *hard* and German *hart*.

hard cash /ˈhärd ˈkæSH/ ▶ n. negotiable coins and paper money as opposed to other forms of payment.

hard cur•ren•cy /ˈhärd ˈkərənsē/ ▶ n. currency that is not likely to depreciate suddenly or to fluctuate greatly in value.

hard•en /ˈhärdn/ ▶ v. [intrans.] (of prices of stocks, commodities, etc.) rise and remain steady at a higher level.

hard sell /ˈhärd ˈsel/ ▶ n. a policy or technique of aggressive salesmanship or advertising.

har•mo•nized sales tax /ˈhärməˌnīzd ˈsälz ˌtæks/ (abbr.: **HST**) ▶ n. Canadian a value-added tax on goods and services combining·the GST and the provincial sales tax in Nova Scotia, New Brunswick, and Newfoundland and Labrador..

haul•age /ˈhôlij/ ▶ n. the commercial transport of goods: *road haulage.*
■ a charge for such transport.

head count /ˈked ˌkownt/ ▶ n. a total number of people, esp. the number of people employed in a particular organization: *you may decide that by reducing your head count you can reach this quarter's goals.*

head•hunt•er /'hed₁həntər/ ▸ n. a person who identifies and approaches suitable candidates employed elsewhere to fill business positions.

heav•y in•dus•try /'hevē 'indəstrē/ ▸ n. the manufacture of large, heavy articles and materials in bulk.

hedge /hej/ ▸ n. a contract entered into or asset held as a protection against possible financial loss: *inflation hedges such as real estate and gold.*

▸ v. [trans.] protect (one's investment or an investor) against loss by making balancing or compensating contracts or transactions: *the company hedged its investment position on the futures market.*

ORIGIN Old English *hegg*, of Germanic origin.

hid•den re•serves /'hidn ri'zərvz/ ▸ plural n. a company's funds that are not declared on its balance sheet.

high-end /'hī 'end/ ▸ adj. denoting the most expensive of a range of products.

high fi•nance /'hī 'fīnæns/ ▸ n. financial transactions involving large amounts of money.

hire /hīr/ ▸ v. [trans.] employ (someone) for wages.

■ employ for a short time to do a particular job. ■ (**hire oneself out**) make oneself available for temporary employment: *he hired himself out as a laborer.*

▸ n. **1** the action of hiring someone or something.

2 a recently recruited employee: *new hires go through six months of training.*

ORIGIN Old English *hȳrian* 'employ (someone) for wages,' *hȳr* 'payment under contract for the use of something,' of West Germanic origin.

hold•back /'hōl(d)₁bæk/ ▸ n. a sum of money withheld under certain conditions.

hold•ing com•pa•ny /'hōldiNG ₁kəmpənē/ ▸ n. a company created to buy and possess the shares of other companies, which it then controls.

hold•ings /'hōldinNGz/ ▸ plural n. stocks, property, and other financial assets in someone's possession: *commercial property holdings.*

hon•or /'änər/ ▸ v. [trans.] accept (a bill) or pay (a check) when due: *the bank informed him that the check would not be honored.*

ORIGIN Middle English: from Old French *onor* (noun), *onorer* (verb), from Latin *honor* .

hon•o•rar•i•um /ˌänə're(ə)rēəm/ ▸ n. (pl. **hon•o•rar•i•ums** or **hon•o• rar•i•a**) a payment given for professional services that are rendered nominally without charge.

ORIGIN mid 17th cent.: from Latin, denoting a gift made on being admitted to public office, from *honorarius* 'honorary.'

hor•i•zon•tal /ˌhôrə'zäntl; ˌhär-/ ▸ adj. combining companies engaged in the same stage or type of production: *a horizontal merger.*

ORIGIN mid 16th cent.: from French, or from modern Latin *horizontalis*, from late Latin *horizon, horizont-* 'horizon.'

hos•tile /'hästl; -ˌstīl/ ▸ adj. (of a takeover bid) opposed by the company to be bought.

ORIGIN late 16th cent.: from French, or from Latin *hostilis*, from *hostis* 'stranger, enemy.'

hot-desk•ing /'hät 'deskiNG/ ▸ n. the practice in an office of allocating desks to workers when they are required or on a rotating system, rather than giving each worker their own desk.

hot mon•ey /'hät 'mənē/ ▸ n. capital that is frequently transferred between financial institutions in an attempt to maximize interest or capital gain.

house /hows/ ▸ n. a business or institution: *a publishing house.*

ORIGIN Old English *hūs* (noun), *hūsian* (verb), of Germanic origin.

HST ▸ abbr. Canadian see **harmonized sales tax**.

hu•man cap•i•tal /'(h)yo͞omən 'kæpitl/ ▸ n. the skills, knowledge, and experience possessed by an individual or population, viewed in terms of their value or cost to an organization or country.

hy•poth•e•cate /hi'päтHiˌkāt; hī-/ ▸ v. [trans.] pledge (money) by law to a specific purpose.

ORIGIN early 17th cent.: from medieval Latin *hypothecat-* 'given as a pledge,' from the verb *hypothecare*, based on Greek *hupothēkē* .

WHAT YOU NEED TO
KNOW ABOUT INSURANCE

Insurance is one of the few products you'll ever buy that you hope you never have to use. For this reason, many people ignore it until they need it. By then, unfortunately, it's too late.

You can insure just about anything, from your car and your house to your favorite painting or even your dog. But there are four basic types of insurance that all of us may need at one time or another:

- Health

- Life

- Disability

- Long-term care.

Health insurance: There are basically two types of health insurance programs to choose from these days: fee-for-service plans and managed care. Fee-for-service (also known as an indemnity plan) allows patients the kind of health care most of us grew up with. Unfortunately, because of the cost, fewer and fewer companies now offer it to their employees.

Managed care is less expensive and, as a result, far more popular. Examples of managed care include health maintenance organizations (HMOs), preferred-provider organizations (PPOs) and point-of-service plans (POS). An HMO is basically a group of health care providers who have joined together to provide comprehensive health care coverage for subscribers.

They are the oldest managed care system around, and the most restrictive. A PPO usually consists of a group of individual physicians, medical practices, and hospitals that have joined together in a loose coalition to create a group network. Although PPOs resemble HMOs, there are some differences. You can visit a PPO specialist on your own, for example, without a referral. You can also use a specialist who's not part of your PPO's group network and the PPO will still cover at least part of the bill. Point-of-service plans combine elements of both and give you the widest choice of options. You can either stay within the POS plan's network of doctors (and save money) or go beyond it and pay a deductible (as with a PPO).

My recommendation is that, when in doubt over a health care provider, err by spending a little bit more a month and getting the best health care provider you can afford. The additional cost between an HMO and the top-of-the-line PPO or POS may be $50 to $100 a month if you're an employee. If you ever become seriously ill, I think you'll be happy you invested the additional dollars a month for top-of-the-line health care coverage.

Here are some Web sites where you can get more information:

AllBusiness
www.allbusiness.com

e-Insure Services Inc.
www.einsurance.com

InsWeb Corp.
www.insweb.com

MasterQuote of America Inc.
www.masterquote.com

Quotesmith.com Inc.
www.insure.com

eHealth Insurance.com
www.ehealthinsurance.com

Life insurance: If you have dependents—children or other relatives who depend on you financially—you must consider protecting them by buying life insurance. Most people hate to talk about life insurance, but if someone depends on you and your income, then you need to have some sort of protection plan in place in case something happens to you. And that's all life insurance is—a protection plan.

Whether you're part of a couple with a family of children or a single parent, you should have life insurance coverage. In fact, as a single parent, getting adequate life insurance could be the most important thing you ever do for your children.

To determine how much coverage you need, you should ask yourself the following questions:

- Who will be hurt financially if I should die? In other words, who relies on my income?

- What does it cost those who depend on me to live for a year? (This figure should include everything—mortgage, taxes, college costs, etc.)

- Are there any major debts, such as a home or business loan, that would need to be paid immediately if I or my significant other were to pass away?

Now you should determine the minimum amount of life insurance you need. To do this, you take your gross annual income (that is, your total earnings before taxes) and multiply it by six. Some people prefer even more coverage. If you do, multiply your gross annual income by the number of years that you want to cover your family's living expenses.

Although insurance companies give their products a variety of fancy names, there are really two primary types of life insurance: term insurance and permanent insurance.

Term insurance provides you with a set amount of protection for a set period. Permanent insurance combines term insurance with a forced savings plan that can help you build a nice nest egg, although it can cost up to eight times as much as term.

Here are some great online sources of life insurance and information that will help you decide what to buy:

Ameritas
www.veritas.ameritas.com

e-Insure Services Inc.
www.einsurance.com

InsWeb Corp.
www.insweb.com

MasterQuote of America Inc.
www.masterquote.com

Quotesmith.com Inc.
www.insure.com

USAA Life Insurance Company
www.usaa.com

Disability insurance: One in eight people can expect to become so injured or seriously ill that he or she would qualify for long-term disability during his or her working life. To protect yourself against this risk, you need insurance, especially if you're self-employed or if you work for a company that doesn't provide it as part of your benefit package.

Most disability plans offer a benefit equal to about 60 percent of your gross (or before-tax) income. That may not sound like much, but 60 percent of the gross is about what most of us actually take home after taxes.

You should apply for disability insurance now while you're healthy. If you wait until something goes wrong, it's too late.

For quotes on disability insurance and information about what's available, check the following Web sites:

Aetna U.S. Healthcare
www.aetna.com

Continental General Insurance Company
www.continentalgeneral.com

Mutual of Omaha Insurance Company
www.mutualofomaha.com

Northwestern Mutual Life Insurance Company
www.northwesternmutual.com

State Farm Mutual Automobile Insurance Company
www.statefarm.com

UnumProvident Corp. (formerly **Paul Revere**)
www.unumprovident.com

USAA Insurance
www.usaa.com

Long-term care (LTC): With families spread out all over the country, aging people often have no support system. With average life expectancies climbing, more elderly people thus find themselves in need of either home care or a long-term care facility.

The cost of such care can be staggering—as much as $30,000 to $70,000 a year for residence in a long-term care facility. LTC insurance will cover the kind of care you get in a nursing home, a residential care facility, a convalescent facility, an extended facility, a community hospice or adult care center, or, in some cases, your own home.

Most people start thinking about LTC coverage in their 50s and purchase it in their 60s. If you wait until you're in your 70s or 80s, it can become prohibitively expensive. Unless you're in terrible shape, you can still get a pretty good deal in your early 60s. When purchasing a disability policy, look for companies that have been in the business of LTC for at least ten years (that means they are committed and should have deeper cash reserves).

Here are some resources for researching LTC insurance:

GE Financial Assurance
www.gefn.com

John Hancock Life Insurance Co.
www.jhancock.com

LTCinsurance.com
www.ltcinsurance.com

I

i•dle /'īdl/ ▸ adj. (**i•dler, i•dlest**) (esp. of a machine or factory) not active or in use: *assembly lines standing idle for lack of spare parts.* ■ (of a person) not working; unemployed. ■ (of money) held in cash or in accounts paying no interest.

▸ v. [trans.] take out of use or employment: *he will close the newspaper, idling 2,200 workers.*

ORIGIN Old English *īdel* 'empty, useless,' of West Germanic origin.

il•liq•uid /i(l)'likwid/ ▸ adj. (of assets) not easily converted into cash: *illiquid assets.*

■ (of a market) with few participants and a low volume of activity.

im•age-mak•er /'imij ˌmākər/ ▸ n. a person employed to identify and create a favorable public image for a person, organization, or product.

IMF ▸ abbr. International Monetary Fund.

im•per•fect com•pe•ti•tion /im'pərfikt ˌkämpi'tisHən/ ▸ n. the situation prevailing in a market in which elements of monopoly allow individual producers or consumers to exercise some control over market prices.

im•port /im'pôrt/ ▸ v. [trans.] bring (goods or services) into a country from abroad for sale.

▸ n. (usu. **imports**) a commodity, article, or service brought in from abroad for sale.

■ (**imports**) sales of goods or services brought in from abroad, or the revenue from such sales: *this surplus pushes up the yen, which ought to boost imports.* ■ the action or process of importing goods or services.

ORIGIN late Middle English: from Latin *importare* 'bring in' (in medieval Latin 'imply, mean, be of consequence'), from *in-* 'in' + *portare* 'carry.'

im•po•si•tion /ˌimpəˈziSHən/ ▸ n. a tax or duty.

ORIGIN late Middle English: from Latin *impositio(n-)*, from the verb *imponere* 'inflict, deceive,' from *in-* 'upon, in' + *ponere* 'put.'

im•post /ˈimˌpōst/ ▸ n. a tax or similar compulsory payment.

ORIGIN mid 16th cent.: from French (earlier form of *impôt*), from medieval Latin *impostus*, from Latin *impositus*, past participle of *imponere* (see **IMPOSITION**).

im•prest /ˈimˌprest/ ▸ n. a fund used by a business for small items of expenditure and restored to a fixed amount periodically.

■ an advance of money made to someone engaged in some business with the state, enabling them to carry out the business. ■ a sum of money advanced to a person for a particular purpose.

ORIGIN mid 16th cent.: from the earlier phrase *in prest* 'as a loan,' influenced by Italian or medieval Latin *imprestare* 'lend.'

im•pute /imˈpyo͞ot/ ▸ v. [trans.] assign (a value) to something by inference from the value of the products or processes to which it contributes: [as adj.] (**imputed**) *recovering the initial outlay plus imputed interest.*

ORIGIN late Middle English: from Old French *imputer*, from Latin *imputare* 'enter in the account,' from *in-* 'in, toward' + *putare* 'reckon.'

Inc. /iNGk/ ▸ abbr. incorporated: *Motorola, Inc.*

in•come /ˈinˌkəm; ˈiNG-/ ▸ n. money received, esp. on a regular basis, for work or through investments: *he has a nice home and an adequate income | figures showed an overall increase in income this year.*

ORIGIN Middle English (in the sense 'entrance, arrival,' now only Scots): in early use from Old Norse *innkoma*, later from **IN** + **COME**. The current sense dates from the late 16th cent.

in•come tax /ˈinˌkəm ˌtaks; ˈiNGˌkəm/ ▸ n. tax levied directly on personal income.

in•con•vert•i•ble /ˌinkənˈvərtəbəl/ ▸ adj. (of currency) not able to be converted into another form on demand.

ORIGIN mid 17th cent.: from French, or from late Latin *inconvert-ibilis*, from *in-* 'not' + *convertibilis* (see CONVERTIBLE).

in•cor•po•rate /in'kôrpə‚rāt/ ▶ v. [trans.] (often **be incorporated**) constitute (a company, city, or other organization) as a legal corpo-ration.■ [intrans.] to become incorporated: *my accountant has ad-vised me to incorporate.*
DERIVATIVES **in•cor•po•ra•tion** n.
ORIGIN late Middle English: from late Latin *incorporat-* 'embod-ied,' from the verb *incorporare*, from *in-* 'into' + Latin *corporare* 'form into a body' (from *corpus, corpor-* 'body').

in•cor•po•rat•ed /in'kôrpə‚rātid/ (abbr.: **Inc.**) ▶ adj. (of a company or other organization) formed into a legal corporation.

in•dem•ni•ty /in'demnitē/ ▶ n. (pl. **in•dem•ni•ties**) security or protec-tion against a loss or other financial burden: *no indemnity will be given for loss of cash.*
ORIGIN late Middle English: from French *indemnite*, from late Latin *indemnitas*, from *indemnis* 'unhurt, free from loss.'

in•dex /'in‚deks/ ▶ n. (pl. **in•dex•es** or esp. in technical use **in•di•ces** /'indəsēz/) a figure in a system or scale representing the average value of specified prices, shares, or other items as compared with some reference figure: *the 100-shares index closed down 9.3.*
▶ v. [trans.] link the value of (prices, wages, or other payments) auto-matically to the value of a price index: *legislation indexing wages to prices.*
▶ adj. denoting a category of (usually) low-cost mutual fund that invests in a stock-market index such as the Standard & Poor's 500.
DERIVATIVES **in•dex•a•tion** n.
ORIGIN late Middle English: from Latin *index, indic-* 'forefinger, informer, sign,' from *in-* 'toward' + a second element related to *dicere* 'say' or *dicare* 'make known.'

USAGE: The original meaning of **index**, 'index finger' (with which one points), came to mean 'pointer' (late 16th cent.), and figura-tively something that serves to point to a fact or conclusion; hence a list of topics in a book ('pointing' to their location).

in•dif•fer•ence curve /in'dif(ə)rəns ‚kərv/ ▶ n. a curve on a graph (the axes of which represent quantities of two commodities) linking those combinations of quantities that the consumer regards as of equal value.

in•di•rect /ˌində'rekt/ ▸ **adj.** (of costs) deriving from overhead charges or subsidiary work.

■ (of taxation) levied on goods and services rather than income or profits.

ORIGIN late Middle English (in the sense 'not in full grammatical concord'): from medieval Latin *indirectus*, from *in-* 'not' + *directus*, past part. of *dirigere*, from *di-* 'distinctly' or *de-* 'down' + *regere* 'put straight.'

in•di•vid•u•al re•tire•ment ac•count /ˌində'vijōōəl ri'tīrmənt ə,kownt/ (abbr.: **IRA**) ▸ **n.** a savings or investment plan in which a person can set aside a certain amount of earned income every year; contributions and earnings on contributions are tax-free until retirement.

ORIGIN 1930s: abbreviation.

in•dul•gence /in'dəljəns/ ▸ **n.** an extension of the time in which a bill or debt has to be paid.

ORIGIN late Middle English: via Old French from Latin *indulgentia*, from the verb *indulgere* 'give free rein to.'

in•dus•tri•al es•pi•o•nage /in'dəstrēəl 'espēə,näzн/ ▸ **n.** spying directed toward discovering the secrets of a rival manufacturer or other industrial company.

in•dus•tri•als /in'dəstrēəlz/ ▸ plural **n.** shares in industrial companies.

ORIGIN early 17th cent.: from French, from *finance* (see **FINANCE**).

in•fla•tion /in'flāsнən/ ▸ **n.** a general increase in prices and fall in the purchasing value of money.

ORIGIN Middle English (in the sense 'the condition of being inflated with a gas'): from Latin *inflatio(n-)*, from *inflare* 'blow into,' from *in-* 'into' + *flare* 'blow.'

in•fla•tion•ar•y /in'flāsнə,nerē/ ▸ **adj.** of, characterized by, or tending to cause monetary inflation: *policies aimed at controlling inflation* | [as adj.] *high inflation rates.*

in•fo•mer•cial /'infō,mərsнəl/ ▸ **n.** a television program that promotes a product in an informative and supposedly objective way.

ORIGIN 1980s: blend of *information* and *commercial.*

in•her•it•ance tax /in'heritəns ˌtæks/ ▶ n. a tax imposed on someone who inherits property or money.

in•i•tial pub•lic of•fer•ing /i'nishəl 'pəblik 'ôf(ə)riNG/ (abbr.: **IPO**) ▶ n. a company's flotation on the stock exchange.

in-serv•ice /'in ˌsərvis/ ▶ adj. (of training) intended for those actively engaged in the profession or activity concerned.

in•sid•er trad•ing /'in,sīdər 'trādiNG/ ▶ n. the illegal practice of trading on the stock exchange to one's own advantage through having access to confidential information.

in•sol•vent /in'sälvənt/ ▶ adj. unable to pay debts owed.

in•stall•ment /in'stôlmənt/ ▶ n. a sum of money due as one of several equal payments for something, spread over an agreed period of time: *the first installment of a grant for housing | the purchase price is paid in installments.*

ORIGIN mid 18th cent.: alteration of obsolete *estalment* (probably by association with *installation*), from Anglo-Norman French *estalement*, from Old French *estaler* 'to fix.'

in•stall•ment plan /in'stôlmənt ˌplæn/ ▶ n. an arrangement for payment by installments.

In•stant Tell•er /'instənt 'telər/ ▶ n. Canadian trademark an automated banking machine.

in•sti•tu•tion /ˌinsti't(y)o͞oSHən/ ▶ n. a large company or other institution involved in financial trading: *the interest rate that financial institutions charge one another.*

ORIGIN late Middle English: via Old French from Latin *institutio(n-)*, from the verb *instituere* 'establish,' from *in-* 'in' + *statuere* 'set up.'

in•sti•tu•tion•al /ˌinsti't(y)o͞oSHənl/ ▶ adj. (of advertising) intended to create prestige rather than immediate sales.

in•sti•tu•tion•al in•ves•tor /ˌinsti't(y)o͞oSHənl in'vestər/ ▶ n. a large organization such as a bank, pension fund, labor union, or insurance company, that makes substantial investments on the stock exchange.

in•sur•a•ble earn•ings /in'SHo͞orəbəl 'ərniNGz/ ▶ n.pl. Canadian income on which employment insurance premiums are paid.

in•sur•ance /in'SHo͞orəns/ ▶ n. a practice or arrangement by which a company or government agency provides a guarantee of compensation for specified loss, damage, illness, or death in return for payment of a premium: *many new borrowers take out insurance against disability or sickness.* ■ the business of providing such an arrangement: *Howard is in insurance.* ■ money paid for this: *my insurance has gone up.* ■ money paid out as compensation under such an arrangement: *when will I be able to collect the insurance?* ■ an insurance policy. ORIGIN late Middle English: from Old French *enseurance*, from *enseurer*, alteration of *aseurer*, based on Latin *ad-* 'to' (expressing change) + *securus*, from *se-* 'without' + *cura* 'care.'

in•sur•ance a•gent /in'sHŏŏrəns ˌājənt/ ▶ n. a person employed to sell insurance policies.

in•sur•ance car•ri•er /in'sHŏŏrəns ˌkærēər/ ▶ n. an insurer; an insurance company.

in•sur•ance pol•i•cy /in'sHŏŏrəns ˌpäləsē/ ▶ n. a document detailing the terms and conditions of a contract of insurance.

in•sure /in'sHŏŏr/ ▶ v. [trans.] arrange for compensation in the event of damage to or loss of (property), or injury to or the death of (someone), in exchange for regular advance payments to a company or government agency: *the table should be* **insured for** *$2,500* | *the company had* **insured** *itself* **against** *a fall of the dollar* | [intrans.] *businesses can* **insure against** *exchange rate fluctuations.* ■ provide insurance coverage with respect to: *subsidiaries set up to insure the risks of a group of companies.* ORIGIN late Middle English: alteration of *ensure* .

USAGE: There is considerable overlap between the meaning and use of **insure** and **ensure.** In both US and British English, the primary meaning of **insure** is the commercial sense of providing financial compensation in the event of damage to property; **ensure** is not used at all in this sense. For the more general senses, **ensure** is more likely to be used, but **insure** and **ensure** are often interchangeable, particularly in US English: *bail is posted to* **insure** *that the defendant appears for trial;* | *the system is run to* **ensure** *that a good quality of service is maintained.*

in•sured /in'SHŏŏrd/ ▸ **adj.** covered by insurance: *the insured car | a privately insured patient | an insured risk.*
▸ **n.** (**the insured**) (pl. same) a person or organization covered by insurance.

in•sur•er /in'SHŏŏrər/ ▸ **n.** a person or company that underwrites an insurance risk; the party in an insurance contract undertaking to pay compensation.

in•tan•gi•ble /in'tænjəbəl/ ▸ **adj.** (of an asset or benefit) not constituting or represented by a physical object and of a value not precisely measurable: *intangible business property like trademarks and patents.*
ORIGIN early 17th cent.: from French, or from medieval Latin *intangibilis*, from *in-* 'not' + late Latin *tangibilis* (from *tangere* 'touch').

in•ter•bank /'intər,bæNGk/ ▸ **adj.** agreed, arranged, or operating between banks: *trading opportunities in the interbank market.*

in•ter•est /'int(ə)rist/ ▸ **n. 1** money paid regularly at a particular rate for the use of money lent, or for delaying the repayment of a debt: *the monthly rate of interest |* [as adj.] *interest payments.*
2 a stake, share, or involvement in an undertaking, esp. a financial one: *holders of voting rights must disclose their interests.*
PHRASES **declare an** (or **one's**) **interest** make known one's financial interests in an undertaking before it is discussed. **with interest** with interest charged or paid: *loans that must be paid back with interest.*
ORIGIN late Middle English (originally as *interess*): from Anglo-Norman French *interesse*, from Latin *interesse* 'differ, be important,' from *inter-* 'between' + *esse* 'be.' The *-t* was added partly by association with Old French *interest* 'damage, loss,' apparently from Latin *interest* 'it is important.'

In•ter•na•tion•al Mon•e•tar•y Fund /,intər'næSH(ə)nl 'mäni,terē ,fənd/ (abbr.: **IMF**) an international organization established in 1945 that aims to promote international trade and monetary cooperation and the stabilization of exchange rates.

USAGE: Member countries contribute in gold and in their own currencies to provide a reserve on which they may draw to meet foreign obligations during periods of deficit in their international balance of payments. It is affiliated with the UN.

in•tra•pre•neur /ˌintrəprəˈnər; -ˈno͝or/ ▶ n. a manager within a company who promotes innovative product development and marketing.

ORIGIN 1970s (originally US): from *intra-* 'within' + a shortened form of ENTREPRENEUR.

in•ven•to•ry /ˈinvənˌtôrē/ ▶ n. (pl. **in•ven•to•ries**) a complete list of items such as property, goods in stock, or the contents of a building.

■ a quantity of goods held in stock: *in our warehouse you'll find a large inventory of new and used bicycles.* ■ (in accounting) the entire stock of a business, including materials, components, work in progress, and finished products.

ORIGIN late Middle English: from medieval Latin *inventorium,* alteration of late Latin *inventarium,* literally 'a list of what is found,' from Latin *invenire* 'come upon.'

in•vest /inˈvest/ ▶ v. [intrans.] expend money with the expectation of achieving a profit or material result by putting it into financial schemes, shares, or property, or by using it to develop a commercial venture: *getting workers to **invest in** private pension funds* | [trans.] *the company is to **invest** $12 million **in** its new manufacturing site.*

DERIVATIVES **in•ves•tor** n.

ORIGIN mid 16th cent.: from French *investir* or Latin *investire,* from *in-* 'into, upon' + *vestire* 'clothe' (from *vestis* 'clothing').

in•vest•ment /inˈvestmənt/ ▶ n. the action or process of investing money for profit or material result: *a debate over private **investment in** road-building* | *a total investment of $50,000.*

■ a thing that is worth buying because it may be profitable or useful in the future: *a used car is rarely a good investment.*

in•vest•ment bank /inˈvestmənt ˌbaNGk/ ▶ n. a bank that purchases large holdings of newly issued shares and resells them to investors.

in•vest•ment deal•er /inˈvestmənt ˌdēlər/ ▶ n. Canadian **1** see **investment company**.

2 a person working as a broker for an investment company.

in•vest•ment grade /in'vestmənt ˌgrād/ ▸ n. a level of credit rating (usually A or higher) for stocks regarded as carrying a minimal risk to investors.

in•vest•ment trust /in'vestmənt ˌtrəst/ ▸ n. a limited company whose business is the investment of shareholders' funds, the shares being traded like those of any other public company.

in•voice /'inˌvois/ ▸ n. a list of goods sent or services provided, with a statement of the sum due for these; a bill.
▸ v. [trans.] send an invoice to (someone).
■ send an invoice for (goods or services provided).
ORIGIN mid 16th cent.: originally the plural of obsolete *invoy*, from obsolete French *envoy*, from *envoyer* 'send,' from *en voie* 'on the way,' based on Latin *via* 'way.'

IPO ▸ abbr. initial public offering.

IRA /'īrə; 'īˌär'ā/ ▸ abbr. individual retirement account.

ir•re•deem•a•ble /ˌiri'dēməbəl/ ▸ adj. (of paper currency) for which the issuing authority does not undertake ever to pay coin.

J

---

jaw•bone /ˈjôˌbōn/ ▶ n. Canadian slang deferred payment; credit.

Jay•cee /ˈjāˈsē/ ▶ n. a member of a Junior Chamber of Commerce, a civic organization for business and community leaders.

ORIGIN 1940s: representing the initials of *Junior Chamber*.

JIT ▶ abbr. (of manufacturing systems) just-in-time.

job /jäb/ ▶ n. **1** a paid position of regular employment.

2 a task or piece of work, esp. one that is paid.

▶ v. (**jobbed, jobbing**) [trans.] buy and sell (stocks) as a broker-dealer, esp. on a small scale.

ORIGIN mid 16th cent.: of unknown origin.

job an•a•lyst /ˈjäb ˌænl-ist/ ▶ n. a person employed to assess the essential factors of particular jobs and the qualifications needed to carry them out.

job•ber /ˈjäbər/ ▶ n. **1** a wholesaler.

2 a person who does casual or occasional work.

ORIGIN late 17th cent. (in the sense 'broker, middleman,' originally not derogatory): from **JOB**.

job ro•ta•tion /ˈjäb rōˌtāsнən/ ▶ n. the practice of moving employees between different tasks to promote experience and variety.

joint ac•count /ˈjoint əˈkownt/ ▶ n. a bank account held by more than one person, each individual having the right to deposit and withdraw funds.

joint stock /ˈjoint ˈstäk/ ▶ n. a portion of capital held jointly; a common fund.

joint-stock com•pa•ny /ˈjoint ˈstäk ˌkəmpənē/ ▶ n. a company whose stock is owned jointly by the shareholders.

joint ven•ture /ˈjoint ˈvenCHər/ ▶ n. a commercial enterprise undertaken jointly by two or more parties that otherwise retain their distinct identities.

jour•nal /'jərnl/ ▸ n. (in bookkeeping) a daily record of business transactions with a statement of the accounts to which each is to be debited and credited.

ORIGIN late Middle English (originally denoting a book containing the appointed times of daily prayers): from Old French *jurnal*, from late Latin *diurnalis,* from *diurnus* 'daily,' from *dies* 'day.'

junk bond /'jəNGk ˌbänd/ ▸ n. a high-yield, high-risk security (often referred to as 'B-rated'), typically issued by a company seeking to raise capital quickly in order to finance a takeover.

just-in-time /'jəst in 'tīm/ (abbr.: **JIT**) ▸ adj. denoting a manufacturing system in which materials or components are delivered immediately before they are required in order to minimize inventory costs.

K

kai•zen /ˈkīzən/ ▸ n. a Japanese business philosophy of continuous improvement of working practices, personal efficiency, etc.
ORIGIN Japanese, literally 'improvement.'

kan•ban /ˈkänˌbän/ ▸ n. (also **kan•ban sys•tem**) a Japanese manufacturing system in which the supply of components is regulated through the use of a card displaying a sequence of specifications and instructions, sent along the production line.
■ a card of this type.
ORIGIN late 20th cent.: Japanese, literally 'billboard, sign.'

kei•ret•su /kāˈretsoō/ ▸ n. (pl. same) (in Japan) a conglomeration of businesses linked together by cross-shareholdings to form a robust corporate structure.
ORIGIN Japanese, from *kei* 'systems' + *retsu* 'tier.'

HOW TO BUY A HOME

Many people don't realize that the same amount of money they spend on rent today could buy them a home tomorrow. As of this writing (in mid-2003), interest rates are near a 40-year low. They may be higher by the time you read this, but let's use the math we have at the moment. To put it simply, for every $1,000 you pay in monthly rent, you could support $125,000 worth of mortgage (including taxes and insurance). In other words, if your rent is currently $2,000 a month, you could afford to make payments on a $250,000 mortgage. In most parts of the country, that would buy you a lot of home!

The number one reason people put off buying a home is because they think they can't afford it. More often than not, they are wrong.

In particular, would-be home buyers are scared off by the down payment. People often think they need to come up with thousands if not tens of thousands of dollars in cash in order to get a mortgage. This is simply not true. There are all sorts of programs sponsored by developers, lenders, and even the government that can enable first-time home buyers to finance as much as 95, 97, or even 100 percent of the purchase price. While borrowing so much can be risky (if you can't afford the monthly payments), it's also a way of getting renters into their own homes much faster than if they had saved up enough money to make a big down payment.

According to the FHA, a good rule of thumb is that most people can afford to spend 29 percent of their gross income on housing expenses—as much as 41 percent if they have no debt.

If you earn $50,000 a year, you should be able to afford to spend at least $1,208, or even up to $1,712 a month on housing in the form of rent or mortgage payments. At 6 percent interest, that means you could afford a mortgage of $200,000 to almost $300,000.

But it's not enough to just buy a house. In fact, buying the house is often the easiest part. The real challenge comes in figuring out how you're going to pay for it. Indeed, the key to making it all work financially is getting the right kind of mortgage.

There are many types of mortgages. Each type has its advantages and disadvantages. If you are conservative and planning on being in your home a long time (at least seven to ten years), a 30-year mortgage offers the most benefits and flexibility. Alternatively, if you're looking for low rates and lower monthly payments, and you're not planning on keeping the property very long, you might choose an intermediate adjustable rate mortgage.

Here are some of the agencies and companies that can help you buy a home:

U.S. Department of Housing and Urban Development
www.hud.gov
If you are a first-time homebuyer, visit this Web site. It offers a wealth of resources on how to buy, what kind of help HUD offers, and how to qualify for assistance.

National Council of State Housing Finance Agencies
www.ncsha.org
The NCSHA Web site contains links to housing finance agencies in every state, many of which offer programs that allow you to buy a home with a down payment of less than 5 percent.

Fannie Mae
(800) 832-2345
www.fanniemae.com
Fannie Mae provides the financing that makes it possible for banks to lend money to consumers. Its free reports—*Opening*

the Door to a Home of Your Own, Choosing a Mortgage, Knowing Your Credit, and *Borrowing Basics*—are all available simply for the asking. Just call (800) 688-4663 and they'll send you one or all of them.

Freddie Mac
(800) 373-3343
www.freddiemac.com
In the Homebuyers section of the Freddie Mac Web site (at *www.freddiemac.com/homebuyers*), you'll find a wonderful tool called "The Road to Home Ownership."

Here are some loan programs to consider:

FHA Loans. Federal Housing Administration (FHA) loans can cover up to 97 percent of the purchase price of a home and can be used to buy a second or third home. To get one, you need to work with a lender who is approved to do FHA loans. For more information, visit *www.fhaloan.com*.

VA Loans. For veterans of the U.S. armed services, the Department of Veterans Affairs offers loans to both first- and second-time homebuyers. In addition to visiting the VA's own Web site at *www.va.gov*, where you'll find a resource center and referrals to VA-approved lenders, you might also want to check out *www.valoans.com*.

Here are some Web sites to help you find and finance a home:

www.citimortgage.com	*www.lendingtree.com*
www.eloan.com	*www.pueblo.gsa.gov*
www.homebuying.about.com	*www.quickenloan.com*
www.homebuyingguide.org	*www.realtor.com*
www.homepath.com	*www.smartmoney.com/home/buying*

L

la•bor mar•ket /'lābər ˌmärkit/ ▸ n. the supply of available workers with reference to the demand for them: *a diverse workforce in a tight labor market.*

Laf•fer curve /'læfər ˌkərv/ ▸ n. a supposed relationship between economic activity and the rate of taxation that suggests the existence of an optimum tax rate that maximizes tax revenue.
ORIGIN 1970s: named after Arthur *Laffer* (born 1942), American economist.

lais•sez-faire /ˌlesā 'fe(ə)r/ ▸ n. abstention by governments from interfering in the workings of the free market: [as adj.] *laissez-faire capitalism.*
ORIGIN French, literally 'allow to do.'

land bank /'lænd ˌbæNGk/ ▸ n. a bank whose main function is to provide loans for land purchase, esp. by farmers.

large-cap /'lärj 'kæp/ ▸ adj. denoting or relating to the stock of a company with a large capitalization.

Latte factor /'lätā ˌfæktər/ ▸ n. trademark a concept that represents the amount people spend every day on items such as coffee, cigarettes, soft drinks, and candy bars, which they could instead save and invest.
USAGE: In purchasing a $3.50 latte every day for a year, one would spend $1,260. If that money were invested at 10 percent over 10 years, it would grow to $21,870. The **Latte factor** is a metaphor for how people waste money.

laun•der /'lôndər; 'län-/ ▸ v. [trans.] conceal the origins of (money obtained illegally) by transfers involving foreign banks or legitimate businesses.

ORIGIN Middle English (as a noun denoting a person who washes linen): contraction of *lavender*, from Old French *lavandier*, based on Latin *lavanda* 'things to be washed,' from *lavare* 'to wash.'

lay•off /'lā͜ôf; -͜äf/ ▸ n. a discharge, esp. temporary, of a worker or workers.

■ a period when this is in force.

LBO ▸ abbr. leveraged buyout.

l.c. ▸ abbr. letter of credit.

lead time /'lēd ͜tīm/ ▸ n. the time between the initiation and completion of a production process.

ledg•er /'lejər/ ▸ n. a book or other collection of financial accounts of a particular type: *the total balance of the purchases ledger.*

ORIGIN late Middle English *legger*, *ligger* (denoting a large bible or breviary), probably from variants of *lay* and *lie*, influenced by Dutch *legger* and *ligger* . This sense dates from the 16th cent.

lend /lend/ ▸ v. (past and past part. **lent**) [trans.] allow (a person or organization) the use of (a sum of money) under an agreement to pay it back later, typically with interest: *no one would lend him the money* | *the bank lends only to its current customers* | [as n.] (**lending**) *balance sheets weakened by unwise lending.*

ORIGIN Old English *lǣnan*, of Germanic origin; related to Dutch *lenen*, also to LOAN. The addition of the final -*d* in late Middle English was due to association with verbs such as *bend* and *send*.

USAGE: See usage at LOAN.

lend•er /'lendər/ ▸ n. an organization or person that lends money: *a mortgage lender.*

let•ter of cred•it /'letər əv 'kredit/ (abbr.: **lc.**) ▸ n. a letter issued by a bank to another bank (typically in a different country) to serve as a guarantee for payments made to a specified person under specified conditions.

lev•er•age /'lev(ə)rij; 'lē-/ ▸ n. the ratio of a company's loan capital (debt) to the value of its ordinary shares (equity).

▸ v. [trans.] [usu. as adj.] (**leveraged**) use borrowed capital for (an investment), expecting the profits made to be greater than the interest payable: *a leveraged takeover bid.*

lev•er•aged buy•out /'lev(ə)rijd 'bī,owt/ (abbr.: **LBO**) ▸ n. the purchase of a controlling share in a company by its management, using outside capital.

li•a•bil•i•ty /ˌlīə'bilətē/ ▸ n. (pl. **li•a•bil•i•ties**) (usu. **liabilities**) a thing for which someone is responsible, esp. a debt or financial obligation: *valuing the company's liabilities and assets.*

LIF /lif/ ▸ abbr. Canadian see **life income fund.**

life in•come fund /'līf 'inkəm ˌfənd/ (abbr.: **LIF**) ▸ n. Canadian a tax-sheltered fund providing annual income to its holder, not falling below an established minimum percentage of the fund, but also not exceeding a maximum payment..

life in•sur•ance /'līf in,SHŏŏrəns/ ▸ n. insurance that pays out a sum of money either on the death of the insured person or after a set period.

LIFO /'līfō/ ▸ abbr. last in, first out (chiefly with reference to methods of stock valuation and data storage).

light in•dus•try /'līt 'indəstrē/ ▸ n. the manufacture of small or light articles.

Lim•it•ed /'limiṯid/ (abbr.: **Ltd.**) ▸ adj. Brit. denoting a company whose owners are legally responsible for its debts only to the extent of the amount of capital they invested (used after a company name): *Times Newspapers Limited.*

lim•it•ed part•ner /'limitid 'pärtnər/ ▸ n. a partner in a company or venture who receives limited profits from the business and whose liability toward its debts is legally limited to the extent of his or her investment.

DERIVATIVES **lim•it•ed part•ner•ship** n.

line /līn/ ▸ n. 1 a company that provides ships, aircraft, or buses on particular routes on a regular basis.

2 a range of commercial goods.

PHRASES **above the line** denoting or relating to money spent on items of current expenditure. **below the line** denoting or relating to money spent on items of capital expenditure. **line of credit** an amount of credit extended to a borrower.

ORIGIN Old English *līne* 'rope, series,' probably of Germanic origin, from Latin *linea (fibra)* 'flax (fiber),' from *linum* 'flax,' reinforced in Middle English by Old French *ligne*, based on Latin *linea*.

liq•uid /'likwid/ ▸ adj. (of assets) held in cash or easily converted into cash.

■ having ready cash or liquid assets. ■ (of a market) having a high volume of activity.

ORIGIN late Middle English: from Latin *liquidus*, from *liquere* 'be liquid.'

liq•ui•date /'likwi‚dāt/ ▸ v. [trans.] wind up the affairs of (a company or firm) by ascertaining liabilities and apportioning assets.

■ [intrans.] (of a company) undergo such a process. ■ [trans.] convert (assets) into cash: *a plan to liquidate $10,000,000 worth of property over seven years.* ■ pay off (a debt).

ORIGIN mid 16th cent. (in the sense 'set out (accounts) clearly'): from medieval Latin *liquidat-* 'made clear,' from the verb *liquidare*, from Latin *liquidus* (see LIQUID).

liq•ui•da•tion /‚likwi'dāsHən/ ▸ n. the process of liquidating a company or firm.

■ the conversion of assets into cash (i.e., by selling them). ■ the clearing of a debt.

PHRASES **go into liquidation** (of a company or firm) be closed and have its assets apportioned.

liq•ui•da•tor /'likwi‚dātər/ ▸ n. a person appointed to wind up the affairs of a company or firm.

liq•uid•i•ty /li'kwiditē/ ▸ n. the availability of liquid assets to a market or company.

■ liquid assets; cash. ■ a high volume of activity in a market.

ORIGIN early 17th cent.: from French *liquidité* or medieval Latin *liquiditas*, from Latin *liquidus* (see LIQUID).

li•quid•i•ty ra•tio /li'kwiditē ‚rāsH(ē)‚ō/ ▸ n. the ratio between the liquid assets and the liabilities of a bank or other institution.

LIRA /'li(ə)rə/ ▸ abbr. Canadian see **locked-in retirement account**.

list•ed /'listid/ ▸ adj. admitted for trading on a stock exchange: *listed securities.*

list price /'list ‚prīs/ ▸ n. the price of an article as shown in a list issued by the manufacturer or by the general body of manufacturers of the particular class of goods: *all items 30 percent off list price.*

liv•ing wage /'liviNG ‚wāj/ ▸ n. [in sing.] a wage that is high enough to maintain a normal standard of living.

Lloyd's /loidz/ an incorporated society of insurance underwriters in London, made up of private syndicates. Founded in 1871, Lloyd's originally dealt only in marine insurance.
ORIGIN named after the coffeehouse of Edward *Lloyd* (*fl.* 1688–1726), in which underwriters and merchants congregated and where *Lloyd's List* was started in 1734.

load /lōd/ ▸ v. [trans.] add an extra charge to (an insurance premium) in the case of a poorer risk.
▸n. a commission that is charged on an investment product, esp. a mutual fund.
▸adj. denoting a type of mutual fund that charges a commission, usually deducted from the amount invested.
ORIGIN Old English *lād* 'way, journey, conveyance,' of Germanic origin.

USAGE: There are basically two types of mutual funds: **load funds** and **no-load funds**. However, both types charge a management fee. The average management fee for a no-load fund is about 1.3 percent a year. **Load fund** management fees are about one-half to one percent higher.

load•ing /'lōdiNG/ ▸ n. an increase in an insurance premium due to a factor increasing the risk involved.

loan /lōn/ ▸ n. a thing that is borrowed, esp. a sum of money that is expected to be paid back with interest: *he wants to take out a loan for $84,000.*
▸v. [trans.] (often **be loaned**) borrow (a sum of money or item of property).
ORIGIN Middle English (also denoting a gift from a superior): from Old Norse *lán*, of Germanic origin; related to Dutch *leen*, German *Lehn*, also to LEND.

USAGE: Traditionally, **loan** was a noun and **lend** was a verb: *I went to ask for a loan; I can you lend me twenty dollars?* But **loan** is now widely used as a verb, esp. in financial contexts: *the banks were loaning money to speculators.*

locked-in re•tire•ment ac•count /'läkt 'in ri'tīrmənt ə‚kownt/ (abbr.: **LIRA**) ▸ n. Canadian a retirement savings account created with money transferred out of a registered pension plan and from which funds can only be transferred to a life income fund, a locked-in retirement income fund, or a life annuity.

locked-in re•tire•ment in•come fund /'läkt 'in ri'tīrmənt 'inkəm ˌfənd/ (abbr.: **LRIF**) ▸ n. Canadian a tax-sheltered savings plan which provides retirement income. .

lock-in /'läk ˌin/ ▸ n. an arrangement according to which a person or company is obliged to negotiate or trade only with a specific company.

lock•up /'läk,əp/ ▸ n. an investment in assets that cannot readily be realized or sold in the short term: *When a company goes public, most employees cannot sell their stock for a specified period, called a* **lockup period.**

lodg•ment /'läjmənt/ (also **lodge•ment**) ▸ n. the depositing of money in a particular bank, account, etc.

ORIGIN late 16th cent.: from French *logement* 'dwelling,' from Old French *loge* 'arbor, hut,' from medieval Latin *laubia, lobia,* of Germanic origin.

lo•go /'lōgō/ ▸ n. (pl. **lo•gos**) a symbol or other small design adopted by an organization to identify its products, uniform, vehicles, etc.

ORIGIN 1930s: abbreviation of *logogram* or *logotype.*

long /lôNG/ ▸ adj. (**long•er, long•est**) (of shares, bonds, or other assets) bought in advance, with the expectation of a rise in price. ■ (of a broker or their position in the market) buying or based on long stocks. ■ (of a security) maturing at a distant date.
▸ n. (**longs**) long-dated securities, esp. gilt-edged securities. ■ assets held in a long position.

ORIGIN Old English *lang, long,* of Germanic origin; related to Dutch and German *lang* .

loon•ie /'lōōnē/ (also **loon•y**) ▸ n. Canadian informal **1** the Canadian one-dollar coin. **2** the Canadian dollar.

ORIGIN from the image on the coin.

loss-lead•er /'lôs ˌlēdər/ ▸ n. a product sold at a loss to attract customers.

loss-mak•ing /'lôs ˌmākiNG/ ▸ adj. (esp. of a business) losing money, rather than making a profit.

low•ball /'lō,bôl/ ▸ **adj.** informal (of an estimate, bid, etc.) deceptively or unrealistically low.

▸ **v.** [trans.] offer a deceptively or unrealistically low estimate, bid, etc: *are you being lowballed by somebody who hopes to make money on extras later?*

low-end /'lō 'end/ ▸ **adj.** denoting the least expensive of a range of products.

LRIF /'elrif/ ▸ **abbr.** Canadian see **locked-in retirement income fund.**

Ltd. Brit. ▸ **abbr.** (after a company name) Limited: *Trimble Navigation Ltd.*

lump sum /'ləmp ,səm/ ▸ **n.** a single payment made at a particular time, as opposed to a number of smaller payments or installments.

USAGE: Many people who retire select a benefit in the form of a **lump sum** payment rather than a guaranteed monthly payment.

M

mac•ro•ec•o•nom•ics /ˈmækrō͵ekəˈnämiks; -͵ēkə-/ ▶ **plural n.** [treated as sing.] the part of economics concerned with large-scale or general economic factors, such as interest rates and national productivity.

DERIVATIVES **mac•ro•ec•o•nom•ic adj.**

mac•ro•e•con•o•my /ˈmækrō-iˈkänəmē/ ▶ n. (pl. **mac•cro•e•cib•o• mies**) a large-scale economic system.

mail or•der /ˈmāl ͵ôrdər/ ▶ n. the selling of goods to customers by mail, generally involving selection from a special catalog: *available by mail order only* | [as adj.] *a mail-order distributor of generic drugs.*

man•aged cur•ren•cy /ˈmænijd ˈkərənsē/ ▶ n. a currency whose exchange rate is regulated or controlled by the government.

man•aged fund /ˈmænijd ˈfənd/ ▶ n. an investment fund run on behalf of an investor by an agent (typically an insurance company).

man•age•ment ac•count•ing /ˈmænijmənt əˈkowntiNG/ ▶ n. the provision of financial data and advice to a company for use in the organization and development of its business.

man•age•ment com•pa•ny /ˈmænijmənt ͵kəmpənē/ ▶ n. a company that is set up to manage a group of properties, a mutual fund, an investment fund, etc.

mar•gin /ˈmärjin/ ▶ n. a profit margin.
- a sum deposited with a broker to cover the risk of loss on a transaction or account.

▶ v. (**mar•gined, mar•gin•ing**) [trans.] deposit an amount of money with a broker as security for (an account or transaction): [as adj.] (**margined**) *a margined transaction.*

ORIGIN late Middle English: from Latin *margo, margin-* 'edge.'

mar•gin•al /'märjənl/ ▸ adj. (chiefly of costs or benefits) relating to or resulting from small or unit changes.

■ (of taxation) relating to increases in income. ■ close to the limit of profitability, esp. through difficulty of exploitation: *marginal farmland.*

ORIGIN late 16th cent.: from medieval Latin *marginalis*, from Latin *margo, margin-* 'edge.'

mar•gin•al cost /'märjənl 'kôst/ ▸ n. the cost added by producing one extra item of a product.

mar•gin call /'märjin ˌkôl/ ▸ n. a demand by a broker that an investor deposit further cash or securities to cover possible losses.

mark•down /'märkˌdown/ ▸ n. a reduction in price.

mar•ket /'märkit/ ▸ n. an area or arena in which commercial dealings are conducted: *the sale of cruisers in the American market continues to plummet | the labor market.*

■ a demand for a particular commodity or service: *there is a market for ornamental daggers.* ■ the state of trade at a particular time or in a particular context: *the bottom's fallen out of the market.* ■ the free market; the operation of supply and demand: *future development cannot simply be left to the market | [as adj.] a market economy* ■ a stock market.

▸ v. (**mar•ket•ed, mar•ket•ing**) [trans.] advertise or promote (something).

■ offer for sale: *sheep farmers unable to market their lambs.* ■ buy or sell provisions in a market: [as n.] (**marketing**) *some people like to do their marketing early in the morning.*

PHRASES **make a market** take part in active dealing in particular shares or other assets.

ORIGIN Middle English, via Anglo-Norman French from Latin *mercatus*, from *mercari* 'buy.'

mar•ket forc•es /'märkit ˌfôrsəz/ ▸ plural n. the economic factors affecting the price, demand, and availability of a commodity: *leaving oil prices to be determined purely by market forces.*

mar•ket•ing /'märkiṯiNG/ ▸ n. the action or business of promoting and selling products or services, including market research and advertising.

mar•ket•ing mix /'märkiṯiNG ˌmiks/ ▶ n. a combination of factors that can be controlled by a company to influence consumers to purchase its products.

mar•ket•i•za•tion /ˌmärkiṯə'zāsHən/ ▶ n. the exposure of an industry or service to market forces.

■ the conversion of a national economy from a planned to a market economy: *the marketization of the Russian economy.*

mar•ket mak•er /'märkit ˌmākər/ (also **mar•ket-mak•er**) ▶ n. a dealer in securities or other assets who undertakes to buy or sell at specified prices at all times.

mar•ket price /'märkit ˌprīs/ ▶ n. the price of a commodity when sold in a given market: *the world market price for nonfat dry milk.*

mar•ket re•search /'märkit 'rēˌsərCH; ri'sərCH/ ▶ n. the action or activity of gathering information about consumers' needs and preferences.

mar•ket share /'märkit ˌsHer/ ▶ n. the portion of a market controlled by a particular company or product.

mar•ket tim•er /'märkit ˌtīmər/ ▶ n. a person or organization that makes decisions to buy or sell investments based on economic and other factors that might affect the direction of the market.

DERIVATIVES **mar•ket tim•ing** n.

USAGE: Market timers look at such things as investor sentiment, earnings reports, direction of interest rates, trading volume, GDP, and whether the country is at war.

mar•ket val•ue /'märkit ˌvælyo͞o/ ▶ n. the amount for which something can be sold on a given market.

mark-to-mar•ket /'märk tə 'märkit / ▶ adj. denoting or relating to a system of valuing assets by the most recent market price.

mark•up /'märˌkəp/ ▶ n. the amount added to the cost price of goods to cover overhead and profit.

mass mar•ket /'mæs 'märkit/ ▶ n. the market for goods that are produced in large quantities.

▶ v. (**mass-mar•ket**) [trans.] market (a product) on a large scale.

ma•trix /'mātriks/ ▶ n. (pl. **ma•tr•ices** /'mātrəsēz/ or **ma•trix•es**) an organizational structure in which two or more lines of command, responsibility, or communication may run through the same individual.

ORIGIN late Middle English (in the sense 'womb'): from Latin, 'breeding female,' later 'womb,' from *mater, matr-* 'mother.'

ma•ture /mə'CHŏŏr; -'t(y)ŏŏr/ ▸ **adj.** (**ma•tur•er, ma•tur•est**) **1** denoting an economy, industry, or market that has developed to a point where substantial expansion and investment no longer takes place. **2** (of a bill) due for payment.

▸**v.** [intrans.] (of an insurance policy, security, etc.) reach the end of its term and hence become payable.

ORIGIN late Middle English: from Latin *maturus* 'timely, ripe.'

ma•tu•ri•ty /mə'CHŏŏriṯē; mə't(y)ŏŏr-/ ▸ **n.** the time when an insurance policy, security, etc., matures.

ORIGIN late Middle English: from Latin *maturitas,* from *maturus* (see **MATURE**).

MBA ▸ **abbr.** Master of Business Administration.

meg•a•store /'megə,stôr/ ▸ **n.** a very large store, typically one specializing in a particular type of product.

mel•on /'melən/ ▸ **n.** a large profit, esp. a stock dividend, to be divided among a number of people: *you can just see them sitting around the room* **cutting up the melon** *in advance.*

ORIGIN late Middle English: via Old French from late Latin *melo, melon-,* contraction of Latin *melopepo,* from Greek *mēlopepōn,* from *mēlon* 'apple' + *pepōn* 'gourd.'

melt•down /'melt,down/ ▸ **n.** a rapid fall in share prices: *the 1987 stock market meltdown.*

merg•er /'mərjər/ ▸ **n.** a combination of two companies into one: *a* **merger between** *two supermarket chains* | *local companies ripe for merger or acquisition.*

ORIGIN early 18th cent.: from Anglo-Norman French *merger* 'dip, plunge.'

met•age /'meṯij/ ▸ **n.** the official weighing of loads of coal, grain, or other material.

■ the duty paid for this.

ORIGIN early 16th cent.: from Old English *metan* 'measure, determine the quantity of' (of Germanic origin) + *-age.*

mez•za•nine /'mezə,nēn; ,mezə'nēn/ ▶ adj. relating to or denoting unsecured, higher-yielding loans that are subordinate to bank loans and secured loans but rank above equity: *mezzanine loans* | *a provider of mezzanine and buy-out capital.*
ORIGIN early 18th cent.: from French, from Italian *mezzanino*, diminutive of *mezzano* 'middle,' from Latin *medianus* 'median.'

MFN ▶ abbr. most favored nation.

mi•cro•ec•o•nom•ics /'mīkrō,ekə'nämiks; -,ēkə-/ ▶ plural n. [treated as sing.] the part of economics concerned with single factors and the effects of individual decisions.
DERIVATIVES **mi•cro•ec•o•nom•ic** adj.

mid•dle•man /'midl,mæn/ ▶ n. (pl. **mid•dle•men**) a person who buys goods from producers and sells them to retailers or consumers: *we aim to maintain value for money by cutting out the middleman and selling direct.*
■ a person who arranges business between other people.

mid•dle man•age•ment /'midl 'mänijmənt/ ▶ n. the level in an organization just below that of senior administrators.
■ the managers at this level regarded collectively.

mill /mil/ ▶ n. a monetary unit used only in calculations, worth one thousandth of a dollar.
ORIGIN late 18th cent.: from Latin *millesimum* 'thousandth part.'

mint par /'mint ,pär/ (also **mint par•i•ty** /'mint ,pæritē/) ▶ n. the ratio between the gold equivalents of currency in two countries.
■ their rate of exchange based on such a ratio.

mixed e•con•o•my /'mikst i'känəmē/ ▶ n. an economic system combining private and public enterprise.

MLR ▶ abbr. minimum lending rate, influenced by the overnight rate established by the Federal Reserve.

mon•e•ta•rism /'mänitə,rizəm; 'mən-/ ▶ n. the theory or practice of controlling the supply of money as the chief method of stabilizing the economy:
DERIVATIVES **mon•e•ta•rist** n. & adj.

mon•e•tar•y /'mäni,terē; 'mən-/ ▶ adj. of or relating to money or currency: *documents with no monetary value.*
ORIGIN early 19th cent.: from French *monétaire* or late Latin *monetarius*, from Latin *moneta* 'money.'

mon•e•tize /'mäni͵tīz; 'mən-/ ▶ v. [trans.] convert into or express in the form of currency.■ [usu. as adj.] (**monetized**) adapt (a society) to the use of money: *a fully monetized society.*
DERIVATIVES **mon•e•ti•za•tion** n.
ORIGIN late 19th cent.: from French *monétiser*, from Latin *moneta* 'money.'

mon•ey•chang•er /'mənē͵CHānjər/ (also **mon•ey-chang•er**) ▶ n. a person whose business is the exchanging of one currency for another, and who charges a percentage or earns a fee on each transaction.

mon•ey•lend•er /'mənē͵lendər/ (also **mon•ey-lend•er**) ▶ n. a person whose business is lending money to others who pay interest.

mon•ey mar•ket /'mənē ͵märkit/ ▶ n. the trade in short-term loans between banks and other financial institutions.

mon•ey mar•ket fund /'mənē ͵märkit ͵fənd/ ▶ n. a mutual fund that invests in very short-term government bonds and, in some cases, short-term, high-grade corporate bonds, certificates of deposit, bank paper, and other safe, short-term securities.

USAGE: The goal of a **money market fund** is to protect principal by maintaining a consistent value per unit, while paying a low rate of interest. Some **money market funds** also offer checkwriting and debit card privileges.

mon•ey of ac•count /'mənē əv ə'kownt/ ▶ n. a denomination of money used in reckoning, but not issued as actual coins or paper money, as the mill.

mon•ey or•der /'mənē ͵ôrdər/ ▶ n. a printed order for payment of a specified sum, issued by a bank or post office.

mon•ey sup•ply /'mənē sə͵plī/ ▶ n. the total amount of money in circulation or in existence in a country.

mon•ey wag•es /'mənē ͵wājiz/ ▶ plural n. income expressed in terms of its monetary value, with no account taken of its purchasing power.

mo•nop•o•list /mə'näpəlist/ ▶ n. a person or business that has a monopoly.

mo•nop•o•ly /mə'näpəlē/ ▶ n. (pl. **mo•nop•o•lies**) the exclusive possession or control of the supply or trade in a commodity or service: *his likely motive was to protect his regional* **monopoly on** *furs.*

■ a company or group having exclusive control over a commodity or service: *areas where cable companies act as monopolies.* ■ a commodity or service controlled in this way: *electricity, gas, and water were considered to be natural monopolies.*

ORIGIN mid 16th cent.: via Latin from Greek *monopōlion,* from *monos* 'single' + *pōlein* 'sell.'

mo•nop•so•ny /məˈnäpsənē/ ▶ n. (pl. **mo•nop•so•nies**) a market situation in which there is only one buyer.

ORIGIN 1930s: from *mono-* 'one' + Greek *opsōnein* 'buy provisions' + *-y* .

mort•gage /ˈmôrgij/ ▶ n. the charging of real (or personal) property by a debtor to a creditor as security for a debt (esp. one incurred by the purchase of the property), on the condition that it shall be returned on payment of the debt within a certain period.

■ a deed effecting such a transaction. ■ a loan obtained through the conveyance of property as security: *I put down a hundred thousand in cash and took out a mortgage for the rest.*

▶v. [trans.] (often **be mortgaged**) convey (a property) to a creditor as security on a loan: *the estate was mortgaged up to the hilt.*

ORIGIN late Middle English: from Old French, literally 'dead pledge,' from *mort* (from Latin *mortuus* 'dead') + *gage* 'pledge.'

mort•ga•gee /ˌmôrgəˈjē/ ▶ n. the lender in a mortgage, typically a bank.

mort•gage rate /ˈmôrgij ˌrāt/ ▶ n. the rate of interest charged by a mortgage lender.

mort•ga•gor /ˈmôrgijər; ˌjôr/ ▶ n. the borrower in a mortgage, typically a homeowner.

most fa•vored na•tion /ˈmōstˈfāvərd ˈnāsHən/ (abbr.: **MFN**) ▶ n. a country that has been granted the most favorable trading terms available by another country.

moun•tain /ˈmowntn/ ▶ n. a large surplus stock of a commodity: *this farming produced huge food mountains.*

ORIGIN Middle English: from Old French *montaigne,* based on Latin *mons, mont-* 'mountain.'

move /mо̄о̄v/ ▸ **v.** [intrans.] (of merchandise) be sold: *despite the high prices, goods are moving.*
■ [trans.] sell (merchandise).
▸**n.** a change of job, career, or business direction.
ORIGIN Middle English: from Old French *moveir*, from Latin *movere* .

mul•ti•na•tion•al /ˌməlti'næsHənl; ˌməltī-/ ▸ **adj.** (of a business organization) operating in several countries: *multinational corporations.*
▸**n.** a company operating in several countries.

mul•ti•pli•er /'məltə,plīər/ ▸ **n.** a factor used to calculate the total income generated by an investment, taking into consideration all the people affected (employees, suppliers, distributors, etc.) and the percentage of their income that each recipient saves.

mu•ni /'myо̄о̄nē/ ▸ **n.** (pl. **mu•nis**) short for MUNICIPAL BOND.

mu•nic•i•pal bond /myо̄о̄'nisəpəl 'bänd/ ▸ **n.** a security issued by or on behalf of a local authority.

USAGE: A *municipal bond* is also called a *tax-free bond* because the interest is exempt from federal taxes.

mu•tu•al /'myо̄о̄CHо̄о̄əl/ ▸ **adj.** denoting an insurance company or other corporate organization owned by its members and dividing some or all of its profits between them.
ORIGIN late 15th cent.: from Old French *mutuel*, from Latin *mutuus* 'mutual, borrowed'; related to *mutare* 'to change.'

mu•tu•al fund /'myо̄о̄CHо̄о̄əl ˌfənd/ ▸ **n.** an investment program funded by shareholders that trades in diversified holdings and is professionally managed.

mu•tu•al in•sur•ance /'myо̄о̄CHо̄о̄əl in'sHо̄о̄rəns/ ▸ **n.** insurance in which some or all of the profits are divided among the policyholders.

mu•tu•al•ize /'myо̄о̄CHо̄о̄ə,līz/ ▸ **v.** [trans.] organize (a company or business) on mutual principles.
■ divide (something, esp. insurance losses) between involved parties.

MVA ▸ **abbr.** Canadian market value assessment (of property values for tax purposes).

THE TOP TEN MONEY
MISTAKES PEOPLE MAKE

When it comes to money, many of us experiment ignorantly and wind up making a horrendous mistake that sends us reeling across the room in financial shock. Here are the ten most shocking mistakes you could make.

Mistake #1: Becoming an investor before you are organized and have specific goals in mind.
In order to become a successful investor, you first have to get your values and goals written down on paper and get your finances organized. You absolutely must do a family financial inventory and balance sheet and determine your current net worth precisely. You also must get a good handle on what you earn and what you spend. Until you know where you stand financially, you should not invest in anything. To help you get your financial documents organized at home, visit *www.finishrich.com* and download the free FinishRich Quickstart Program (found in the Resource Center).

Mistake #2: Not taking credit card debt seriously.
Credit card debt can be incredibly destructive. If you're single, it can keep you from achieving your goals and make you miserable. If you're part of a couple, it can destroy your relationship to boot. Knowing that you owe a company money and that you're being charged as much as 20 percent interest on the outstanding balance will make even the most laid-back person anxious. One of the easiest things to do today is call your

credit-card company and negotiate with them to lower your interest rate on your debt. First, visit *www.bankrate.com* to see the rates available from competing cards. Then, call your credit card company and advise them that unless they lower your interest rate to match a competitor, you are going to transfer your debt. You should be able to get the interest rate lowered dramatically with one phone call; just make sure you always ask to speak to a supervisor.

Mistake #3: Having a 30-year mortgage.

A typical 30-year mortgage at 8 percent inflates the real cost of a $250,000 home to more than $660,000. If you paid off your mortgage in 15 years, the total cost of your house would come to just under $493,000. That's nearly $168,000 less than it would have been with a 30-year mortgage.

Make a small extra payment each month or fork over a larger lump sum at the end of the year. By making an extra 10-percent payment each month and then adding an extra month's payment at the end of the year, for example, you can pay off your 30-year mortgage in about 18 years.

Mistake #4: Waiting to buy a house.

When you own your own home, you are building equity for yourself. When you rent, you are building someone else's equity.

The number-one reason people put off buying a home is because they think they can't afford it. But you don't need tens of thousands of dollars in the bank for a down payment. All lenders will provide 75 percent of the purchase price of your house or condominium, and many banks will lend as much as 95 percent.

You can probably get a substantial home for the equivalent of your current rental payment. Say you pay $2,000 a month in rent. For that kind of money, you could get a $250,000 mortgage. In most of the country, $250,000 can buy you a lot of house.

Mistake #5: Putting off saving for retirement.
Almost 95 percent of Americans age 65 or older have an income of less than $25,000 a year. That means only 5 percent of us are in a position of financial security, much less comfort, when we reach our so-called golden years.

The best way to get started saving for retirement is to arrange to have your monthly contribution either deducted directly from your paycheck or automatically transferred from your checking account each month. If you're not yet using your retirement account at work, go in to the office and sign up for your plan today. Make it a goal to save 10 percent or more of your gross income. If you can't imagine saving 10 percent, start with 3 percent and make it a goal to increase that amount by a small percentage every month (you'll barely feel it). By the end of the year, you'll be contributing the maximum allowable amount to your retirement account at work.

Mistake #6: Speculating with your investment money.
A speculator, like a gambler, is someone who is looking for a fast buck. Over the long haul, nothing will more effectively prevent you from ever becoming financially secure than speculating with your investment money.

Here are the most common ways to speculate. (Avoid them!):

- Investing in options. With options, you bet that the price of a certain stock will reach a certain point by a certain date. If you bet wrong, you lose the money you paid for the option.

- Investing in companies that don't make a profit. As long as you are investing to secure your future, you should stick to solid companies that have proven track records.

- Actively trading your account. Invest for the long term, with the goal of owning a particular company's stock for years.

- Throwing good money after bad. When a stock price falls through the floor, and the company doesn't have a convincing explanation for the collapse, the stock's not a bargain, it's a disaster.

Mistake #7: Building a portfolio that's not diversified.

History has shown that no asset class will always outperform every other asset class. Because of human nature, strong asset classes inevitably become "overbought" (that is, overenthusiastic investors bid up prices too high). At that point, people panic and values plunge. The best way to diversify your account is to build what is commonly known as a "balanced account." A balanced account is an investment account that is 40 percent fixed income (bonds and cash) and 60 percent equities (stocks). A balanced account will allow you to ride out the bumps and volatility of the stock market while earning a solid return. There are many solid mutual funds that will do all of this for you. A great example of solid balanced mutual fund is the Vanguard Balanced Fund (*www.vanguard.com*).

Mistake #8: Paying too much in taxes.

When you are building an investment portfolio, it is absolutely imperative that you take into consideration your potential tax liability. Financial advisors call this "looking for the real rate of return." The more you seek to minimize your taxes when investing, the more money you'll keep. Start by making it a goal to fully invest in your 401(k) plan or retirement plan at work. No plan at work? Make sure you use an IRA account. Once you've maxed out your retirement accounts, look to investments that grow tax-free (like tax-free bonds).

Mistake #9: Buying an investment that is illiquid.

An illiquid investment is one that you cannot sell in less than five business days. Limited partnerships, for example, which pool investors' money to purchase certain types of investments—typically real estate—are not liquid. Neither are collectible coins, second mortgages, paintings by your cousin, or antique cars.

Ask yourself: "If I absolutely had to, could I sell this and get my money back within five business days?" If the answer is no, think hard before you put any money into the investment.

Mistake #10: Giving up.
People often make a financial mistake, get bad advice, and then give up on their dream of financial security. Don't let this happen to you.

Yes, you should be careful, but don't become overcautious. By learning to avoid the common pitfalls investors make, you can minimize your risk and put yourself on the road to financial security. The biggest mistake you can make is to not become an investor.

N

NAFTA /'næftə/ ▸ **abbr.** North American Free Trade Agreement.

nar•row mon•ey /'nærō 'mənē/ ▸ **n.** money in forms that can be used as a medium of exchange, generally banknotes, coins, and certain balances held by banks.

NASDAQ /'næz‚dæk/ ▸ **abbr.** National Association of Securities Dealers Automated Quotations, a computerized system for trading in securities.

na•tion•al bank /'næsH(ə)nl 'bæNGk/ ▸ **n.** a commercial bank that is chartered under the federal government and is a member of the Federal Reserve System.

Na•tion•al Child Ben•e•fit /'næsH(ə)nl 'CHīld ‚benəfit/ (abbr.: **NCB**) ▸ **n.** Canadian a joint program of the Canadian federal, provincial, and territorial governments and First Nations to increase income support and child-welfare services for low-income working families..

na•tion•al debt /'næsH(ə)nl 'det/ ▸ **n.** the total amount of money that a country's government has borrowed, by various means.

na•tion•al in•come /'næsH(ə)nl 'in‚kəm; 'iNG‚kəm/ ▸ **n.** the total amount of money earned within a country.

na•tion•al•ize /'næsH(ə)nl‚īz / ▸ **v.** [trans.] transfer (a major branch of industry or commerce) from private to state ownership or control.
  DERIVATIVES **na•tion•al•i•za•tion n.**

NAV ▸ **abbr.** net asset value.

near mon•ey /'ni(ə)r 'mənē/ ▸ **n.** assets that can readily be converted into cash, such as government bonds.

neg•a•tive eq•ui•ty /'negətiv 'ekwitē/ ▸ **n.** potential indebtedness arising when the market value of a property falls below the out-standing amount of a mortgage secured on it.

neg•a•tive in•come tax /'negətiv 'in,kəm ,taks; 'iNG,kəm/ ▸ n. money credited as allowances to a taxed income, and paid as a benefit when it exceeds debited tax.

ne•go•ti•ate /ni'gōsHē,āt/ ▸ v. [trans.] transfer (a check, bill, or other document) to the legal ownership of another person.

■ convert (a check) into cash.

ORIGIN early 17th cent.: from Latin *negotiat-* 'done in the course of business,' from the verb *negotiari*, from *negotium* 'business,' from *neg-* 'not' + *otium* 'leisure.'

ne•go•ti•a•tion /ni,gōsHē'āsHən/ ▸ n. (also **ne•go•ti•a•tions**) the action or process of transferring ownership of a document.

ORIGIN late 15th cent. (denoting an act of dealing with another person): from Latin *negotiatio(n-)*, from the verb *negotiari* (see NEGOTIATE).

net /net/ ▸ adj. (of an amount, value, or price) remaining after a deduction, such as tax or a discount, has been made: *net earnings per share rose* | *the net worth of the business.* Often contrasted with GROSS .

■ (of a price) to be paid in full; not reducible.

▸ v. (**net•ted, net•ting**) [trans.] acquire or obtain (a sum of money) as clear profit.

■ return (profit or income) for (someone): *the land netted its owner a turnover of $800,000.* ■ (**net something down/off/out**) exclude a nonnet amount, such as tax, when making a calculation, in order to reduce the amount left to a net sum: *the scrap or salvage value should be netted off against the original purchase price.*

ORIGIN Middle English: from French *net* 'neat,' from Latin *nitidus* 'shining,' from *nitere* 'shine.'

net asset value /'net 'æsit ,vælyoo/ (abbr.: **NAV**) ▸ n. the value of a mutual fund that is reached by deducting the fund's liabilities from the market value of all of its shares and then dividing by the number of issued shares.

net book val•ue /'net 'book ,vælyoo/ ▸ n. the value of an asset as recorded in the accounts of its owner.

net na•tion•al prod•uct /'net 'næsH(ə)nl 'prädəkt/ (abbr.: **NNP**) ▸ n. the total value of goods produced and services provided in a country during one year, after depreciation of capital goods has been allowed for.

net pres•ent val•ue /'net 'prezənt ˌvælyo͞o/ (abbr.: **NPV**) ▶ n. see PRESENT VALUE.

net prof•it /'net 'präfit/ ▶ n. the actual profit after working expenses not included in the calculation of gross profit have been paid.

NIC ▶ abbr. newly industrialized country.

niche /nicH/ ▶ n. a specialized but profitable corner of the market: [as adj.] *important new niche markets.*

ORIGIN early 17th cent.: from French, literally 'recess,' from *nicher* 'make a nest,' based on Latin *nidus* 'nest.'

night shift /'nīt ˌsHift/ ▶ n. the period of time scheduled for work at night, as in a factory or other institution.

■ the group of people working during this period.

Nik•kei in•dex /'nēkā ˌindeks/ a figure indicating the relative price of representative shares on the Tokyo Stock Exchange. Also called **Nik•kei av•er•age.**

ORIGIN 1970s: *Nikkei,* abbreviation of *Ni(hon) Kei(zai Shimbun)* 'Japanese Economic Journal.'

NNP ▶ abbr. net national product.

no-fault /'nō 'fôlt/ ▶ adj. denoting an insurance policy that is valid regardless of whether the policyholder was at fault: *no-fault auto insurance.*

no-load /'nō 'lōd/ ▶ adj. **1** (of shares in a mutual fund) sold without a commission being charged at the time of purchase or sale.
2 denoting a mutual fund that does not charge a commission.

nom•i•nal /'nämənl/ ▶ adj. **1** (of a price or amount of money) very small; far below the real value or cost: *some firms charge only a nominal fee for the service.*
2 (of a quantity or dimension, esp. of manufactured articles) stated or expressed but not necessarily corresponding exactly to the real value: *legislation allowed variation around the nominal weight (that printed on each packet).*

■ (of a rate or other figure) expressed in terms of a certain amount, without making allowance for changes in real value over time: *the nominal exchange rate.*

ORIGIN late 15th cent.: from Latin *nominalis*, from *nomen*, *nomin-* 'name.'

nom•i•nal ac•count /'nämənl ə'kownt/ ▸ n. an account recording the financial transactions of a business in a particular category, rather than with a person or other organization.

nom•i•nal ledg•er /'nämənl 'lejər/ ▸ n. a ledger containing nominal accounts, or one containing both nominal and real accounts.

nom•i•nal val•ue /'nämənl 'vælyōō/ ▸ n. the value that is stated on currency; face value.

■ the price of a share, bond, or security when it was issued, rather than its current market value.

nom•i•nee /,nämə'nē/ ▸ n. a person or company whose name is given as having title to a stock, real estate, etc., but who is not the actual owner.

ORIGIN mid 17th cent.: from *nominate* + *-ee*.

non•con•trib•u•to•ry /,nänkən'tribyə,tôrē/ ▸ adj. (of a pension or pension plan) funded by regular payments by the employer, not the employee.

non•earn•ing /,nän 'ərniNG/ ▸ adj. (esp. of a person or an investment) not earning a regular income.

non•ne•go•ti•a•ble /,nä(n)nə'gōsHəbəl/ ▸ adj. (of a document) not able to be transferred or assigned to the legal ownership of another person.

non•par•tic•i•pat•ing /,nänpər'tisə,pātiNG/ ▸ adj. (of an insurance policy) not allowing the holder a share of the profits, typically in the form of a bonus, made by the company.

non•pay•ment /,nän'pāmənt/ ▸ n. failure to pay an amount of money that is owed: *homes repossessed for nonpayment of mortgages.*

non•prof•it /,nän'präfit/ ▸ adj. not making or conducted primarily to make a profit: *charities and other nonprofit organizations.*

North A•mer•i•can Free Trade A•gree•ment /'nôrTH ə'merikən 'frē 'trād ə,grēmənt/ (abbr.: **NAFTA**) an agreement that came into effect in January 1994 between the US, Canada, and Mexico to remove barriers to trade between the three countries over a ten-year period.

not-for-prof•it /'nät fər 'präfit/ ▸ adj. another term for **NONPROFIT**.

NPV ▸ abbr. net present value. See **PRESENT VALUE**.

num•bered ac•count /ˈnəmbərd əˈkownt/ ▸ n. a bank account, esp. in a Swiss bank, identified only by a number and not bearing the owner's name.

nu•me•raire /ˈn(y)o͞omə͵re(ə)r/ ▸ n. an item or commodity acting as a measure of value or as a standard for currency exchange.

ORIGIN 1960s: from French *numéraire*, from late Latin *numerarius*, from Latin *numerus* 'a number.'

NYSE ▸ abbr. New York Stock Exchange.

USAGE: The **New York Stock Exchange** was started more than 200 years ago by 24 New York City stockbrokers and merchants. It remains the world's foremost securities marketplace, listing nearly 2,800 companies, valued at close to $16 trillion in market capitalization. Its Web site is *www.nyse.com*.

O

OAS ▸ abbr. Canadian see **old age security.**

oc•troi /'äktroi; äk'trwä/ ▸ n. a tax levied in some countries on various goods entering a town or city.
ORIGIN late 16th cent.: from French *octroyer* 'to grant,' based on medieval Latin *auctorizare*, from *auctor* 'originator, promoter.'

odd lot /'äd 'lät/ ▸ n. a transaction involving less than the usual round number of shares.

OECD ▸ abbr. Organization for Economic Cooperation and Development.

OEM ▸ abbr. original equipment manufacturer (an organization that makes devices from component parts bought from other organizations).

off-brand /'ôf ˌbrænd/ ▸ adj. denoting or relating to an item of retail goods of an unknown, unpopular, or inferior brand.
▸ n. an unknown, unpopular, or inferior brand.

of•fer /'ôfər/ ▸ v. [trans.] (usu. **be offered**) make available for sale: *the product is offered at a very competitive price.*
▸ n. an amount of money that someone is willing to pay for something: *the prospective purchaser who made the highest offer.*
■ a specially reduced price or terms for something on sale: *the offer runs right up until Christmas Eve.*
ORIGIN Old English *offrian* 'sacrifice (something) to a deity,' of Germanic origin, from Latin *offerre* 'bestow, present,' reinforced by French *offrir* . The noun (late Middle English) is from French *offre* .

of•fer doc•u•ment /'ôfər ˌdäkyəmənt/ ▸ n. a document containing details of a takeover bid that is sent to the shareholders of the target company.

of•fer•ing price /'ôfəriNG ˌprīs/ ▸ n. the price at which a dealer or institution is prepared to sell securities or other assets.

of•fi•cer /'ôfisər/ ▸ n. a holder of a post in a society, company, or other organization, esp. one who is involved at a senior level in its management: *a chief executive officer.*

ORIGIN Middle English: via Anglo-Norman French from medieval Latin *officiarius*, from Latin *officium* 'performance of a task,' based on *opus* 'work' + *facere* 'do.'

off-price /'ôf ˌprīs/ ▸ n. a method of retailing in which brand-name goods (esp. clothing) are sold for less than the usual retail price. ▸ **adv.** using this method: *selling goods off-price.*

off•set /'ôfˌset/ ▸ n. a consideration or amount that diminishes or balances the effect of a contrary one: *an offset against taxable profits.*

off•shore /'ôf'sHôr/ ▸ adj. & adv. **1** of or relating to the business of extracting oil or gas from the seabed: *offshore drilling.*
2 made, situated, or conducting business abroad, esp. in order to take advantage of lower costs or less stringent regulation: *deposits in offshore accounts.*

old age se•cu•ri•ty /'ōld 'āj siˌkyo͞oritē/ (abbr.: **OAS**) ▸ n. Canadian a system of government-funded pensions for those over the age of 65.

ol•i•gop•o•ly /ˌäli'gäpəlē/ ▸ n. (pl. **ol•i•gop•o•lies**) a state of limited competition, in which a market is shared by a small number of producers or sellers.

ORIGIN late 19th cent.: from *oligo-* 'small number,' on the pattern of *monopoly.*

ol•i•gop•so•ny /ˌäli'gäpsənē/ ▸ n. (pl. **ol•i•gop•so•nies**) a state of the market in which only a small number of buyers exists for a product.

ORIGIN 1940s: from *oligo-* 'small number' + Greek *opsōnein* 'buy provisions,' on the pattern of *monopsony.*

OPEC /'ōpek/ ▸ abbr. Organization of Petroleum Exporting Countries.

o•pen /'ōpən/ ▸ adj. (of a bank account) available for transactions: *the minimum required to keep the account open.*

ORIGIN Old English, of Germanic origin, from the root of the adverb *op(p), uppe* 'up.'

o•pen en•roll•ment /ˈōpən enˈrōlmənt/ ▸ n. a period during which employees may change, add, or drop benefits coverage.

o•pen in•ter•est /ˈōpən ˈint(ə)rist/ ▸ n. the number of contracts or commitments outstanding in futures and options that are trading on an official exchange at any one time.

o•pen mar•ket /ˈōpən ˈmärkit/ ▸ n. (often **the open market**) an unrestricted market with free access by and competition of buyers and sellers.

o•pen out•cry /ˈōpən ˈowt‚krī/ ▸ n. a system of financial trading in which dealers shout their bids and contracts aloud.

op•er•at•ing prof•it /ˈäpə‚rātiNG ‚präfit/ ▸ n. profit from business operations (gross profit less operating expenses) before deduction of fixed costs.

op•er•a•tions re•search /‚äpəˈrāsHənz ‚rēsərCH; ri‚sərCH/ ▸ n. the application of scientific principles to business management, providing a quantitative basis for complex decisions.

OPM ▸ abbr. other people's money.

USAGE: Individuals and companies often use **OPM** raised from banks, investors, and other sources to invest in or build a business.

op•por•tu•ni•ty cost /‚äpərˈt(y)o͞onitē ‚kôst/ ▸ n. the loss of potential gain from other alternatives when one alternative is chosen: *idle cash balances represent an opportunity cost in terms of lost interest.*

op•tion /ˈäpsHən/ ▸ n. a right to buy or sell a particular thing at a specified price within a set time: *Columbia Pictures **has an option on** the script | an option to buy the land.*
▸v. [trans.] buy or sell an option on (something): *his second script will have been optioned by the time you read this.*
ORIGIN mid 16th cent.: from French, or from Latin *optio(n-)*, from the stem of *optare* 'choose.' The verb dates from the 1930s.

Or•gan•i•za•tion of the Pe•tro•le•um Ex•port•ing Coun•tries /‚ôrgəniˈzāsHən əv pəˈtrōlēəm ‚ekspôrtiNG ‚kəmpənēz/ (abbr.: **OPEC**) an association of major oil-producing countries, founded in 1960 to coordinate policies and prices. Members are Algeria, Gabon, Indonesia, Iran, Iraq, Kuwait, Libya, Nigeria, Qatar, Saudi Arabia, the United Arab Emirates, and Venezuela.

o•rig•i•na•tion fee /ə‚rijəˈnāsHən ‚fē/ ▸ n. a fee charged by a lender on entering into a loan agreement to cover the cost of processing the loan.

out•let /'owt₁let/ ▶ n. a place from which goods are sold or distributed: *a fast-food outlet.*
■ a retail store that sells the goods of a specific manufacturer or brand: [as adj.] *an outlet store.* ■ a retail store offering discounted merchandise, esp. overstocked or irregular items. ■ a market for goods: *the indoor markets in Moscow were an outlet for surplus collective-farm produce.*
ORIGIN Middle English: from *out-* + the verb *let* .

out•place•ment /'owt₁plāsmənt/ ▶ n. the provision of assistance to laid-off employees in finding new employment, either as a benefit provided by the employer directly, or through a specialist service.

out•sert /'owt₁sərt/ ▶ n. a piece of promotional material that is placed on the outside of a package, publication, or other product.
ORIGIN 1960s: from *out* + *insert* .

out•side di•rec•tor /'owt₁sīd də'rektər/ ▶ n. a director of a company who is not employed by that company, typically an employee of an associated company.

out•side mon•ey /'owt₁sīd 'mənē/ ▶ n. money held in a form such as gold that is an asset for the holder and does not represent a corresponding liability for someone else.
■ money or investment from an indpendent source.

out•source /'owt₁sôrs/ ▶ v. [trans.] obtain (goods or a service) from an outside supplier, esp. in place of an internal source.
■ contract (work) out: *you may choose to **outsource** this function **to** another company or do it yourself.*

out•turn /'ow(t)₁tərn/ ▶ n. the amount of something produced, esp. money; output: *the financial outturn.*

o•ver•age /'ōv(ə)rij/ ▶ n. an excess or surplus, esp. the amount by which a sum of money is greater than a previous estimate.

o•ver•buy /₁ōvər'bī/ ▶ v. (past and past part. **o•ver•bought**) [trans.] buy more of (something) than one needs: *the tendency to overbuy software.*

o•ver•ca•pac•i•ty /₁ōvərkə'pæsitē/ ▶ n. the situation in which an industry or factory cannot sell as much as it can produce.

o•ver•cap•i•tal•ize /₁ōvər'kæpitl₁īz/ ▶ v. [trans.] [usu. as adj.] (**over-**

capitalized) provide (a company) with more capital than is advisable or necessary: *a bleak time for the overcapitalized firm.*
■ estimate or set the capital value of (a company) at too high an amount.

o•ver•draft /'ōvər‚dræft/ ▶ n. a deficit in a bank account caused by drawing more money than the account holds.

o•ver•draw /‚ōvər'drô/ ▶ v. (past **o•ver•drew**; past part. **o•ver•drawn**) [trans.] (usu. **be overdrawn**) draw money from (one's bank account) in excess of what the account holds: *you only pay interest if your account is overdrawn.*
■ **(be overdrawn)** (of a person) have taken money out of an account in excess of what it holds: *I'm already overdrawn this month.*

o•ver•ful•fill /‚ōvər‚fo͝ol'fil/ ▶ v. (**o•ver•ful•filled, o•ver•ful•fill•ing**) [trans.] fulfill (a contract or quota) earlier or in greater quantity than required: *he overfulfilled the quota by forty percent.*

o•ver•head /'ōvər‚hed/ ▶ adj. (of a cost or expense) incurred in the general upkeep or running of a plant, premises, or business, and not attributable to specific products or items.
▶ n. overhead cost or expense: *research conducted in space requires more overhead.*

o•ver•heat /‚ōvər'hēt/ ▶ v. [intrans.] ■ (of a country's economy) show marked inflation when increased demand results in rising prices rather than increased output.

o•ver•in•sured /‚ōvərin'sho͝ord/ ▶ adj. having insurance coverage beyond what is necessary.

o•ver•is•sue /‚ōvər'isho͞o/ ▶ v. (**o•ver•is•sues, o•ver•is•sued, o•ver•is•su•ing**) [trans.] issue (bonds, shares of stock, etc.) beyond the authorized amount or the issuer's ability to pay them on demand.
▶ n. the action of overissuing bonds, shares of stock, etc.

o•ver•pro•duce /‚ōvərprə'd(y)o͞os/ ▶ v. [trans.] produce more of (a product or commodity) than is wanted or needed.

o•ver•sell /‚ōvər'sel/ ▶ v. (past and past part. **o•ver•sold**) [trans.] sell more of (something) than exists or can be delivered: *a surge in airlines overselling flights.*

o•ver•stock /‚ōvər'stäk/ ▶ n. (esp. in a manufacturing or retailing context) a supply or quantity in excess of demand or requirements: *factory overstock | publishers' overstocks and remainders.*

o•ver•sub•scribed /ˌōvərsəb'skrībd/ ▶ adj. applied for in greater quantities than are available or expected: *those bonds were said to be 12 to 14 times oversubscribed.*

o•ver•trade /ˌōvər'trād/ ▶ v. [intrans.] engage in more business than can be supported by the market or by the funds or resources available.

o•ver•val•ue /ˌōvər'vælyōō/ ▶ v. (**o•ver•val•ues, o•ver•val•ued, o•ver•val•u•ing**) [trans.] fix the value of (something, esp. a currency) at too high a level: *sterling was overvalued against the dollar.*

HOW TO CREATE A
FINANCIAL PLAN
THAT WILL REALLY
WORK FOR YOU

Planning involves more than just setting objectives and then finding ways to achieve them. For one thing, you have to make sure that your objectives correspond with your own values. Some people would like to spend time at the beach doing nothing but listening to the waves lapping the shore. Other people would go nuts if they had to spend more than an hour in such an environment. Your plan has to reflect you, your values and your nature.

You can do this by designing a **Purpose-Focused Financial Plan™**. A Purpose-Focused Financial Plan is nothing more than a list of things to do (your goals) to enable you to live a life in line with the values that are most important to you. Here are seven tips on how to define those goals.

1. Make sure your goals are based on your values. By identifying your top five values, you can then base your goals on them. The more you base your goals on your values, the more likely it is that you will achieve them. After all, can you think of anything better or more exciting around which to plan your spending and investing than the things that really matter to you? And what could matter more than the values by which you and your partner want to live and grow?

Ideally, each of these top five values should lead you to a specific key goal. You'll write down a value and then, right next to it, a related goal on which you want to focus your time and energy.

2. Make your goals specific, detailed, and with a finish line. Wanting something and getting it are two different things. In order to achieve a goal, you must know precisely what it is that you're after. In other words, you need to take those vague ideas and thoughts you have about what sort of life you'd like and make them specific.

Your goal could be to buy a dream house by a lake. Or it could be getting your credit card bills paid off over the next 12 months, going to Hawaii on a dream vacation sometime in the next two years, or cleaning out the house from top to bottom in the next three months.

3. Put your top five goals in writing. Study after study has shown that writing down your goals makes it much more likely that you'll achieve them. Writing down goals does something to you subconsciously that often brings the goal to you. For one thing, writing down your goals helps you make them more specific. For another, it makes your goals seem more real to you.

4. Start taking action toward your goals within 48 hours. If you don't get moving immediately toward your goal, even if only in a small way, chances are you'll never get moving at all. Even if it will take years to achieve a particular goal, there are still things you can do to start moving toward that goal right away. And you can do it within the next 48 hours. By taking this sort of specific, immediate action, your goal becomes even more real to you and, thus, even more exciting.

5. Enlist help. There's no such thing as a "self-made" person. No one ever reaches a really important goal without some sort of help from some other person. It's important to share your dreams and goals with the people you love and trust, but it also doesn't hurt to share them with strangers, too. You never know—the person you're sitting next to at a dinner party or a lecture may be in the perfect position to help you make your dream a reality. If you keep your goals to yourself, you could miss your big chance.

6. Get a rough idea of how much it will cost to achieve your goals. You need to get a sense of what it will take in dollars and cents to achieve your various goals. This will enable you to do two things: (1) understand how realistic (or unrealistic) your goals may be, and (2) get yourself started on a systematic savings and investment plan to accumulate the money you'll need to achieve them. Some goals will take almost no time to save for, and some goals may take a lot of time and investing to reach. Since it's important to know which is which, part of creating a Purpose-Focused Financial Plan involves estimating how much money you think you will ultimately need to pay for your top five goals. So ask yourself, What is this goal going to cost? How much do I need to start putting aside each week or month to help me get there?

7. If you live with a partner, make sure your goals match both your values. What's the point of being with someone if you don't share your most intimate dreams and thoughts with them? If you've got kids, share your dreams with them, too. Ask them what they'd like to see the family doing over the next three years. Ask them about their values, and then work together on a family list of five things that you all want to accomplish together.

P

---

pack•er /'pækər/ ▸ n. a person or machine that packs something, esp. someone who prepares and packs food for transportation and sale.

paid-up /'pād 'əp/ ▸ adj. denoting the part of the subscribed capital of an undertaking that has actually been paid: *paid-up capital.*

■ denoting an endowment policy in which the policyholder has stopped paying premiums, resulting in the surrender value being used to purchase single-premium whole-life insurance.

P & L ▸ abbr. profit and loss account.

par /pär/ ▸ n. the face value of a stock or other security, as distinct from its market value.

■ (also **par of ex•change**) the recognized value of one country's currency in terms of another's.

ORIGIN late 16th cent.: from Latin, 'equal,' also 'equality.'

par•cel /'pärsəl/ ▸ n. 1 a piece of land, esp. one considered as part of an estate.

2 a quantity dealt with in one commercial transaction: *a parcel of shares.*

ORIGIN late Middle English: from Old French *parcelle*, from Latin *particula* 'small part.'

Par•is club /'pæris ˌkləb/ a group of the major creditor nations of the International Monetary Fund whose representatives meet informally in Paris to discuss the financial relations of the IMF member nations.

par•i•ty /'pærite͞/ ▸ n. the value of one currency in terms of another at an established exchange rate.

ORIGIN late 16th cent.: from late Latin *paritas*, from *par* 'equal.'

part•ner /'pärtnər/ ▸ n. a person who takes part in an undertaking with another or others, esp. in a business or company with shared risks and profits.

ORIGIN Middle English: alteration of *parcener* 'partner, joint heir,' from Anglo-Norman French *parcener*, based on Latin *partitio(n-)* 'partition.' The change in the first syllable was due to association with *part* .

part•ner•ship /'pärtnər, SHip/ ▶ n. an association of two or more people as partners: *an increase in partnerships with housing associations.* ■ a business or firm owned and run by two or more partners. ■ a position as one of the partners in a business or firm.

pass /pæs/ ▶ v. [trans.] (of a company) not declare or pay (a dividend). ORIGIN Middle English: from Old French *passer*, based on Latin *passus* 'pace.'

pass•book /'pæs,bŏŏk/ ▶ n. a booklet issued by a bank to an account holder for recording sums deposited and withdrawn.

pas•sive /'pæsiv/ ▶ adj. denoting a style of investing in which an individual buys units of an index fund that replicates a market index, thus ensuring investment performance that is no better and no worse than the market itself. Compare with ACTIVE (def. 2). ORIGIN late Middle English: from Latin *passivus*, from *pass-* 'suffered,' from the verb *pati* .

USAGE: Because index funds charge a lower management fee than actively managed funds, **passive** investing is a less expensive style of investing.

pat•ent /'pætnt/ ▶ n. a government authority to an individual or organization conferring a right or title, esp. the sole right to make, use, or sell some invention: *he took out a patent for an improved steam hammer.*
▶ adj. made and marketed under a patent; proprietary: *patent milk powder.*
▶ v. [trans.] obtain a patent for (an invention): *an invention is not your own until it is patented.*
ORIGIN late Middle English: from Old French, from Latin *patent-* 'lying open,' from the verb *patere* 'stand wide open.'

pat•ent•ee /,pætn'tē/ ▶ n. a person or organization that obtains or holds a patent for something.

Pa•tri•ot bond /'pātrēət ˌbänd/ ▸ n. a US savings bond introduced on December 11, 2001, and made available through financial institutions or over the Internet.

USAGE: These bonds are specially inscribed with the words **Patriot Bond** to enable investors to show their support for the nation's antiterrorism efforts. They are available at the Savings Bonds Direct Web site.

pay•a•ble /'pāəbəl/ ▸ adj. 1 (of money) required to be paid; due: *interest is payable on the money owing.*
2 able to be paid: *it costs just $195, payable in five monthly installments.*
▸ n. (**payables**) debts owed by a business; liabilities.

pay-as-you-go /'pā əz ˌyoō 'gō/ ▸ adj. relating to a system of paying debts or meeting costs as they arise.

pay•back /'pāˌbæk/ ▸ n. financial return or reward, esp. profit equal to the initial outlay of an investment: *a long time lag between investment and payback.*

pay•back pe•ri•od /'pāˌbæk ˌpi(ə)rēəd/ ▸ n. the length of time required for an investment to recover its initial outlay in terms of profits or savings.

pay•ee /ˌpā'ē/ ▸ n. a person to whom money is paid or is to be paid, esp. the person to whom a check is made payable.

pay•roll /'pāˌrōl/ ▸ n. a list of a company's employees and the amount of money they are to be paid: *there are just three employees* **on the payroll.**
■ the total amount of wages and salaries paid by a company to its employees: *small employers with a payroll of less than $45,000.*

peg /peg/ ▸ n. a point or limit on a scale, esp. of exchange rates.
▸ v. (**pegged, peg•ging**) [trans.] fix (a price, rate, or amount) at a particular level.
ORIGIN late Middle English: probably of Low German origin; compare with Dutch dialect *peg* 'plug, peg.' The verb dates from the mid 16th cent.

pen•e•tra•tion /ˌpeni'trāsHən/ ▸ n. the successful selling of a company's or country's products in a particular market or area: *Japanese import penetration.*

■ the extent to which a product is recognized and bought by customers in a particular market: *the software has attained a high degree of market penetration.*

ORIGIN late Middle English: from Latin *penetratio(n-)*, from the verb *penetrare* 'place within or enter.'

pen•ny stock /'penē ˌstäk/ ▶ n. a common stock valued at less than one dollar, and therefore highly speculative.

pen•sion /'pensHən/ ▶ n. a regular payment made during a person's retirement from an investment fund to which that person or their employer has contributed during their working life.

■ a regular payment made by the government to people of or above the official retirement age and to some widows and disabled people.

▶v. [trans.] (**pension someone off**) dismiss someone from employment, typically because of age or ill health, and pay them a pension: *he was pensioned off from the army at the end of the war.*

DERIVATIVES **pen•sion•ar•y** adj.

ORIGIN late Middle English: from Old French, from Latin *pensio(n-)* 'payment,' from *pendere* 'to pay.' The current verb sense dates from the mid 19th cent.

pen•sion•a•ble /'pensHənəbəl/ ▶ adj. entitling to or qualifying for a pension.

pen•sion fund /'pensHən ˌfənd/ ▶ n. a fund from which pensions are paid, accumulated from contributions from employers, employees, or both.

per an•num /pər 'ænəm/ ▶ adv. for each year (used in financial contexts): *an average growth rate of around 2 percent per annum.*

ORIGIN early 17th cent.: Latin.

p/e ra•tio /'pē 'ē ˌrāsH(ē)ˌō/ ▶ abbr. price–earnings ratio.

per con•tra /pər 'käntrə/ ▶ n. the opposite side of an account or an assessment.

ORIGIN mid 16th cent.: from Italian.

per di•em /pər 'dēəm/ ▶ adv. & adj. for each day (used in financial contexts).

▶n. an allowance or payment made for each day.

ORIGIN early 16th cent.: Latin.

per•fect com•pe•ti•tion /'pərfikt ˌkämpi'tisHən/ ▶ n. the situation prevailing in a market in which buyers and sellers are so numerous and well informed that all elements of monopoly are absent and the market price of a commodity is beyond the control of individual buyers and sellers.

per•form /pər'fôrm/ ▸ v. [intrans.] (of an investment) yield a profitable return.

ORIGIN Middle English: from Anglo-Norman French *parfourmer*, alteration (by association with *forme* 'form') of Old French *parfournir*, from *par* 'through, to completion' + *fournir* 'furnish, provide.'

per•for•mance /pər'fôrməns/ ▸ n. the extent to which an investment is profitable, esp. in relation to other investments.

per•for•mance bond /pər'fôrməns ˌbänd/ ▸ n. a bond issued by a bank or other financial institution, guaranteeing the fulfillment of a particular contract.

per•pet•u•al /pər'peCHo͞oəl/ ▸ adj. (of an investment) having no fixed maturity date; irredeemable: *a perpetual bond.*

ORIGIN Middle English: from Old French *perpetuel*, from Latin *perpetualis*, from *perpetuus* 'continuing throughout,' from *perpes*, *perpet-* 'continuous.'

per•pe•tu•i•ty /ˌpərpi't(y)o͞oi̱tē/ ▸ n. (pl. **per•pe•tu•i•ties**) a bond or other security with no fixed maturity date.

ORIGIN late Middle English: from Old French *perpetuite*, from Latin *perpetuitas*, from *perpetuus* 'continuing throughout' (see **PERPETUAL**).

per•son•al i•den•ti•fi•ca•tion num•ber /'pərsənl īˌdentəfi'kāsHən ˌnəmbər/ (abbr.: **PIN**) (also **PIN number**) ▸ n. a number allocated to an individual and used to validate electronic transactions.

per•son•al shop•per /'pərsənl 'sHäpər/ ▸ n. an individual who is paid to help another to purchase goods, either by accompanying them while shopping or by shopping on their behalf.

per•son•nel de•part•ment /ˌpərsə'nel diˌpärtmənt/ ▸ n. the part of an organization concerned with the appointment, training, and welfare of employees.

pet•ro•dol•lar /'petrōˌdälər/ ▸ n. a notional unit of currency earned by a country from the export of petroleum: *petrodollars were pouring into the kingdom.*

pet•ty cash /'petē 'kæSH/ ▶ n. an accessible store of money kept by an organization for expenditure on small items.

phan•tom /'fæntəm/ ▶ n. denoting a financial arrangement or transaction that has been invented for fraudulent purposes but that does not really exist: *he diverted an estimated $1,500,000 into "phantom" bank accounts.*

ORIGIN Middle English (also in the sense 'illusion, delusion'): from Old French *fantosme,* based on Greek *phantasma,* from *phantazein* 'make visible,' from *phanein* 'show.'

phar•ma•ceu•ti•cals /ˌfärməˈsoo͞otikəlz/ ▶ plural n. companies manufacturing medicinal drugs.

Phil•lips curve /'filəps ˌkərv/ ▶ n. a supposed inverse relationship between the level of unemployment and the rate of inflation.

ORIGIN 1960s: named after Alban W. H. *Phillips* (1914–75), New Zealand economist.

piece rate /'pēs ˌrāt/ ▶ n. a rate of payment for piecework.

piece•work /'pēs,wərk/ ▶ n. work paid for according to the amount produced.

PIN /pin/ (also **PIN num•ber**) ▶ abbr. personal identification number.

pi•rate /'pīrət/ ▶ n. ■ a person who appropriates or reproduces the work of another for profit without permission, usually in contravention of patent or copyright.

▶ v. [trans.] [often as adj.] (**pirated**) use or reproduce (another's work) for profit without permission, usually in contravention of patent or copyright: *he sold pirated tapes of Hollywood blockbusters | a competing company cannot pirate its intellectual achievements.*

DERIVATIVES **pi•ra•cy n.**

ORIGIN Middle English: from Latin *pirata,* from Greek *peiratēs,* from *peirein* 'to attempt, attack' (from *peira* 'an attempt').

pit /pit/ ▶ n. a part of the floor of an exchange in which a particular stock or commodity is traded, typically by open outcry.

ORIGIN Old English *pytt,* of West Germanic origin; related to Dutch *put* and German *Pfütze,* based on Latin *puteus* 'well, shaft.'

place /plās/ ▶ v. [trans.] dispose of (something, esp. shares) by selling to a customer.

ORIGIN Middle English: from Old French, from an alteration of

Latin *platea* 'open space,' from Greek *plateia (hodos)* 'broad (way).'

planned ob•so•les•cence /'plænd ˌäbsə'lesəns/ ▸ n. a policy of producing consumer goods that rapidly become obsolete and so require replacing, achieved by frequent changes in design, termination of the supply of spare parts, and the use of nondurable materials.

plas•tic /'plæstik/ ▸ n. informal credit cards or other types of plastic card that can be used as money: *he pays with cash instead of with plastic.*

ORIGIN mid 17th cent. (in the sense 'characteristic of molding'): from French *plastique* or Latin *plasticus*, from Greek *plastikos*, from *plassein* 'to mold.'

plat•i•num card /'plætn-əm ˌkärd/ ▸ n. a credit card made available to individuals with high credit ratings, which carries certain privileges that are unavailable to holders of other cards.

USAGE: There are currently more than 120 million **platinum cards** in use in the US.

plc (also **PLC**) Brit. ▸ abbr. public limited company.

PO ▸ abbr. purchase order.

po•gey /'pōgē/ (also **po•gy**) ▸ n. Canadian informal **1** unemployment insurance benefits.
2 welfare benefits.

ORIGIN origin unknown.

point /point/ ▸ n. a percentage of the profits from a movie or recording offered to certain people involved in its production.
■ a unit of varying value, used in quoting the price of stocks, bonds, or futures. ■ a one-percent increment in the interest rate on a loan, typically in connection with financing a home mortgage: *She lowered her mortgage rate by two points.*

ORIGIN Middle English: from Old French *point*, from Latin *punctum* 'something that is pricked,' and from Old French *pointe*, from Latin *puncta* 'pricking.'

point of sale /'point əv 'sāl/ (abbr.: **POS**) ▸ n. the place at which goods are retailed.

poi•son pill /'poizən ˌpil/ ▸ n. a tactic used by a company threatened with an unwelcome takeover bid to make itself unattractive to the bidder.

pol•i•cy /'päləsē/ ▶ n. (pl. **pol•i•cies**) a contract of insurance: *they took out a joint policy.*

ORIGIN mid 16th cent.: from French *police* 'bill of lading, contract of insurance,' from Provençal *poliss(i)a*, probably from medieval Latin *apodissa*, *apodixa*, based on Greek *apodeixis* 'evidence, proof,' from *apodeiknunai* 'demonstrate, show.'

pool /pо̄ol/ ▶ n. a group of people available for work when required: *the typing pool.*

■ a group of people considered as a resource: *a nationwide pool of promising high-school students.* ■ an arrangement, illegal in many countries, between competing parties to fix prices or rates and share business in order to eliminate competition. ■ a common fund into which all contributors pay and from which financial backing is provided: *big public investment pools.* ■ a source of common funding for speculative operations on financial markets: *a huge pool of risk capital.*

▶ v. [trans.] (of two or more people or organizations) put (money or other assets) into a common fund: *they entered a contract to pool any gains and invest them profitably.*

ORIGIN late 17th cent.: from French *poule* in the sense 'stake, kitty.'

port•fo•li•o /pôrt'fōlē͜ˌō/ ▶ n. (pl. **port•fo•li•os**) a range of investments held by a person or organization: *better returns on its investment portfolio.*

■ a range of products or services offered by an organization, esp. when considered as a business asset: *an unrivaled portfolio of quality brands.*

ORIGIN early 18th cent.: from Italian *portafogli*, from *portare* 'carry' + *foglio* 'leaf' (from Latin *folium*).

POS ▶ abbr. point of sale.

po•si•tion /pə'zisHən/ ▶ n. an investor's net holdings in one or more markets at a particular time; the status of an individual or institutional trader's open contracts: *traders were covering short positions.*

▶v. [trans.] promote (a product, service, or business) within a particular sector of a market, or as the fulfillment of that sector's specific requirements: *a comprehensive development plan that will* **position** *the city* **as** *a major economic force in the region.*
ORIGIN late Middle English: from Old French, from Latin *positio(n-)*, from *ponere* 'to place.'

post[1] /pōst/ ▶ v. [trans.] announce or publish (a financial result): *the company posted a $460,000 loss.*
ORIGIN Old English, from Latin *postis* 'doorpost,' later 'rod, beam.'

post[2] /pōst/ ▶ v. [trans.] (in bookkeeping) enter (an item) in a ledger: *post the transaction in the second column.*
■ complete (a ledger) in this way.
ORIGIN early 16th cent.: from French *poste*, from Italian *posta*, from a contraction of Latin *posita*, feminine past participle of *ponere* 'to place.'

post[3] /pōst/ ▶ n. a position of paid employment; a job: *he resigned from the post of foreign minister* | *a teaching post.*
ORIGIN mid 16th cent.: from French *poste*, from Italian *posto*, from a contraction of popular Latin *positum*, neuter past participle of *ponere* 'to place.'

post•in•dus•tri•al /ˌpōstin'dəstrēəl/ ▶ adj. of or relating to an economy that no longer relies on heavy industry.

post-tax /'pōst 'taks/ ▶ adj. (of income or profits) remaining after the deduction of taxes.

pov•er•ty line /'pävertē ˌlīn/ ▶ n. the estimated minimum level of income needed to secure the necessities of life.

PPP ▶ abbr. purchasing power parity (a way of measuring what an amount of money will buy in different countries).

PR ▶ abbr. public relations.

pred•a•to•ry pric•ing /'predəˌtôrē 'prīsiNG/ ▶ n. the pricing of goods or services at such a low level that other suppliers cannot compete and are forced to leave the market.

pre•emp•tive /prē'emptiv/ ▶ adj. relating to the purchase of goods or shares by one person or party before the opportunity is offered to others: *preemptive rights.*

pref. ▶ **abbr.** preferred (with reference to a preferred stock).

pref•er•en•tial /ˌprefə'renCHəl/ ▶ **adj.** (of a union shop) giving employment preference to union members: *a preferential shop.*
■ (of a creditor) having a claim on the receipt of payment from a debtor that will be met before those of other creditors.
ORIGIN mid 19th cent.: from *preference*, on the pattern of *differential.*

pre•ferred stock /pri'fərd 'stäk/ ▶ **n.** stock that entitles the holder to a fixed dividend, whose payment takes priority over that of common-stock dividends.

pre•mi•um /'prēmēəm/ ▶ **n. 1** an amount to be paid for an insurance policy.
2 a sum added to an ordinary price or charge: *customers are reluctant to pay a premium for organic fruit.*
■ a sum added to interest or wages; a bonus. ■ [as adj.] relating to or denoting a commodity or product of superior quality and therefore a higher price: *premium beers.* ■ the amount by which the price of a share or other security exceeds its issue price, its nominal value, or the value of the assets it represents: *the fund has traded at a premium of 12 percent.*
ORIGIN early 17th cent.: from Latin *praemium* 'booty, reward,' from *prae* 'before' + *emere* 'buy, take.'

pre•need /'prē'nēd/ ▶ **adj.** denoting a scheme in which one pays in advance for a service or facility: *preneed funeral sales.*

pres•ent val•ue /'prezənt 'vælyo͞o/ (also **net pres•ent val•ue**) ▶ **n.** the value in the present of a sum of money, in contrast to some future value it will have when it has been invested at compound interest.

pres•tige pric•ing /pres'tēZH ˌprīsiNG; -tēj/ ▶ **n.** the practice of pricing goods at a high level in order to give the appearance of quality.

pre•tax /'prē'tæks/ ▶ **adj.** (of income or profits) considered or calculated before the deduction of taxes: *pretax profits rose 23 percent.*

price con•trol /'prīs kənˌtrōl/ ▶ **n.** a government regulation establishing a maximum price to be charged for specified goods and services, esp. during periods of war or inflation.

price dis•crim•i•na•tion /'prīs diskriməˌnāSHən/ ▶ **n.** the action of selling the same product at different prices to different buyers, in order to maximize sales and profits.

price-earn•ings ra•tio /'prīs 'ərniNGz ‚rāSH(ē),ō/ (abbr.: **p/e ratio**) (also **price-earn•ings mul•ti•ple**) ▶ n. the current market price of a company share divided by the earnings per share of the company.

price-fix•ing /'prīs ‚fiksiNG/ (also **price fix•ing**) ▶ n. the maintaining of prices at a certain level by agreement between competing sellers.

price point /'prīs ‚point/ ▶ n. a point on a scale of possible prices at which something might be marketed.

price-sen•si•tive /'prīs ‚sensitiv/ ▶ adj. denoting a product whose sales are greatly influenced by the price.

■ (of information) likely to affect share prices if it were made public.

price sup•port /'prīs sə‚pôrt/ ▶ n. government assistance in maintaining the levels of market prices regardless of supply or demand.

price-tak•er /'prīs ‚tākər/ ▶ n. a company that must accept the prevailing prices in the market of its products, its own transactions being unable to affect the market price.

DERIVATIVES **price-tak•ing** n. & adj.

price war /'prīs ‚wôr/ ▶ n. a fierce competition in which retailers cut prices in an attempt to increase their share of the market.

pri•ma•ry in•dus•try /'prī‚merē 'indəstrē/ ▶ n. industry, such as mining, agriculture, or forestry, that is concerned with obtaining or providing natural raw materials for conversion into commodities and products for the consumer.

prime /prīm/ ▶ n. short for PRIME RATE.

ORIGIN Late Middle English, via Old French from Latin *primus* 'first.'

prime cost /'prīm 'kôst/ ▶ n. the direct cost of a commodity in terms of the materials and labor involved in its production, excluding fixed costs.

prime rate /'prīm 'rāt/ ▶ n. the lowest rate of interest at which money may be borrowed commercially.

prin•ci•pal /'prinsəpəl/ ▶ adj. (of money) denoting an original sum invested or lent: *the principal amount of your investment.*

▶n. **1** a sum of money lent or invested on which interest is paid: *the winners are paid from the interest without even touching the principal.*

2 a person for whom another acts as an agent or representative: *stockbrokers in Tokyo act as agents rather than as principals.*

ORIGIN Middle English: via Old French from Latin *principalis* 'first, original,' from *princeps, princip-* 'first, chief.'

USAGE: Is it **principal** or **principle**? **Principal** means 'most important' or 'person in charge': *my principal reason for coming tonight*; | *the high school principal.* It also means 'a capital sum': *the principal would be repaid in five years.* **Principle** means 'rule, basis for conduct': *her principles kept her from stealing despite her poverty.*

pri•vate en•ter•prise /ˈprīvit ˈentər͵prīz/ ▶n. business or industry that is managed by independent companies or private individuals rather than by the state.

pri•vate sec•tor /ˈprīvit ˈsektər/ ▶n. the part of the national economy that is not under direct government control.

pri•vate trea•ty /ˈprīvit ˈtrētē/ ▶n. the agreement for the sale of a property at a price negotiated directly between the vendor and purchaser or their agents.

pri•va•tize /ˈprīvə͵tīz/ ▶v. [trans.] transfer (a business, industry, or service) from public to private ownership and control: *a plan for privatizing education.*

pro•duc•er /prəˈd(y)o͞osər/ ▶n. **1** a person, company, or country that makes, grows, or supplies goods or commodities for sale: *an oil producer.*

2 a person responsible for the financial and managerial aspects of making of a movie or broadcast or for staging a play, opera, etc.

pro•duc•tion line /prəˈdəksHən ͵līn/ ▶n. an arrangement in a factory in which a thing being manufactured is passed through a set linear sequence of mechanical or manual operations.

pro•duc•tiv•i•ty /͵prōdəkˈtivətē/ ▶n. the state or quality of producing something, esp. crops: *the long-term productivity of land* | *agricultural productivity.*

■ the effectiveness of productive effort, esp. in industry, as measured in terms of the rate of output per unit of input: *workers have boosted productivity by 30 percent.*

prod•uct li•a•bil•i•ty /'prädəkt ˌlīə'bilitē/ ▶ n. the legal liability a manufacturer or trader incurs for producing or selling a faulty product.

prod•uct life-cy•cle /'prädəkt ˌlīf ˌsīkəl/ ▶ n. the series of four stages (introduction, growth, maturity, and decline) through which the levels of sales of a product pass during its market life.

prod•uct mix /'prädəkt ˌmiks/ ▶ n. the total range of products offered by a company.

prof•it /'präfit/ ▶ n. a financial gain, esp. the difference between the amount earned and the amount spent in buying, operating, or producing something.

▶v. (**prof•it•ed, prof•it•ing**) [intrans.] obtain a financial advantage or benefit, esp. from an investment.

PHRASES **at a profit** making more money than is spent buying, operating, or producing something: *fixing up houses and selling them at a profit.*

ORIGIN Middle English (in the sense 'advantage, benefit'): from Old French, from Latin *profectus* 'progress, profit,' from *proficere* 'to advance,' from *pro-* 'on behalf of' + *facere* 'do.' The verb is from Old French *profiter* .

prof•it•a•ble /'präfiṭəbəl/ ▶ adj. (of a business or activity) yielding profit or financial gain.

ORIGIN Middle English: from Old French, from the verb *profiter* (see **PROFIT**).

prof•it and loss ac•count /'präfit ən 'lôs əˌkownt/ (abbr.: **P & L**) ▶ n. an account in the books of an organization to which incomes and gains are credited and expenses and losses debited, so as to show the net profit or loss over a given period.

■ a financial statement showing a company's net profit or loss in a given period.

prof•it cen•ter /'präfit ˌsentər/ ▶ n. a part of an organization with assignable revenues and costs and hence ascertainable profitability.

prof•it mar•gin /'präfit ˌmärjin/ ▶ n. the amount by which revenue from sales exceeds costs in a business.

prof•it-tak•ing /'präfit ͵tākiNG/ (also **prof•it tak•ing**) ▶ n. the sale of securities that have risen in price.

pro for•ma /prō 'fôrmə/ ▶ adj. denoting a standard document or form, esp. an invoice sent in advance of or with goods supplied.
■ (of a financial statement) showing potential or expected income, costs, assets, or liabilities, esp. in relation to some planned or expected act or situation.
▶ n. a standard document or form or financial statement of such a type.
ORIGIN early 16th cent.: from Latin.

pro•gram trad•ing /'prōgræm ͵trādiNG/ ▶ n. the simultaneous purchase and sale of many different stocks, or of stocks and related futures contracts, with the use of a computer program to exploit price differences in different markets.

prom•is•so•ry note /'prämə͵sôrē 'nōt/ ▶ n. a signed document containing a written promise to pay a stated sum to a specified person or the bearer at a specified date or on demand.

pro•mote /prə'mōt/ ▶ v. [trans.] **1** give publicity to (a product, organization, or venture) so as to increase sales or public awareness: *they are using famous personalities to promote the library nationally.*
2 (often **be promoted**) advance or raise (someone) to a higher position or rank: *she was **promoted to** general manager.*
ORIGIN late Middle English: from Latin *promot-* 'moved forward,' from the verb *promovere*, from *pro-* 'forward, onward' + *movere* 'to move.'

pro•mot•er /prə'mōtər/ ▶ n. a person or company that finances or organizes a sporting event or theatrical production: *a boxing promoter.*
■ a person involved in setting up and funding a new company.
ORIGIN late Middle English: from Anglo-Norman French *promotour*, from medieval Latin *promotor* (see **PROMOTE**).

pro•mo•tion /prə'mōsHən/ ▶ n. **1** the publicization of a product, organization, or venture so as to increase sales or public awareness.
■ a publicity campaign for a particular product, organization, or venture: *the paper is reaping the rewards of a series of promotions.*
■ [often as adj.] (**promotions**) the activity or business of organizing such publicity or campaigns: *she's the promotions manager for the museum.*

2 the action of raising someone to a higher position or rank or the fact of being so raised: *a promotion to divisional sales director.*
ORIGIN late Middle English: via Old French from Latin *promotio(n-)*, from *promovere* 'move forward' (see **PROMOTE**).

prop•er•ty /'präpərtē/ ▸ n. (pl. **prop•er•ties**) a building or buildings and the land belonging to it or them: *he's expanding now, buying property | the renovation of commercial properties.*
ORIGIN Middle English: from an Anglo-Norman French variant of Old French *propriete*, from Latin *proprietas*, from *proprius* 'one's own, particular.'

pro•pri•e•tar•y /prə'prīi,terē/ ▸ adj. of or relating to an owner or ownership: *the company has a proprietary right to the property.*
■ (of a product) marketed under and protected by a registered trade name: *proprietary brands of insecticide.*
ORIGIN late Middle English (as a noun denoting a member of a religious order who held property): from late Latin *proprietarius* 'proprietor,' from *proprietas* (see **PROPERTY**).

pro•pri•e•tar•y name /prə'prīi,terē 'nām/ ▸ n. a name of a product or service registered by its owner as a trademark and not usable by others without permission.

pro•pri•e•tor /prə'prīitər/ ▸ n. the owner of a business.

pro•tect /prə'tekt/ ▸ v. [trans.] (often **be protected**) (of an insurance policy) promise to pay (someone) an agreed amount in the event of loss, injury, fire, theft, or other misfortune: *in the event of your death, your family will be protected against any financial problems that may arise.*
■ shield (a domestic industry) from competition by imposing import duties on foreign goods. ■ provide funds to meet (a bill of exchange or commercial draft).
ORIGIN late Middle English: from Latin *protect-* 'covered in front,' from the verb *protegere*, from *pro-* 'in front' + *tegere* 'to cover.'

pro•tec•tion•ism /prə'teksHə,nizəm/ ▸ n. the theory or practice of shielding a country's domestic industries from foreign competition by taxing imports.

pro•tec•tive /prə'tektiv/ ▸ adj. of or relating to the protection of domestic industries from foreign competition: *protective tariffs.*

pro•vi•sion /prə'vizHən/ ▸ n. (**provision for/against**) financial or other arrangements for future eventualities or requirements: *farmers have been slow to **make provision for** their retirement.*
■ an amount set aside out of profits in the accounts of an organization for a known liability, esp. a bad debt or the diminution in value of an asset.
▸v. [intrans.] set aside an amount in an organization's accounts for a known liability: *financial institutions have to **provision against** loan losses.*
ORIGIN late Middle English: via Old French from Latin *provisio(n-)*, from *providere* 'foresee, attend to,' from *pro-* 'before' + *videre* 'see.' The verb dates from the early 19th cent.

psy•chic in•come /'sīkik 'in‚kəm; 'iNG‚kəm/ ▸ n. the nonmonetary or nonmaterial satisfactions that accompany an occupation or economic activity.

pub•lic /'pəblik/ ▸ adj. of or provided by the government rather than an independent, commercial company: *public spending.*
PHRASES **go public** become a public company.
ORIGIN late Middle English: from Old French, from Latin *publicus*, blend of *poplicus* 'of the people' (from *populus* 'people') and *pubes* 'adult.'

pub•lic com•pa•ny /'pəblik 'kəmpənē/ ▸ n. a company whose shares are traded freely on a stock exchange.

pub•lic good /'pəblik 'go͞od/ ▸ n. a commodity or service that is provided without profit to all members of a society, either by the government or a private individual or organization: *a conviction that library informational services are a public good, not a commercial commodity.*

pub•lic•i•ty /pə'blisitē/ ▸ n. the giving out of information about a product, person, or company for advertising or promotional purposes: *head of publicity and marketing.*
■ material or information used for such a purpose: *we distributed publicity from a stall in the marketplace.*
ORIGIN late 18th cent.: from French *publicité*, from *public* 'public' (see **PUBLIC**).

pub•lic re•la•tions /'pəblik ri'lāsHənz/ ▸ plural n. [also treated as sing.]

the professional maintenance of a favorable public image by a company or other organization or a famous person.

■ the state of the relationship between the public and a company or other organization or a famous person: *companies justify the cost in terms of improved public relations.*

pub•lic sec•tor /'pəblik 'sektər/ ▶ n. the part of an economy that is controlled by the government.

pull•back /'po͞ol,bæk/ ▶ n. a reduction in price or demand: *there is no sign of a consumer pullback.*

pump-prim•ing /'pəmp 'prīmiNG/ ▶ n. the stimulation of economic activity by investment.

put op•tion /'po͞ot ,äpsHən/ (also **put**) ▶ n. an option to sell assets at an agreed price on or before a particular date.

Pvt. (also **PVT**) ▶ abbr. (in company names) private: *Waves Electronic Pvt. Ltd.*

pyr•a•mid /'pirəmid/ ▶ n. a system of financial growth achieved by a small initial investment, with subsequent investments being funded by using unrealized profits as collateral.

▶ v. [trans.] achieve a substantial return on (money or property) after making a small initial investment.

ORIGIN late Middle English (in the geometric sense): via Latin from Greek *puramis*, *puramid-*, of unknown ultimate origin.

Q

Q ▸ **abbr.** quarter (used to refer to a specified quarter of the fiscal year): *we expect to have an exceptional Q4.*

QPP ▸ **abbr.** Canadian Quebec Pension Plan.

QST ▸ **n.** Canadian Quebec Sales Tax.

qual•i•ty as•sur•ance /'kwälitē ə‚sHŏŏrəns/ ▸ **n.** the maintenance of a desired level of quality in a service or product, esp. by means of attention to every stage of the process of delivery or production.

qual•i•ty cir•cle /'kwälitē ‚sərkəl/ ▸ **n.** a group of employees that meets regularly to consider ways of resolving problems and improving production in their organization.

quant /kwänt/ ▸ **n.** *informal* a specialist in the use of statistics and mathematical analyses in business, esp. in investing.

ORIGIN late 20th cent.: abbreviation of *quantative analyst.*

quan•ti•ty the•o•ry /'kwäntitē ‚THi(ə)rē/ (also **the quan•ti•ty the•o• ry of mon•ey**) ▸ **n.** the hypothesis that changes in prices correspond to changes in the monetary supply.

quo•ta /'kwōt̬ə/ ▸ **n.** a limited quantity of a particular product that under official controls can be produced, exported, or imported: *the country may be exceeding its OPEC quota of 1,100,000 barrels of oil per day.*

ORIGIN early 17th cent.: from medieval Latin *quota (pars)* 'how great (a part),' feminine of *quotus*, from *quot* 'how many.'

quo•ta•tion /‚kwō'tāsHən/ ▸ **n.** a price offered by a broker for the sale or purchase of a stock or other security.

■ a registration granted to a company enabling their shares to be officially listed and traded.

ORIGIN mid 16th cent. (denoting a marginal reference to a passage of text): from medieval Latin *quotatio(n-)*, from the verb *quotare* (see **QUOTE**).

quote /kwōt/ ▸ v. [trans.] give someone (the estimated price of a job or service).

■ (usu. **be quoted**) give (a company) a quotation or listing on a stock exchange: *an organization that is **quoted on** the Stock Exchange.*

▸n. a price offered by a broker for the sale or purchase of a stock or other security.

■ a quotation or listing of a company on a stock exchange.

ORIGIN late Middle English: from medieval Latin *quotare*, from *quot* 'how many,' or from medieval Latin *quota* (see **QUOTA**).

USAGE: The original sense of the verb **quote** was 'mark a book with numbers, or with marginal references,' later 'give a reference by page or chapter,' hence 'cite a text or person' (late 16th cent.).

R

R ▸ **abbr.** (also ®) registered as a trademark.

rack rent /'ræk ˌrent/ ▸ **n.** an extortionate or very high rent, esp. an annual rent equivalent to the full value of the property to which it relates.

▸ **v.** (**rack-rent**) [trans.] exact an excessive or extortionate rent from (a tenant) or for (a property).

ORIGIN late 16th cent. (as *rack-rented*): from the verb *rack* (in the sense 'cause stress') + the noun *rent*.

raid /rād/ ▸ **n.** a hostile attempt to buy a major or controlling interest in the shares of a company.

ORIGIN late Middle English: Scots variant of *road* in the early senses 'journey on horseback,' 'foray.' The noun became rare from the end of the 16th cent. but was revived by Sir Walter Scott.

ral•ly /'rælē/ ▸ **v.** (**ral•lies, ral•lied**) [intrans.] (of share, currency, or commodity prices) increase after a fall: *prices of metals such as aluminum and copper have rallied.*

▸ **n.** a quick or marked recovery after a reverse or period of weakness: *the market staged a late rally.*

ORIGIN early 17th cent.: from French *rallier*, from *re-* 'again' + *allier* 'to ally.'

rate /rāt/ ▸ **n.** a fixed price paid or charged for something, esp. goods or services: *the basic rate of pay | advertising rates.*

■ the amount of a charge or payment expressed as a percentage of some other amount, or as a basis of calculation: *you'll find our current interest rate very competitive.*

ORIGIN late Middle English: from Old French, from medieval

Latin *rata* (from Latin *pro rata parte* (or *portione*) 'according to the proportional share'), from *ratus* 'reckoned,' past participle of *reri* .

rate of ex•change /'rāt əv iks'CHānj/ ▶ n. another term for EXCHANGE RATE.

rate of re•turn /'rāt əv ri'tərn/ ▶ n. the annual income from an investment expressed as a proportion (usually a percentage) of the original investment.

ra•ti•o /'rāSH(ē),ō/ ▶ n. (pl. **ra•ti•os**) the relative value of silver and gold in a bimetallic system of currency.

ORIGIN mid 17th cent.: from Latin, literally 'reckoning,' from *rat-* 'reckoned,' from the verb *reri* .

ra•tion•al ex•pec•ta•tions hy•poth•e•sis /'ræSHənl ,ekspek'tāSHənz hī,päTHəsis/ ▶ n. the hypothesis that an economic agent will make full use of all available information when forming expectations, esp. with regard to inflation, and not just past values of a particular variable.

re•act /rē'ækt/ ▶ v. [intrans.] (of stock prices) fall after rising.

ORIGIN mid 17th cent.: from *re-* (expressing intensive force or reversal) + *act*, originally suggested by medieval Latin *react-* 'done again,' from the verb *reagere* .

read•y mon•ey /'redē 'mənē/ (also **read•y cash**) ▶ n. money in the form of cash that is immediately available.

re•al /'rē(ə)l/ ▶ adj. adjusted for changes in the value of money; assessed by purchasing power: *real incomes had fallen by 30 percent* | *an increase in real terms of 11.6 percent.*

ORIGIN late Middle English: from Anglo-Norman French, from late Latin *realis*, from Latin *res* 'thing.'

re•al es•tate a•gent /'rē(ə)l i,stāt ,ājənt/ ▶ n. a person who sells and rents out buildings and land for clients.

DERIVATIVES **re•al es•tate a•gen•cy** n.

re•al•i•za•ble /,rēə'līzəbəl/ ▶ adj. in or able to be converted into cash: *10 percent of realizable assets.*

re•al•i•za•tion /,rēələ'zāSHən/ ▶ n. the action of converting an asset into cash.

■ a sale of goods: *auction realizations.*

re•al•ize /'rēə‚līz/ ▸ v. [trans.] make (money or a profit) from a transaction: *she realized a profit of $100,000.*

■ (of goods) be sold for (a specified price); fetch: *the drawings are expected to realize $500,000.* ■ convert (an asset) into cash: *he realized all the assets in her trust fund.*

ORIGIN early 17th cent.: from REAL, on the pattern of French *réaliser* .

re•al•tor /'rē(ə)ltər/ ▸ n. a person who acts as an agent for the sale and purchase of buildings and land; a real estate agent.

ORIGIN early 20th cent.: from *realty* + *-or.*

re•badge /rē'bæj/ ▸ v. [trans.] relaunch (a product) under a new name or logo.

re•base /rē'bās/ ▸ v. [trans.] establish a new base level for (a tax level, price index, etc.).

re•bate /'rē‚bāt/ ▸ n. a partial refund to someone who has paid too much money for tax, rent, or a utility.

■ a deduction or discount on a sum of money due.

▸ v. [trans.] pay back (such a sum of money).

ORIGIN late Middle English (as a verb in the sense 'diminish (a sum or amount)'): from Anglo-Norman French *rebatre* 'beat back,' also 'deduct.'

re•brand /rē'brænd/ ▸ v. [trans.] change the corporate image of (a company or organization).

re•cap•i•tal•ize /rē'kæpitl‚īz/ ▸ v. [trans.] provide (a business) with more capital, esp. by replacing debt with stock.

re•ceipt /ri'sēt/ ▸ n. a written or printed statement acknowledging that something has been paid for or that goods have been received.

■ (**receipts**) an amount of money received during a particular period by an organization or business: *box-office receipts.*

▸ v. [trans.] [usu. as adj.] (**receipted**) mark (a bill) as paid: *the receipted hotel bill.*

■ write a receipt for (goods or money): *all fish shall be receipted at time of purchase.*

ORIGIN late Middle English: from Anglo-Norman French *receite,* from medieval Latin *recepta* 'received,' feminine past participle of Latin *recipere* . The *-p-* was inserted in imitation of the Latin spelling.

re•ceiv•a•bles /ri'sēvəbəlz/ ▸ **plural n.** amounts owed to a business, regarded as assets.

re•ceiv•er /ri'sēvər/ ▸ **n.** a person or company appointed by a court to manage the financial affairs of a business or person that has gone bankrupt: *the company is in the hands of the receivers.*

re•ceiv•er•ship /ri'sēvər,sнip/ ▸ **n.** the state of being dealt with by an official receiver: *the company went into receivership last week.*

re•ces•sion /ri'sesнən/ ▸ **n.** a period of temporary economic decline during which trade and industrial activity are reduced, generally identified by a fall in GDP in two successive quarters.

D E R I V A T I V E S **re•ces•sion•ar•y adj.**

O R I G I N mid 17th cent.: from Latin *recessio(n-),* from *recess-* 'gone back,' from the verb *recedere,* from *re-* 'back' + *cedere* 'go.'

re•ces•sive /ri'sesiv/ ▸ **adj.** undergoing an economic recession: *the recessive housing market.*

O R I G I N late 17th cent.: from *recess,* on the pattern of *excessive.*

rec•on•cile /'rekən,sīl/ ▸ **v.** [trans.] (often **be reconciled**) make (one account) consistent with another, esp. by allowing for transactions begun but not yet completed: *it is not necessary to reconcile the cost accounts to the financial accounts.*

O R I G I N late Middle English: from Old French *reconcilier* or Latin *reconciliare,* from Latin *re-* 'back' (also expressing intensive force) + *conciliare* 'bring together.'

rec•on•cil•i•a•tion state•ment /,rekən,silē'āsнən ,stātmənt/ ▸ **n.** an account statement in which discrepancies are adjusted so that different accounts balance.

re•coup /ri'ko͞op/ ▸ **v.** [trans.] regain (money spent or lost), esp. through subsequent profits: *oil companies are keen to recoup their investment.*

■ reimburse or compensate (someone) for money spent or lost.

■ deduct or keep back (part of a sum due).

O R I G I N early 17th cent.: from French *recouper* 'retrench, cut back,' from *re-* 'back' + *couper* 'to cut.'

re•course /'rē,kôrs; ri'kôrs/ ▸ **n.** [in sing.] the legal right to demand compensation or payment: *the bank has recourse against the exporter for losses incurred.*

P H R A S E S **without recourse** a formula used to disclaim responsibility for future nonpayment, esp. of a negotiable financial instrument.

ORIGIN late Middle English: from Old French *recours*, from Latin *recursus*, from *re-* 'back, again' + *cursus* 'course, running.'

re•cov•er•y stock /ri'kəvərē ˌstäk/ ▸ n. a stock that has fallen in price but is thought to have the potential of climbing back to its original level.

re•deem /ri'dēm/ ▸ v. [trans.] gain or regain possession of (something) in exchange for payment: *his best suit had been redeemed from the pawnbrokers.*
■ repay (a stock, bond, or other instrument) at the maturity date.
■ exchange (a coupon, voucher, or trading stamp) for merchandise, a discount, or money. ■ pay the necessary money to clear (a debt): *owners were unable to redeem their mortgages.* ■ exchange (paper money) for gold or silver.

ORIGIN late Middle English: from Old French *redimer* or Latin *redimere*, from *re(d)-* 'back' + *emere* 'buy.'

re•demp•tion /ri'dempsʜən/ ▸ n. the action of regaining or gaining possession of something in exchange for payment, or clearing a debt.

ORIGIN late Middle English: from Old French, from Latin *redemptio(n-)*, from *redimere* 'buy back' (see **REDEEM**).

re•demp•tion yield /ri'dempsʜən ˌyēld/ ▸ n. the yield of a stock calculated as a percentage of the redemption price with an adjustment made for any capital gain or loss the price represents relative to the current price.

re•dis•count /rē'disˌkownt/ ▸ v. [trans.] (of a central bank) discount (a bill of exchange or similar instrument) that has already been discounted by a commercial bank.

re•en•gi•neer /ˌrēenjə'ni(ə)r/ ▸ v. [trans.] restructure (a company or part of its operations), esp. by exploiting information technology.

re•ex•port /rē'ekspôrt; ˌrē-ik'spôrt/ ▸ v. [trans.] export (imported goods), typically after they have undergone further processing or manufacture.

re•fi•nance /ˌrēfə'næns; rē'fīnæns/ ▸ v. [trans.] finance (something) again, typically with a new loan at a lower rate of interest.

re•flate /ri'flāt/ ▸ v. [trans.] expand the level of output of (an economy) by government stimulus, using either fiscal or monetary policy.
ORIGIN 1930s: from *re-* 'again,' on the pattern of *inflate*, *deflate*.

Reg•is•tered Home Own•er•ship Sav•ings Plan /'rejistərd 'hōm ˌōnərsHip 'sāviNGz ˌplæn/ ▸ n. Canadian see **RHOSP**.

Reg•is•tered Re•tire•ment In•come Fund /'rejistərd 'ritīrmənt ˌinkəm ˌfənd/ ▸ n. Canadian see **RRIF**.

Reg•is•tered Re•tire•ment Sav•ings Plan /'rejistərd 'ritīrmənt ˌsāviNGz ˌplæn/ ▸ n. Canadian see **RRSP**.

reg•u•late /'regyəˌlāt/ ▸ v. [trans.] control or supervise (a company or business activity) by means of rules and regulations: *the organization that regulates fishing in the region.*
ORIGIN late Middle English: from late Latin *regulat-* 'directed, regulated,' from the verb *regulare*, from Latin *regula* 'rule.'

reg•u•la•tor /'regyəˌlātər/ ▸ n. [trans.] a person or body that supervises a particular industry or business activity.

re•im•port /ˌrē-im'pôrt/ ▸ v. [trans.] import (goods processed or made from exported materials).

re•in•sure /ˌrē-in'sHŌŌr/ ▸ v. [trans.] (of an insurer) transfer (all or part of a risk) to another insurer to provide protection against the risk of the first insurance.

re•in•vest /ˌrē-in'vest/ ▸ v. [trans.] put (the profit on a previous investment) back into the same place: *the enterprise had been expanded by reinvesting profits.*

re•mit /ri'mit/ ▸ v. (**re•mit•ted, re•mit•ting**) [trans.] send (money) in payment or as a gift: *the income they remitted to their families.*
DERIVATIVES **re•mit•tance n.**
ORIGIN late Middle English: from Latin *remittere* 'send back, restore,' from *re-* 'back' + *mittere* 'send.'

re•mort•gage /rē'môrgij/ ▸ v. [trans.] take out another or a different kind of mortgage on (a property).
▸ n. a different or additional mortgage.

re•mu•ner•ate /ri'myōŌnəˌrāt/ ▸ v. [trans.] pay (someone) for services rendered or work done: *they should be remunerated fairly for their work.*

DERIVATIVES **re•mu•ner•a•tion n.**
ORIGIN early 16th cent.: from Latin *remunerat-* 'rewarded, recompensed,' from the verb *remunerari*, from *re-* (expressing intensive force) + *munus, muner-* 'gift.'

re•na•tion•al•ize /rēˈnæSHənlˌīz/ ▶ v. [trans.] transfer (a privatized industry) back into state ownership or control.

rent /rent/ ▶ n. a tenant's regular payment to a landlord for the use of property or land.
■ a sum paid for the hire of equipment.
▶v. [trans.] pay someone for the use of (something, typically property, land, or a car).
■ (of an owner) let someone use (something) in return for payment: *he purchased a large tract of land and rented out most of it to local farmers.* ■ [intrans.] be let or hired out at a specified rate: *skis or snowboards rent for $60–80 for six days.*
PHRASES **for rent** available to be rented.
DERIVATIVES **rent•a•ble adj.**
ORIGIN Middle English: from Old French *rente*, from *rendre* 'give back,' from an alteration of Latin *reddere,* from *re-* 'back' + *dare* 'give.'

ren•tal /ˈrentl/ ▶ n. an amount paid or received as rent.
■ the action of renting something: *the office was on weekly rental.*
■ a rented house or car.
▶adj. of, relating to, or available for rent: *rental properties.*
ORIGIN late Middle English: from Anglo-Norman French, or from Anglo-Latin *rentale,* from Old French *rente* (see **RENT**).

re•or•der /rēˈôrdər/ ▶ n. a renewed or repeated order for goods.

rep /rep/ informal ▶ n. a representative: *a union rep.*
■ a sales representative.
▶v. (**repped, rep•ping**) [intrans.] act as a sales representative for a company or product: *at eighteen she was working for her dad, repping on the road.*
ORIGIN late 19th cent.: abbreviation for *representative* and *represent.*

re•pa•tri•ate /rēˈpātrēˌāt; rēˈpæ-/ ▶ v. [trans.] send or bring (money) back to one's own country: *foreign firms would be permitted to repatriate all profits.*

ORIGIN early 17th cent.: from late Latin *repatriat-* 'returned to one's country,' from the verb *repatriare,* from *re-* 'back' + Latin *patria* 'native land.'

re•po /ˈrēˌpō/ informal ▸ n. (pl. **re•pos**) a car or other item that has been repossessed.

▸v. (**re•po's, re•po'd**) [trans.] repossess (a car or other item) when a buyer defaults on payments.

re•pos•sess /ˌrēpəˈzes/ ▸ v. [trans.] retake possession of (something) when a buyer defaults on payments: *565 homes were repossessed for nonpayment of mortgages.*

re•pos•ses•sor /ˌrēpəˈzesər/ ▸ n. a person hired by a credit company to repossess an item when the buyer defaults on payments.

re-pre•sent /ˌrē priˈzent/ ▸ v. [trans.] present (a check or bill) again for payment.

re•pur•chase /rēˈpərCHəs/ ▸ v. [trans.] buy (something) back. ▸n. the action of buying something back.

re•pur•chase a•gree•ment /rēˈpərCHəs əˌgrēmənt/ ▸ n. a contract in which the vendor of a security agrees to repurchase it from the buyer at an agreed price.

re•sale /ˈrēˌsāl/ ▸ n. the sale of a thing previously bought: *he is renovating them for resale.*

re•sell /rēˈsel/ ▸ v. (past and past part. **re•sold**) [trans.] sell (something one has bought) to someone else: *products can be resold on the black market for huge profits.*

re•serve /riˈzərv/ ▸ n. **1** (often **reserves**) a supply of a commodity not needed for immediate use but available if required: *Australia has major coal, gas, and uranium reserves.* ■ funds kept available by a bank, company, or government: *the foreign exchange reserves.* ■ a part of a company's profits added to capital rather than paid as a dividend.
2 short for RESERVE PRICE.

ORIGIN Middle English: from Old French *reserver,* from Latin *reservare* 'keep back,' from *re-* 'back' + *servare* 'keep.'

re•serve bank /riˈzərv ˌbæNGk/ ▸ n. a regional bank operating under and implementing the policies of the US Federal Reserve.

re•serve price /riˈzərv ˌprīs/ ▸ n. the price stipulated as the lowest acceptable by the seller for an item sold at auction.

re•sid•u•al /ri'zijо̄о̄əl/ ▸ n. **1** a royalty paid to a performer, writer, etc., for a repeat of a play, television show, etc. **2** the resale value of a new car or other item at a specified time after purchase, expressed as a percentage of its purchase price.

re•source /'rē¸sôrs; 'rē¸zôrs; ri'sôrs; ri'zôrs/ ▸ n. (usu. **resources**) a stock or supply of money, materials, staff, and other assets that can be drawn on by a person or organization in order to function effectively: *local authorities complained that they lacked resources.* ■ (**resources**) a country's collective means of supporting itself or becoming wealthier, as represented by its reserves of minerals, land, and other assets. ■ (**resources**) available assets. ▸ v. [trans.] provide (a person or organization) with materials, money, staff, and other assets necessary for effective operation: *ensuring that primary health care workers are adequately resourced.* ORIGIN early 17th cent.: from obsolete French *ressourse,* feminine past participle (used as a noun) of Old French dialect *resourdre* 'rise again, recover' (based on Latin *surgere* 'to rise').

re•stock /rē'stäk/ ▸ v. [trans.] replenish (a store) with fresh stock or supplies.

re•straint of trade /ri¸strānt əv 'trād/ ▸ n. action that interferes with free competition in a market.

re•struc•ture /rē'strəkCHər; -SHər/ ▸ v. [trans.] convert (the debt of a business in difficulty) into another kind of debt, typically one that is repayable at a later time.

re•tail /'rē¸tāl/ ▸ n. the sale of goods to the public in relatively small quantities for use or consumption rather than for resale: [as adj.] *the product's retail price.* ▸ adv. being sold in such a way: *it is not yet available retail.* ▸ v. [trans.] sell (goods) to the public in such a way: *the difficulties in retailing the new products.* ■ [intrans.] (**retail at/for**) (of goods) be sold in this way for (a specified price): *the product retails for around $20.* ORIGIN late Middle English: from an Anglo-Norman French use of Old French *retaille* 'a piece cut off,' from *retaillier,* from *re-* (expressing intensive force) + *tailler* 'to cut.'

re•tire /ri'tīr/ ▸ v. [intrans.] leave one's job and cease to work, typically upon reaching the normal age for leaving employment: *he retired from the navy in 1966.*

■ [trans.] withdraw (a bill or note) from circulation or currency.

■ pay off or cancel (a debt): *the debt is to be retired from state gaming-tax receipts.*

DERIVATIVES **re•tire•ment n.**

ORIGIN mid 16th cent.: from French *retirer*, from *re-* 'back' + *tirer* 'draw.'

re•trench /ri'trenCH/ ▸ v. [intrans.] (of a company, government, or individual) reduce costs or spending in response to economic difficulty: *as a result of the recession the company retrenched.*

DERIVATIVES **re•trench•ment n.**

ORIGIN late 16th cent.: from obsolete French *retrencher*, variant of *retrancher*, from *re-* (expressing reversal) + *trancher* 'to cut, slice.'

re•turn /ri'tərn/ ▸ v. [trans.] yield or make (a profit): *the company returned a profit of 4.3 million dollars.*

▸ n. (often **returns**) a profit from an investment: *product areas are being developed to produce maximum returns.*

■ a good rate of return.

ORIGIN Middle English: the verb from Old French *returner*, from Latin *re-* 'back' + *tornare* 'to turn'; the noun via Anglo-Norman French.

re•val•ue /rē'vælyo͞o/ ▸ v. (**re•val•ues, re•val•ued, re•val•u•ing**) [trans.] assess the value of (something) again.

■ adjust the value of (a currency) in relation to other currencies.

rev•e•nue /'revə,n(y)o͞o/ ▸ n. income, esp. when of a company or organization and of a substantial nature.

ORIGIN late Middle English: from Old French *revenu(e)* 'returned,' past participle (used as a noun) of *revenir*, from Latin *revenire* 'return,' from *re-* 'back' + *venire* 'come.'

rev•e•nue tar•iff /'revə,n(y)o͞o ,tærif; ,te(ə)rif/ ▸ n. a tariff imposed principally to raise government revenue rather than to protect domestic industries.

re•verse en•gi•neer•ing /ri'vərs ,enjə'ni(ə)riNG/ ▸ n. the reproduction of another manufacturer's product following detailed examination of its construction or composition.

re•verse take•o•ver /ri'vərs 'tāk,ōvər/ ▸ n. a takeover of a public company by a smaller company.

re•volv•ing cred•it /ri'välviNG ,kredit/ ▸ n. credit that is automatically renewed as debts are paid off.

re•volv•ing fund /ri'välviNG ,fənd/ ▸ n. a fund that is continually replenished as withdrawals are made.

RFP ▸ abbr. request for proposal, a detailed specification of goods or services required by an organization, sent to potential contractors or suppliers.

RHOSP ▸ abbr. Canadian Registered Home Ownership Savings Plan, a tax-sheltered account in which a first-time homebuyer may save money for a down payment.

rig /rig/ ▸ v. (**rigged, rig•ging**) [trans.] cause an artificial rise or fall in prices in (a market, esp. the stock market) with a view to personal profit: *he accused games manufacturers of rigging the market.*
ORIGIN late 18th cent.: of unknown origin.

rights is•sue /'rīts ,isH$\overline{oo}$/ ▸ n. an issue of shares offered at a special price by a company to its existing shareholders in proportion to their holding of old shares.

risk /risk/ ▸ n. the possibility of financial loss: [as adj.] *project finance is essentially an exercise in risk management.* ■ (usu. **risks**) a possibility of harm or damage against which something is insured.
ORIGIN mid 17th cent.: from French *risque* (noun), *risquer* (verb), from Italian *risco* 'danger' and *rischiare* 'run into danger.'

risk cap•i•tal /'risk ,kæpitl/ ▸ n. another term for VENTURE CAPITAL.

ROCE ▸ abbr. return on capital employed.

ROI ▸ abbr. return on investment.

roll•out /'rōl,owt/ (also **roll-out**) ▸ n. the official launch of a new product or service.

roll•o•ver /'rōl,ōvər/ ▸ n. the extension or transfer of a debt or other financial arrangement.

Roth IRA /rôTH 'ī ,är 'ā; 'īrä/ ▸ n. an individual retirement account allowing a person to set aside after-tax income up to a specified amount each year. Both earnings on the account and withdrawals after age 59½ are tax-free.
ORIGIN created in 1997 and named for Senator William Victor Roth II (born 1921) of Delaware, who proposed this in Congress.

RRIF /rif/ ▸ **abbr.** Canadian Registered Retirement Income Fund, a tax-sheltered savings plan which provides retirement income.

RRSP ▸ **abbr.** Canadian Registered Retirement Savings Plan, a tax-sheltered plan for saving for retirement.

RSP ▸ **abbr.** Canadian Retirement Savings Plan.

run /rən/ ▸ **n.** (**a run on**) a widespread and sudden or continuous demand for (a particular currency or commodity): *there's been* **a** *big* **run on** *nostalgia toys this year.*

■ a sudden demand for repayment from a bank made by a large number of lenders: *growing nervousness among investors led to a run on some banks.*

ORIGIN Old English *rinnan, irnan* (verb), of Germanic origin, probably reinforced in Middle English by Old Norse *rinna, renna.* The current form with *-u-* in the present tense is first recorded in the 16th cent.

run-up /ˈrən ˌəp/ ▸ **n.** a marked rise in the value or level of something: *a sharp run-up of land and stock prices.*

HOW TO PLAN FOR
RETIREMENT

Here are seven rules for planning for retirement:

1. Invest for growth. Even with the recent downturn in the stock market, it's still critical that, when you invest in your retirement accounts, you invest for growth. Many people are now making the crucial mistake of thinking that the stock market will never go up again and, as a result, they are putting all of their money in guaranteed investments (like certificates of deposit). The problem with investing in something that is guaranteed is that the return may be less than inflation, which means you are actually losing money each year. The cost of living has been climbing steadily, at an average of slightly more than 3 percent a year. Playing it safe will not allow you to beat that rate. If your retirement account doesn't grow faster than inflation, you're not going to have enough money to live on when you retire, 20, 30, or 40 years from now.

While seeking growth requires you to invest some of your money in stocks (and that means more risk), over the long term, you should come out ahead and be able to build a bigger nest egg.

2. Take advantage of free money. One of the smartest things you can do when it comes to saving for the future is taking advantage of the free money your employer may give you. In many cases, employers will supplement your retirement plan contributions with contributions of their own. These matching contributions usually start at 20 percent of what you've put in and sometimes go as high as 100 percent. At the same time, you should still make the maximum allowable contribution, not just the percentage of your paycheck that your company will match. If your employer stops matching your contributions (as many companies have recently started doing), don't make the critical mistake of stopping your contributions to your retirement account. With or without a match, you want to use your retirement account at work.

3. Don't borrow from your retirement plan. Although your retirement plan may allow you to borrow money from your account without paying taxes or penalties, don't do it. Why? For starters, imagine being laid off from work. At the worst possible time, your company tells you, "You have to pay back your 401(k) loan." Without a paycheck, you can't pay back your loan, right? Your company then reports your loan as a distribution, and now you owe the IRS taxes on the loan, plus a 10 percent penalty fee. But wait, you're not working. How will you pay the IRS? See the problem here? This is happening to thousands of Americans right now. Don't let it happen to you. Leave your retirement money alone until you're ready to retire.

4. Consolidate your accounts. Many people remember Grandma's advice about not putting all your eggs in one basket, but they often misunderstand it. Not putting your eggs in one basket means diversifying your risk—putting your money into different kinds of assets, such as stocks, bonds, mutual funds, and other investment vehicles. It doesn't mean opening an IRA at a different bank or brokerage firm every year.

There is simply no way you can do a good job managing your retirement accounts if they are spread all over the place. If that's what you've done, consider consolidating them into one IRA custodial account. Not only can you completely diversify your investments within a single IRA, but you'll also find it much easier to keep track of everything.

5. Be careful who you list as the beneficiary of your retirement account. Many people follow their lawyer's advice to create a living trust to protect their estate, put all their assets in it, and register the beneficiary of their retirement accounts in their trust's name. This is a big mistake. When you do this, your spouse loses the ability to do what's called a spousal IRA rollover, which allows, for example, a widow to take over her late husband's IRA and put it in her name, without having to pay any taxes on it until she actually starts taking the money out. If the husband has transferred ownership of his IRA to a trust, the wife can't take it over in the event of his death. Instead, the account goes to the trust, and the proceeds become taxable. For much the same reason, you shouldn't make a trust the beneficiary of any of your IRAs or 401(k) plans. You should also make sure that, if you or your partner has been married before, your ex isn't still listed as the beneficiary on any of your retirement accounts. Finally, if you're newly married, make sure that your spouse has put you down as the beneficiary of his or her accounts. Many people when they marry have "Mom" down as a beneficiary. No offense to "Mom" or "Sis," but you want *your* name on that beneficiary statement. Also, make sure you list your kids as contingent beneficiaries.

6. Always take your retirement money with you. When you leave a company where you've been contributing to a 401(k) plan, don't leave your retirement money behind. Rather, immediately inform the benefits department that you want to do an IRA rollover. Your former employer will then transfer your retirement funds either to a new custodial IRA that you've set up for yourself at a bank or brokerage firm, or to the 401(k) plan at your new employer (assuming there is one and it accepts money from other plans). If you leave money in an old 401(k) plan, your beneficiary, upon your death, would have to go back to a company where you may not have worked in years to get your money. The process can take as long as a year, and the money could be subject to taxes before your beneficiary can collect it.

7. Don't shortchange yourself. Whatever else you do in your financial life, take retirement planning seriously. There is nothing you can do that will have more impact on your future financial security than maximizing your contributions to a retirement account and making sure that money works really hard for you.

S

---

sal•a•ry /'sælərē/ ▸ n. (pl. **sal•a•ries**) a fixed regular payment, typically paid on a monthly or biweekly basis but often expressed as an annual sum, made by an employer to an employee, esp. a professional or white-collar worker: *he received a salary of $29,000* | [as adj.] *a 15 percent salary increase.* Compare with WAGE.

ORIGIN Middle English: from Anglo-Norman French *salarie*, from Latin *salarium*, originally denoting a Roman soldier's allowance to buy salt, from *sal* 'salt.'

sales tax /'sālz ˌtæks/ ▸ n. a tax on sales or on the receipts from sales.

Sal•lie Mae /'sælē 'mā/ ▸ n. informal the Student Loan Marketing Association, an agency that makes educational loans more widely available to college students.

USAGE: **Sallie Mae** purchases loans from originating financial institutions and sells them into the secondary market as short- and medium-term notes. It also provides financing to state student loan agencies.

S & L ▸ abbr. savings and loan.

S & P 500 ▸ abbr. Standard & Poor's 500.

sat•u•rate /'sæCHəˌrāt/ ▸ v. [trans.] supply (a market) beyond the point at which the demand for a product is satisfied: *Japan's electronics industry began to saturate the world markets.*

DERIVATIVES **sat•u•ra•tion** n.

ORIGIN late Middle English: from Latin *saturat-* 'filled, glutted,' from the verb *saturare*, from *satur* 'full.'

sav•ings ac•count /'sāviNGz əˌkownt/ ▸ n. a bank account that earns interest.

sav•ings and loan /'sāviNGz ən 'lōn/ (abbr.: **S & L**) (also **sav•ings and loan as•so•ci•a•tion**) ▶ n. an institution that accepts savings at interest and lends money to savers chiefly for home mortgage loans and may offer checking accounts and other services. Also called THRIFT.

sav•ings bank /'sāviNGz ˌbæNGk/ ▶ n. a financial institution that receives savings accounts and pays interest to depositors.

sav•ings bond /'sāviNGz ˌbänd/ ▶ n. a bond issued by the government and sold to the general public.

Say's law /'sāz ˌlô/ a law stating that supply creates its own demand. ORIGIN 1930s: named after Jean Baptiste *Say* (1767–1832), French economist.

SBA ▶ abbr. Small Business Administration.

sci•en•tif•ic man•age•ment /'sīənˌtifik 'mænijmənt; ˌsīən'tifik/ ▶ n. management of a business, industry, or economy according to principles of efficiency derived from experiments in methods of work and production, esp. from time-and-motion studies.

scrip /skrip/ ▶ n. **1** a representation of value such as a receipt, certificate, or document recognized by the payor and payee, even though it is not actual currency.

▪ such representations collectively. ▪ (also **scrip is•sue** or **scrip div•i•dend**) an issue of additional shares to shareholders in proportion to the shares already held.

2 (also **land scrip**) a certificate entitling the holder to acquire possession of certain portions of public land.

ORIGIN mid 18th cent.: abbreviation of *subscription receipt*.

SDR ▶ abbr. special drawing rights.

SEAQ /'sēˌæk/ ▶ abbr. (in the UK) Stock Exchange Automated Quotations, the computer system on which dealers trade shares and seek or provide price quotations on the London Stock Exchange.

SEC ▶ abbr. Securities and Exchange Commission, a US governmental agency that monitors trading in securities and company takeovers.

sec•ond mort•gage /'sekənd 'môrgij/ ▶ n. a mortgage taken out on a property that is already mortgaged.

sec•u•lar /'sekyələr/ ▶ adj. (of a fluctuation or trend) occurring or persisting over an indefinitely long period: *there is evidence that the slump is not cyclical but secular.*

ORIGIN early 19th cent.: from Latin *saecularis* 'relating to an age or period.'

se•cure /si'kyŏŏr/ ▸ v. [trans.] seek to guarantee repayment of (a loan) by having a right to take possession of an asset in the event of nonpayment: *a loan secured on your home.*

ORIGIN mid 16th cent.: from Latin *securus*, from *se-* 'without' + *cura* 'care.'

se•cu•ri•tize /sə'kyŏŏri‚tīz/ ▸ v. [trans.] [often as adj.] (**securitized**) convert (an asset, esp. a loan) into marketable securities, typically for the purpose of raising cash by selling them to other investors: *the use of securitized debt as a major source of corporate finance.*

se•cu•ri•ty /si'kyŏŏritē/ ▸ n. (pl. **se•cu•ri•ties**) 1 a thing deposited or pledged as a guarantee of the fulfillment of an undertaking or the repayment of a loan, to be forfeited in case of default.
2 (often **securities**) a certificate attesting credit, the ownership of stocks or bonds, or the right to ownership connected with tradable derivatives.

ORIGIN late Middle English: from Old French *securite* or Latin *securitas*, from *securus* 'free from care' (see **SECURE**).

seign•ior•age /'sānyərij/ (also **seign•or•age**) ▸ n. profit made by a government by issuing currency, esp. the difference between the face value of coins and their production costs.

ORIGIN late Middle English: from Old French *seignorage*, from *seigneur*, from Latin *senior* 'older, elder.'

self-as•sess•ment /'self ə'sesmənt/ ▸ n. assessment or evaluation of one's performance at a job or learning task considered in relation to an objective standard.

self-fi•nanc•ing /'self 'fīnænsiNG/ ▸ adj. (of an organization or enterprise) having or generating enough income to finance itself.

self-in•sur•ance /'self in'SHŏŏrəns/ ▸ n. insurance of oneself or one's interests by maintaining a fund to cover possible losses rather than by purchasing an insurance policy.

self-liq•ui•dat•ing /'self 'likwi‚dātiNG/ ▸ adj. denoting an asset that earns back its original cost out of income over a fixed period.
■ denoting a loan used to finance a project that will bring a sufficient return to pay back the loan and its interest and leave a profit.

■ denoting a sales promotion offer that pays for itself by generating increased sales.

sell /sel/ ▸ v. (past and past part. **sold**) [trans.] give or hand over (something) in exchange for money. ■ have a stock of (something) available for sale. ■ [intrans.] (of a thing) be purchased: *this magazine of yours won't sell.* ■ [trans.] (of a publication or recording) attain sales of (a specified number of copies): *the album sold 6 million copies in the United States.* ■ [intrans.] (**sell for/at**) be available for sale at (a specified price): *these antiques sell for about $375.* ■ (**sell out**) sell all of one's stock of something: *they had nearly sold out of the initial run of 75,000 copies.* ■ (**sell out**) be all sold: *it was clear that the performances would not sell out.* ■ (**sell through**) (of a product) be purchased by a customer from a retail outlet. ■ (**sell up**) sell all of one's property, possessions, or assets.

ORIGIN Old English *sellan*, of Germanic origin; related to Old Norse *selja* 'give up, sell.'

sell•er /'selər/ ▸ n. **1** a person who sells something.

■ (**the seller**) the party in a legal transaction who is selling: *the seller may accept the buyer's offer.*

2 a product that sells in some specified way: *the game will undoubtedly be the biggest seller of the year.*

PHRASES **seller's** (or **sellers'**) **market** an economic situation in which goods or shares are scarce and sellers can keep prices high.

sell-in /'sel ˌin/ ▸ n. the sale of goods to retail traders prior to public retailing.

sell•ing point /'seliNG ˌpoint/ ▸ n. a feature of a product for sale that makes it attractive to customers.

sell-off /'sel ˌôf/ ▸ n. a sale of assets, typically at a low price, carried out in order to dispose of them rather than as normal trade.

■ a sale of shares, bonds, or commodities, esp. one that causes a fall in price.

sell•out /'selˌowt/ ▸ n. **1** the selling of an entire stock of something, esp. tickets for an entertainment or sports event.

■ an event for which all tickets are sold: *the game is sure to be a sellout.*

2 a sale of a business or company.

sell-through /'sel ˌTHro͞o/ ▶ n. the ratio of the quantity of goods sold by a retail outlet to the quantity distributed to it wholesale: *the sell-through was amazing, 60 percent.*
■ the retail sale of something, typically a prerecorded videocassette, as opposed to its rental.

sen•si•tive /'sensiṯiv/ ▶ adj. (of a market) unstable and liable to quick changes of price because of outside influences.
ORIGIN late Middle English: from Old French *sensitif, -ive* or medieval Latin *sensitivus,* formed irregularly from Latin *sentire* 'feel.' The current senses date from the early 19th cent.

SEP (also **SEP-IRA**) ▶ n. Simplified Employee Pension, a pension plan in which both the employer and employee make contributions to an Individual Retirement Account (IRA).

USAGE: SEPs are for companies with 25 or fewer employees or for self-employed individuals. Total maximum contribution by both employer and employee is $30,000 a year.

serv•ice /'sərvis/ ▶ n. assistance or advice given to customers during and after the sale of goods: *they aim to provide better quality of service.*
■ short for SERVICE INDUSTRY: *a private security service.* ■ work done for a customer other than manufacturing: *scheduled commercial airline service | highly customized goods and services.* ■ short for SERVICE CHARGE: *service is included in the final bill.* ■ a period of employment with a company or organization: *he retired after 40 years' service.*
▶ v. [trans.] perform a service or services for (someone): *the state's biggest health maintenance organization servicing the poor.*
■ pay interest on (a debt): *taxpayers are paying $250 million just to service that debt.*
ORIGIN Old English (denoting religious devotion or a form of liturgy), from Old French *servise* or Latin *servitium* 'slavery,' from *servus* 'slave.'

serv•ice charge /'sərvis ˌCHärj/ (also **serv•ice fee**) ▶ n. an extra charge assessed for a service.

serv•ice con•tract /'sərvis ˌkäntrækt/ ▶ n. a business agreement between a contractor and customer covering the maintenance and servicing of equipment over a specified period.

serv•ice in•dus•try /'sərvis ˌindəstrē/ ▸ n. a business that does work for a customer, and occasionally provides goods, but is not involved in manufacturing.

serv•ice mark /'sərvis ˌmärk/ ▸ n. a legally registered name or designation used in the manner of a trademark to distinguish an organization's services from those of its competitors.

set-off /'set ôf/ ▸ n. an item or amount that is or may be set off against another in the settlement of accounts.

■ a counterbalancing debt pleaded by the defendant in an action to recover money due.

set•tle /'setl/ ▸ v. [trans.] pay (a debt or account): *his bill was settled by charge card.*

DERIVATIVES **set•tle•ment n.**

ORIGIN Old English *setlan* 'to seat, place,' of Germanic origin.

sev•er•ance /'sev(ə)rəns/ ▸ n. dismissal or discharge from employment.

■ short for SEVERANCE PAY.

ORIGIN late Middle English: from Anglo-Norman French, based on Latin *separare* 'disjoin, divide.'

sev•er•ance pay /'sev(ə)rəns ˌpā/ ▸ n. an amount paid to an employee upon dismissal or discharge from employment.

shade /sHād/ ▸ v. [trans.] make a slight reduction in the amount, rate, or price of: *banks may shade the margin over base rate they charge customers.*

ORIGIN Old English *sc(e)adu*, of Germanic origin.

shad•ow price /'sHædō ˌprīs/ ▸ n. the estimated price of a good or service for which no market price exists.

share /sHe(ə)r/ ▸ n. a part or portion of a larger amount that is divided among a number of people, or to which a number of people contribute: *under the proposals, investors would pay a greater share of the annual fees required* | *we gave them all the chance to have a share in the profits.*

■ one of the equal parts into which a company's capital is divided, entitling the holder to a proportion of the profits: *bought 33 shares of American Standard.* ■ part proprietorship of property held by joint owners: *Jake had a share in a large seagoing vessel.*

ORIGIN Old English *scearu* 'division, part into which something may be divided,' of Germanic origin.

share•hold•er /'sHe(ə)r͵hōldər/ ▸ n. an owner of shares in a company.

Sharpe ra•ti•o /'sHärp ͵rāsH(ē)͵ō/ ▸ n. a measure that indicates the average return minus the risk-free return divided by the standard deviation of return on an investment.

USAGE: The **Sharpe ratio** measures the relationship of reward to risk in an investment strategy. The higher the ratio, the safer the strategy.

shelf life /'sHelf ͵līf/ ▸ n. the length of time during which an item remains usable, fit for consumption, or saleable.

shell com•pa•ny /'sHel ͵kəmpənē/ ▸ n. an inactive company used as a vehicle for various financial maneuvers or kept dormant for future use in some other capacity.

shel•ter /'sHeltər/ ▸ v. [trans.] protect (income) from taxation: *only your rental income can be sheltered.*

ORIGIN late 16th cent.: perhaps an alteration of obsolete *sheltron* 'phalanx,' from Old English *scieldtruma*, literally 'shield troop.'

shift /sHift/ ▸ n. one of two or more recurring periods in which different groups of workers do the same jobs in relay: *the night shift.*

■ a group of workers who work in this way.

ORIGIN Old English *sciftan* 'arrange, divide, apportion,' of Germanic origin; related to German *schichten* 'to layer, stratify.'

shift work /'sHift ͵wərk/ ▸ n. work comprising recurring periods in which different groups of workers do the same jobs in rotation.

ship•ment /'sHipmənt/ ▸ n. the action of shipping goods: *logs waiting for shipment | shipments begin this month.*

■ a quantity of goods shipped; a consignment: *coal and oil shipments.*

ship•ping /'sHipiNG/ ▸ n. ships considered collectively, esp. those in a particular area or belonging to a particular country: *the volume of shipping using these ports.*

■ the transport of goods by sea or some other means. ■ a charge imposed by a retail company to send merchandise to a customer: *statues were available at $20 plus $4 for* **shipping and handling.**

shock /SHäk/ ▶ **n.** a disturbance causing instability in an economy: *trading imbalances caused by the two oil shocks.*

ORIGIN mid 16th cent.: from French *choc*, of unknown origin.

short /SHôrt/ ▶ **adj.** (of stocks or other securities or commodities) sold in advance of being acquired, with reliance on the price falling so that a profit can be made.

■ (of a broker, position in the market, etc.) buying or based on such stocks or other securities or commodities. ■ denoting or having a relatively early date for the maturing of a bill of exchange.

▶ **n.** a person who sells short.

■ (**shorts**) short-dated stocks.

ORIGIN Old English *sceort*, of Germanic origin; related to *shirt* and *skirt.*

short cov•er•ing /'SHôrt 'kəvəriNG/ ▶ **n.** the buying of stocks or other securities or commodities that have been sold short, typically to avoid loss when prices move upward.

short-dat•ed /'SHôrt 'dātid/ ▶ **adj.** (of a stock or bond) due for early payment or redemption.

short-term•ism /'SHôrt 'tərmizəm/ ▶ **n.** concentration on short-term projects or objectives for immediate profit at the expense of long-term security.

shrink•age /'SHriNGkij/ ▶ **n.** an allowance made for reduction in the earnings of a business due to wastage or theft.

SIB ▶ **abbr.** Securities and Investment Board, a regulatory body that oversees London's financial markets.

siege e•con•o•my /'sēj i₁känəmē/ ▶ **n.** an economy in which import controls are imposed and the export of capital is curtailed.

sight de•pos•it /'sīt di₁päzit/ ▶ **n.** a bank deposit that can be withdrawn immediately without notice or penalty.

si•lent part•ner /'sīlənt 'pärtnər/ ▶ **n.** a partner not sharing in the actual work of a firm.

sim•ple /'simpəl/ ▶ **adj.** (**sim•pler, sim•plest**) (of interest) payable on the sum loaned only.

ORIGIN Middle English: from Old French, from Latin *simplus.*

sin•gle-en•try /'siNGgəl 'entrē/ ▸ **adj.** denoting a system of bookkeeping in which each transaction is entered in one account only.

sin•gle mar•ket /'siNGgəl 'märkit/ ▸ **n.** an association of countries trading with each other without restrictions or tariffs. The European single market came into effect on January 1, 1993.

sin•gle-source /'siNGgəl 'sôrs/ ▸ **v.** [trans.] give a franchise to a single supplier for (a particular product).

sink•ing fund /'siNGkiNG ,fənd/ ▸ **n.** a fund formed by periodically setting aside money for the gradual repayment of a debt or replacement of a wasting asset.

sin tax /'sin ,taks/ ▸ **n.** informal a tax on items considered undesirable or harmful, such as alcohol or tobacco.

skim /skim/ ▸ **v.** (**skimmed, skim•ming**) [trans.] informal steal or embezzle (money), esp. in small amounts over a period of time.
ORIGIN Middle English: back-formation from *skimmer*, or from Old French *escumer*, from *escume* 'scum, foam.'

skunk•works /'skəNGk,wərks/ (also **skunk works**) ▸ **plural n.** [usu. treated as sing.] informal an experimental laboratory or department of a company or institution, typically smaller than and independent of its main research division.

slack /slæk/ ▸ **adj.** (of business) characterized by a lack of work or activity; quiet: *business was rather slack.*
PHRASES **take** (or **pick**) **up the slack** use up a surplus or improve the use of resources to avoid an undesirable lull in business: *as domestic demand starts to flag, foreign demand will help pick up the slack.*
ORIGIN Old English *slæc* 'inclined to be lazy, unhurried,' of Germanic origin; related to Latin *laxus* 'loose.'

slid•ing scale /'slīdiNG 'skāl/ ▸ **n.** a scale of fees, taxes, wages, etc., that varies in accordance with variation of some standard.

slo•gan /'slōgən/ ▸ **n.** a short and striking or memorable phrase used in advertising.
ORIGIN early 16th cent.: from Scottish Gaelic *sluagh-ghairm*, from *sluagh* 'army' + *gairm* 'shout.'

slow•down /'slō,down/ ▸ **n.** a decline in economic activity.

slump /sləmp/ ▸ **v.** [intrans.] undergo a sudden severe or prolonged fall in price, value, or amount: *land prices slumped.*

▸n. a sudden severe or prolonged fall in the price, value, or amount of something: *a slump in annual profits.*
■ a prolonged period of abnormally low economic activity, typically bringing widespread unemployment.
ORIGIN late 17th cent. (in the sense 'fall into a bog'): probably imitative and related to Norwegian *slumpe* 'to fall.'

small-cap /'smôl ˌkæp/ ▸ **adj.** denoting or relating to the stock of a company with a small capitalization.

smart card /'smärt ˌkärd/ ▸ **n.** a plastic card with a built-in microprocessor, used typically to perform financial transactions.

so•cial cred•it /'sōsHəl 'kredit/ ▸ **n.** the economic theory that consumer purchasing power should be increased either by subsidizing producers so that they can lower prices or by distributing the profits of industry to consumers.

so•cial in•sur•ance num•ber /'sōsHəl in'sHo͞orəns ˌnəmbər/ (abbr.: **SIN**) ▸ **n.** Canadian a nine-digit number by which the Canadian federal government identifies individuals for the purposes of taxation, employment insurance, pensions, etc.

so•cial mar•ket e•con•o•my /'sōsHəl 'märkit i'känəmē/ (also **so• cial mar•ket**) ▸ **n.** an economic system based on a free market operated in conjunction with state provision for those unable to sell their labor, such as the elderly or unemployed.

so•cial se•cu•ri•ty /'sōsHəl si'kyo͞oritē/ ▸ **n.** any government system that provides monetary assistance to people with an inadequate or no income.
■ (**So•cial Se•cu•ri•ty**) a federal insurance program that provides benefits to retired persons, the unemployed, and the disabled.

soft /sôft/ ▸ **adj.** (of a market, currency, or commodity) falling or likely to fall in value.
ORIGIN Old English *sōfte* 'agreeable, calm, gentle,' of West Germanic origin.

soft loan /'sôft ˌlōn/ ▸ **n.** a loan, typically one to a developing country, made on terms very favorable to the borrower.

soft sell /'sôft 'sel/ ▸ **n.** [in sing.] subtly persuasive selling.
▸**v.** (**soft-sell**) (past and past part. **soft-sold**) [trans.] sell (something) by using such a method.

so•go sho•sha /'sōgō 'sHōsHə/ ▸ **n.** (pl. same) a very large Japanese company that trades internationally in a wide range of goods and services.

ORIGIN Japanese, from *sōgō* 'comprehensive' + *shōsha* 'mercantile society.'

sol•vent /'sälvənt/ ▶ adj. having assets in excess of liabilities; able to pay one's debts: *interest rate rises have very severe effects on normally solvent companies.*

ORIGIN mid 17th cent.: from Latin *solvent-* 'loosening, unfastening, paying,' from the verb *solvere* .

spe•cial draw•ing rights /'speSHəl 'drôiNG ˌrīts/ (abbr.: **SDR**) ▶ plural n. a form of international money, created by the International Monetary Fund, and defined as a weighted average of various convertible currencies.

spe•cie /'spēsHē; -sē/ ▶ n. money in the form of coins rather than notes.

PHRASES **in specie** in coin.

ORIGIN mid 16th cent.: from Latin, ablative of *species* 'form, kind,' in the phrase *in specie* 'in the actual form.'

spe•cif•ic /spə'sifik/ ▶ adj. (of a duty or a tax) levied at a fixed rate per physical unit of the thing taxed, regardless of its price.

ORIGIN mid 17th cent.: from late Latin *specificus*, from Latin *species* (see SPECIES).

spec•u•late /'spekyəˌlāt/ ▶ v. [intrans.] invest in stocks, property, or other ventures in the hope of gain but with the risk of loss: *he didn't look as though he had the money to speculate in stocks.*

DERIVATIVES **spec•u•la•tion** n.

ORIGIN late 16th cent.: from Latin *speculat-* 'observed from a vantage point,' from the verb *speculari*, from *specula* 'watchtower,' from *specere* 'to look.'

spec•u•la•tive /'spekyəˌlātiv; -lətiv/ ▶ adj. (of an investment) involving a high risk of loss.

■ (of a business venture) undertaken on the chance of success, without a preexisting contract.

split /split/ ▶ v. (**split•ting**; past and past part. **split**) [trans.] issue new shares of (stock) to existing stockholders in proportion to their current holdings.

▶n. short for STOCK SPLIT.
ORIGIN late 16th cent.: from Middle Dutch *splitten*, of unknown ultimate origin.

split shift /'split 'sHift/ ▶ n. a working shift comprising two or more separate periods of duty in a day.

spot /spät/ ▶ n. [as adj.] denoting a system of trading in which commodities or currencies are delivered and paid for immediately after a sale: *trading in the spot markets | the current spot price.*
ORIGIN Middle English: perhaps from Middle Dutch *spotte* .

Spous•e's Al•low•ance /'spowsiz ə,lowəns/ ▶ n. Canadian a federal benefit paid to low-income 60-64-year-old spouses of Old Age Security pensioners.

spread /spred/ ▶ n. the difference between two rates or prices: *the very narrow spread between borrowing and deposit rates.*
ORIGIN Old English -*sprædan* (used in combinations), of West Germanic origin.

squeeze /skwēz/ ▶ n. a strong financial demand or pressure, typically a restriction on borrowing, spending, or investment in a financial crisis: *industry faced higher costs and a squeeze on profits.*
ORIGIN mid 16th cent.: from earlier *squise*, from obsolete *queise*, of unknown origin.

sta•bi•liz•er /'stābə,līzər/ ▶ n. a financial mechanism that prevents unsettling fluctuation in an economic system.

stag /stæg/ ▶ n. a person who applies for shares in a new issue with a view to selling at once for a profit.
ORIGIN Middle English: related to Old Norse *steggr* 'male bird,' Icelandic *steggi* 'tomcat.'

stag•fla•tion /,stæg'flāsHən/ ▶ n. persistent high inflation combined with high unemployment and stagnant demand in a country's economy.
ORIGIN 1960s: blend of *stagnation* and INFLATION.

stake•hold•er /'stāk,hōldər/ ▶ n. a person with an interest or concern in something, esp. a business.
■ [as adj.] denoting a type of organization or system in which all the members or participants are seen as having an interest in its success: *a stakeholder economy.*

stale /stāl/ ▸ adj. (**stal•er, stal•est**) (of a check or legal claim) invalid because out of date.

ORIGIN Middle English (describing beer in the sense 'clear from long standing, strong'): probably from Anglo-Norman French and Old French, from *estaler* 'halt.'

stand•ard /'stændərd/ ▸ n. a system by which the value of a currency is defined in terms of gold or silver or both.

ORIGIN Middle English: shortening of Old French *estendart*, from *estendre* 'extend.'

Stand•ard & Poor's 500 /'stændərd ən 'pо̄o̅rz ˌfīv'həndrid/ (abbr.: **S&P 500**) ▸ a group of 500 companies whose average daily share prices are used to calculate an index of the day's security prices.

stand•ard de•vi•a•tion /'stændərd ˌdēvē'āsHən/ ▸ n. a quantity calculated to indicate the extent of deviation for a group as a whole.

USAGE: In modern portfolio theory, the past performance of a security is used to determine the range of possible future performances, and a probability is attached to each performance. The greater the degree of dispersion, the greater the risk.

stand•ard of liv•ing /'stændərd əv 'liviNG/ ▸ n. the degree of wealth and material comfort available to a person or community.

stand•ing or•der /'stændiNG 'ôrdər/ ▸ n. an order for goods that remains in effect until cancelled.

stand•still a•gree•ment /'stænd 'stil ə,grēmənt/ ▸ n. an agreement between two countries in which a debt owed by one to the other is held in abeyance for a specified period.

▪ an agreement between a company and a bidder for the company in which the bidder agrees to buy no more shares for a specified period.

state•ment /'stātmənt/ ▸ n. a document setting out items of debit and credit between a bank or other organization and a customer.

ster•ling /'stərliNG/ ▸ n. British money: *prices in sterling are shown.*

ORIGIN Middle English: probably from *steorra* 'star' + the suffix *-ling* (because some early Norman pennies bore a small star). Until recently one popular theory was that the coin was originally made by *Easterling* moneyers (from the "eastern" Hansa towns), but the stressed first syllable would not have been dropped.

stock /stäk/ ▸ n. 1 the goods or merchandise kept on the premises of a business or warehouse and available for sale or distribution: *the store has a very low turnover of stock | buy now, while stocks last!* ▪ a supply or quantity of something accumulated or available for future use: *I need to replenish my* **stock** *of wine | fish stocks are being dangerously depleted.*
2 the capital raised by a business or corporation through the issue and subscription of shares: *between 1982 and 1986, the value of the company's stock rose by 86 percent.*
▪ (also **stocks**) a portion of this as held by an individual or group as an investment: *she owned $3000 worth of stock.* ▪ (also **stocks**) the shares of a particular company, type of company, or industry: *blue-chip stocks.* ▪ securities issued by the government in fixed units with a fixed rate of interest: *government gilt-edged stock.*
▸ **adj.** (of a product or type of product) usually kept in stock and thus regularly available for sale: *25 percent off stock items.*
▸ **v.** [trans.] have or keep a supply of (a particular product or type or product) available for sale: *most supermarkets now stock a range of organic produce.*
PHRASES **in** (or **out of**) **stock** (of goods) available (or unavailable) for immediate sale in a store.
ORIGIN Old English *stoc(c)* 'trunk, block of wood, post,' of Germanic origin. The notion 'store, fund' arose in late Middle English and is of obscure origin.

stock ex•change /ˈstäk iksˌCHānj/ ▸ n. a market in which securities are bought and sold: *the company was floated on the Stock Exchange.*
▪ (**the Stock Exchange**) the level of prices in such a market: *a plunge in the Stock Exchange during the election campaign.*

stock•hold•er /ˈstäkˌhōldər/ ▸ n. a shareholder.

stock in•dex fu•tures /ˈstäk ˌindeks ˌfyōōCHərz/ ▸ plural n. contracts to buy a range of shares at an agreed price but delivered and paid for later.

stock-in-trade /ˈstäk in ˈtrād/ ▸ n. the typical subject or commodity a person, company, or profession uses or deals in: *information is our stock-in-trade.*

■ the goods kept on hand by a business for the purposes of its trade.

stock mar•ket /'stäk ˌmärkit/ ▶ n. (usu. **the stock market**) a stock exchange.

stock op•tion /'stäk ˌäpsHən/ ▶ n. a benefit in the form of an option given by a company to an employee to buy stock in the company at a discount or at a stated fixed price.

stock•out /'stäkˌowt/ ▶ n. a situation in which an item is out of stock.

stock split /'stäk ˌsplit/ ▶ n. an issue of new shares in a company to existing shareholders in proportion to their current holdings.

stop /stäp/ ▶ v. (**stopped, stop•ping**) [trans.] instruct a bank to withhold payment on (a check).

PHRASES **stop payment** instruct a bank to withhold payment on a check.

ORIGIN Old English *(for)stoppian* 'block up (an aperture),' of West Germanic origin; related to German *stopfen*, from late Latin *stuppare* 'to stuff.'

stop-loss /'stäp ˌlôs/ ▶ adj. denoting or relating to an order to sell a security or commodity at a specified price in order to limit a loss.

strad•dle /'strædl/ ▶ n. a simultaneous purchase of options to buy and to sell a security or commodity at a fixed price, allowing the purchaser to make a profit whether the price of the security or commodity goes up or down.

ORIGIN mid 16th cent.: alteration of dialect *striddle*, back-formation from dialect *striddling* 'astride,' from *stride* + the adverbial suffix *-ling*.

straight-line /'strāt 'līn/ ▶ adj. of or relating to a method of depreciation allocating a given percentage of the cost of an asset each year for a fixed period.

straight time /'strāt 'tīm/ ▶ n. normal working hours, paid at a regular rate.

street /strēt/ ▶ n. (**the street**) used to refer to the financial markets and activities on Wall Street.

ORIGIN Old English *strǣt*, of West Germanic origin, from late Latin *strāta (via)* 'paved (way),' feminine past participle of *sternere* 'lay down.'

street name /'strēt ˌnām/ ▸ n. the name of a brokerage firm, bank, or dealer in which stock is held on behalf of a purchaser.

strike /strīk/ ▸ v. (past and past part. **struck**) **1** [intrans.] (of employees) refuse to work as a form of organized protest, typically in an attempt to obtain a particular concession or concessions from their employer: *workers may strike over threatened job losses.*
■ [trans.] undertake such action against (an employer).
2 [trans.] (in financial contexts) reach (a figure) by balancing an account: *last year's loss was struck after allowing for depreciation of $67 million.*
▸ n. a refusal to work organized by a body of employees as a form of protest, typically in an attempt to gain a concession or concessions from their employer: *dockers voted for an all-out strike | local government workers **went on strike**.*
ORIGIN Old English *strīcan* 'go, flow' and 'rub lightly,' of West Germanic origin; related to German *streichen* 'to stroke,' also to *stroke.*

strike pay /'strīk ˌpā/ ▸ n. money paid to strikers by their trade union.

strip /strip/ ▸ v. (**stripped, strip•ping**) [trans.] sell off (the assets of a company) for profit.
■ divest (a bond) of its interest coupons so that it and they may be sold separately.
ORIGIN Middle English: of Germanic origin.

strip mall /'strip ˌmôl/ ▸ n. a shopping mall consisting of stores and restaurants typically in one-story buildings located on a busy main road.

strong /strôNG/ ▸ adj. (**strong•er, strong•est**) in a secure financial position: *the company's chip business remains strong.*
■ (of a market) having steadily high or rising prices.
ORIGIN Old English, of Germanic origin; related to Dutch and German *streng*, also to *string.*

struc•tur•al un•em•ploy•ment /'strəkCHərəl ˌənem'ploimənt/ ▸ n. unemployment resulting from industrial reorganization, typically due to technological change, rather than fluctuations in supply or demand.

sub•con•tract /ˌsəb'käntrækt/ ▸ v. [trans.] employ a business or person

outside one's company to do (work) as part of a larger project: *we would subcontract the translation work out.*
■ [intrans.] (of a business or person) carry out work for a company as part of a larger project.
▶n. a contract for a company or person to do work for another company as part of a larger project.
sub•con•trac•tor /ˌsəb'känˌtræktər/ ▶ n. a business or person that carries out work for a company as part of a larger project.
sub•or•di•nat•ed debt /sə'bôrdnˌātid 'det/ ▶ n. a debt owed to an unsecured creditor that can only be paid, in the event of a liquidation, after the claims of secured creditors have been met.
sub•scribe /səb'skrīb/ ▶ v. [intrans.] apply for or undertake to pay for an offering of shares of stock: *investors would subscribe electronically to the initial stock offerings | yesterday's offering was fully subscribed.*
ORIGIN late Middle English: from Latin *subscribere,* from *sub-* 'under' + *scribere* 'write.'
sub•sid•i•ar•y /səb'sidēˌerē/ ▶ adj. (of a company) controlled by a holding or parent company.
▶n. (pl. **sub•sid•i•ar•ies**) a company controlled by a holding company.
ORIGIN mid 16th cent.: from Latin *subsidiarius,* from *subsidium* 'support, assistance.'
sub•si•dy /'səbsidē/ ▶ n. (pl. **sub•si•dies**) a sum of money granted by the government or a public body to assist an industry or business so that the price of a commodity or service may remain low or competitive: *a farm subsidy | they disdain government subsidy.*
ORIGIN late Middle English: from Anglo-Norman French *subsidie,* from Latin *subsidium* 'assistance.'
sub•ten•ant /ˌsəb'tenənt/ ▶ n. a person who leases property from a tenant.
sun•rise in•dus•try /'sənˌrīz ˌindəstrē/ ▶ n. a new and growing industry, esp. in electronics or telecommunications.
sun•set in•dus•try /'sənˌset ˌindəstrē/ ▶ n. an old and declining industry.
su•per•an•nu•ate /ˌso͞opər'ænyo͞oˌāt/ ▶ v. [trans.] (usu. **be superan-**

nuated) retire (someone) with a pension: *his pilot's license was withdrawn and he was superannuated.* ▪ [as adj.] (**superannuated**) (of a position or employee) belonging to a superannuation scheme: *she is not superannuated and has no paid vacation.* ▪ [usu. as adj.] (**superannuated**) cause to become obsolete through age or new technological or intellectual developments: *superannuated computing equipment.* ORIGIN mid 17th cent.: back-formation from *superannuated*, from medieval Latin *superannuatus*, from Latin *super-* 'over' + *annus* 'year.'

su•per•an•nu•a•tion /ˌso͞opər͡ˌænyo͞oˈāsHən/ ▶ n. regular payment made into a fund by an employee toward a future pension. ▪ a pension of this type paid to a retired person. ▪ the process of superannuating an employee.

su•per•store /ˈso͞opərˌstôr/ ▶ n. a retail store, as a grocery store or bookstore, with more than the average amount of space and variety of stock.

su•per•tax /ˈso͞opərˌtæks/ ▶ n. an additional tax on something already taxed.

sup•ply /səˈplī/ ▶ n. (pl. **sup•plies**) the amount of a good or service offered for sale.

PHRASES **supply and demand** the amount of a good or service available and the desire of buyers for it, considered as factors regulating its price: *by the law of supply and demand the cost of health care will plummet.* ORIGIN late Middle English: from Old French *soupleer*, from Latin *supplere* 'fill up,' from *sub-* 'from below' + *plere* 'fill.'

sup•ply chain /səˈplī ˌcHān/ ▶ n. the sequence of processes involved in the production and distribution of a commodity.

sup•ply-side /səˈplī ˌsīd/ ▶ adj. denoting or relating to a policy designed to increase output and employment by changing the conditions under which goods and services are supplied, esp. by measures that reduce government involvement in the economy and allow the free market to operate.

sur•charge /ˈsərˌcHärj/ ▶ n. an additional charge or payment: *we guarantee that no surcharges will be added to the cost of your trip.*

■ a charge made by assessors as a penalty for false returns of taxable property. ■ the showing of an omission in an account for which credit should have been given.

▶v. [trans.] exact an additional charge or payment from: *retailers will be able to surcharge credit-card users.*

ORIGIN late Middle English: from Old French *surcharger*, from *sur-* 'super-' + *charger* 'load.'

sur•plus /'sər͵pləs/ ▶ n. an amount of something left over when requirements have been met; an excess of production or supply over demand: *exports of food surpluses.*

■ an excess of income or assets over expenditure or liabilities in a given period, typically a fiscal year: *a trade surplus of $1.4 billion.*

■ the excess value of a company's assets over the face value of its stock.

ORIGIN late Middle English: from Old French *sourplus*, from medieval Latin *superplus*, from *super-* 'in addition' + *plus* 'more.'

sur•ren•der /sə'rendər/ ▶ v. [trans.] (of an insured person) cancel (a life insurance policy) and receive back a proportion of the premiums paid.

ORIGIN late Middle English: from Anglo-Norman French.

sur•ren•der val•ue /sə'rendər ͵vælyo͞o/ ▶ n. the amount payable to a person who surrenders a life insurance policy.

sur•tax /'sər͵tæks/ ▶ n. an additional tax on something already taxed, such as a higher rate of tax on incomes above a certain level.

ORIGIN late 19th cent.: from French *surtaxe.*

sus•pense ac•count /sə'spens ə͵kownt/ ▶ n. an account in the books of an organization in which items are entered temporarily before allocation to the correct or final account.

swap /swäp/ ▶ n. an exchange of liabilities between two borrowers, either so that each acquires access to funds in a currency they need or so that a fixed interest rate is exchanged for a floating rate.

ORIGIN Middle English (originally in the sense 'throw forcibly'): probably imitative of a resounding blow. Current senses have arisen from an early use meaning 'clasp hands as a token of agreement.'

swap•tion /'swäpsHən/ ▶ n. an option giving the right but not the obligation to engage in a swap.

ORIGIN 1980s: blend of SWAP and OPTION.

sweat eq•ui•ty /'swet ˌekwiṯē/ ▶ n. informal an interest or increased value in a property earned from labor toward upkeep or restoration.

sweat•shop /'swetˌSHäp/ ▶ n. a factory or workshop, esp. in the clothing industry, where manual workers are employed at very low wages for long hours and under poor conditions.

swipe card /'swīp ˌkärd/ ▶ n. a plastic card such as a credit card or ID card bearing magnetically encoded information that is read when the edge of the card is slid through an electronic device.

syn•di•cate ▶ n. /'sindikit/ a group of individuals or organizations combined to promote some common interest: *large-scale buyouts involving a syndicate of financial institutions* | *a crime syndicate.* ▶ v. [trans.] (usu. **be syndicated**) /'sindiˌkāt/ control or manage by a syndicate: *the loans are syndicated to a group of banks.*
DERIVATIVES **syn•di•ca•tion n.**
ORIGIN early 17th cent.: from French *syndicat*, from medieval Latin *syndicatus*, from late Latin *syndicus* 'delegate of a corporation.'

syn•er•gy /'sinərjē/ (also **syn•er•gism** /'sinərˌjizəm/) ▶ n. the interaction or cooperation of two or more organizations, substances, or other agents to produce a combined effect greater than the sum of their separate effects: *the synergy between artist and record company.*
ORIGIN mid 19th cent.: from Greek *sunergos* 'working together,' from *sun-* 'together' + *ergon* 'work.'

T

tai•pan /'tī,pæn/ ▶ n. a foreigner who is head of a business in China or Hong Kong.
ORIGIN mid 19th cent.: from Chinese (Cantonese dialect) *daaihbāan* .

tare /te(ə)r/ ▶ n. an allowance made for the weight of the packaging in order to determine the net weight of goods.
■ the weight of a motor vehicle, railroad car, or aircraft without its fuel or load.
ORIGIN late Middle English: from French, literally 'deficiency, tare,' from medieval Latin *tara*, based on Arabic *ṭaraḥa* 'reject, deduct.'

tar•iff /'tærəf; 'te(ə)r-/ ▶ n. a tax or duty to be paid on a particular class of imports or exports.
■ a list of these taxes. ■ a table of the fixed charges made by a business, esp. in a hotel or restaurant.
▶ v. [trans.] fix the price of (something) according to a tariff: *these services are tariffed by volume.*
ORIGIN late 16th cent.: via French from Italian *tariffa*, based on Arabic *'arrafa* 'notify.'

tax /tæks/ ▶ n. a compulsory contribution to state revenue, levied by the government on workers' income and business profits or added to the cost of some goods, services, and transactions.
▶ v. [trans.] impose a tax on (someone or something): *hardware and software is **taxed** at 7.5 percent.*
ORIGIN Middle English: from Old French *taxer*, from Latin *taxare* 'to censure, charge, compute,' perhaps from Greek *tassein* 'fix.'

tax•a•tion /tæk'sāsHən/ ▶ n. the levying of tax.
■ money paid as tax.
ORIGIN Middle English: via Old French from Latin *taxatio(n-)*, from *taxare* 'to censure, charge.'

tax a•void•ance /'taks ə‚voidns/ ▶ n. the arrangement of one's financial affairs to minimize tax liability within the law.

tax brack•et /'taks ‚brækit/ ▶ n. a range of incomes taxed at a given rate.

tax break /'taks ‚brāk/ ▶ n. informal a tax concession or advantage allowed by a government.

Tax Court of Can•a•da /'tæks ‚kôrt əv 'kænədə/ ▶ n. Canadian a federal court with jurisdiction to hear appeals on matters involving especially income taxes, employment insurance, the Canada Pension Plan, etc.

tax cred•it /'taks ‚kredit/ ▶ n. an amount of money that can be offset against a tax liability.

tax-de•duct•i•ble /'taks di‚dəktəbəl/ ▶ adj. able to be deducted from taxable income or the amount of tax to be paid.

tax e•va•sion /'taks i‚vāzHən/ ▶ n. the illegal nonpayment or underpayment of tax.

tax ex•ile /'taks ‚egzīl; ‚eksīl/ ▶ n. a person with a high income or considerable wealth who chooses to live in a country or area with low rates of tax.

tax ha•ven /'taks ‚hāvən/ ▶ n. a country or independent area where taxes are levied at a low rate.

tax loss /'taks ‚lôs/ ▶ n. a loss that can be offset against taxable profit earned elsewhere or in a different period.

tax•pay•er /'tæks‚pāər/ ▶ n. a person who pays taxes.

tax re•turn /'taks ri‚tərn/ ▶ n. a form on which a taxpayer makes an annual statement of income and personal circumstances, used by the tax authorities to assess liability for tax.

tax shel•ter /'taks ‚sHeltər/ ▶ n. a financial arrangement made to avoid or minimize taxes.

T-bill /'tē ‚bil/ ▶ n. informal short for TREASURY BILL.

T-bond /'tē ‚bänd/ ▶ n. informal short for TREASURY BOND.

tech•no•struc•ture /'teknō‚strəkCHər/ ▶ n. [treated as sing. or pl.] a group of technologists or technical experts having considerable control over the workings of industry or government. ORIGIN 1960s: coined by J. K. Galbraith (born 1908).

tel•e•mar•ket•ing /ˌtelə'märkiṯiNG/ ▶ n. the marketing of goods or services by means of telephone calls, typically unsolicited, to potential customers.
DERIVATIVES **tel•e•mar•ket•er** n.

tel•e•phone bank•ing /'telə,fōn ˌbæNGkiNG/ ▶ n. a method of banking in which the customer conducts transactions by telephone, typically by means of a computerized system using touch-tone dialing or voice-recognition technology.

tel•e•sales /'telə,sālz/ ▶ plural n. the selling of goods or services over the telephone: *sales personnel work on fully automated telesales systems.*

tell•er /'telər/ ▶ n. a person employed to deal with customers' transactions in a bank.
■ an automated teller machine: *the growing use of automatic tellers.*

temp /temp/ informal ▶ n. a temporary employee, typically an office worker who finds temporary employment through an agency.
▶ v. [intrans.] work as a temporary employee.
ORIGIN 1930s: abbreviation for *temporary employee.*

ten•der /'tendər/ ▶ v. [trans.] offer (money) as payment: *she tendered her fare.*
■ [intrans.] make a formal written offer to carry out work, supply goods, or buy land, shares, or another asset for a stated fixed price: *firms of interior decorators have been **tendering for** the work.*
■ make such an offer giving (a stated fixed price): *what price should we tender for a contract?*
▶ n. an offer to carry out work, supply goods, or buy land, shares, or another asset at a stated fixed price.
PHRASES **put something out to tender** seek offers to carry out work or supply goods at a stated fixed price.
ORIGIN mid 16th cent.: from Old French *tendre,* from Latin *tendere* 'to stretch, hold forth.'

ten•or /'tenər/ ▶ n. the time that must elapse before a bill of exchange or promissory note becomes due for payment.

ORIGIN Middle English: from Old French *tenour*, from Latin *tenor* 'course, substance, import of a law,' from *tenere* 'to hold.'

term de•pos•it /'tərm di‚päzit/ ▸ n. Canadian an amount of money, usually between $1,000 and $5,000, deposited with a financial institution for a fixed term, usually between 30 days and a year, at a fixed interest rate, and which can be withdrawn before term on payment of a penalty.

terms of trade /'tərmz əv 'trād/ ▸ plural n. the ratio of an index of a country's export prices to an index of its import prices.

T4 ▸ n. (in full **T4 slip**) Canadian an official statement issued by an employer, indicating one's employment income for the year, as well as the amount paid in employment insurance premiums and contributions to the Canada Pension Plan etc., used to calculate the amount of taxes owed and submitted with one's tax return.

think tank /'THiNGk ‚tæNGk/ ▸ n. a body of experts providing advice and ideas on specific political or economic problems.

third mar•ket /'THərd 'märkit/ ▸ n. used to refer to over-the-counter trading in listed stocks outside the stock exchange.

third par•ty /'THərd 'pärtē/ ▸ adj. of or relating to a person or group besides the two primarily involved in a situation: *third-party suppliers.*

thrift /THrift/ ▸ n. another term for SAVINGS AND LOAN.

ORIGIN Middle English: from Old Norse, from *thrífa* 'grasp, get hold of.'

tick /tik/ ▸ n. the smallest recognized amount by which a price of a security or future may fluctuate.

ORIGIN Middle English: probably of Germanic origin.

tie-in /'tī ‚in/ ▸ n. a book, movie, or other product produced to take advantage of a related work in another medium.■ [as adj.] denoting sales made conditional on the purchase of an additional item or items from the same supplier.

ti•ger /'tīgər/ ▸ n. (also **ti•ger e•con•o•my**) a dynamic economy of one of the smaller eastern Asian countries, esp. that of Singapore, Taiwan, or South Korea.

ORIGIN Middle English: from Old French *tigre*, from Latin *tigris*, from Greek.

tight mon•ey /'tīt ˌmənē/ ▶ n. money or finance that is available only at high rates of interest.

till /til/ ▶ n. a cash register or drawer for money in a store, bank, or restaurant.

PHRASES **have** (or **with**) **one's fingers** (or **hand**) **in the till** used in reference to theft from one's place of work: *he was caught with his hand in the till.*

ORIGIN late Middle English: of unknown origin.

time-and-mo•tion stud•y /'tīm ən 'mōsHən ˌstədē/ ▶ n. a procedure in which the efficiency of an industrial or other operation is evaluated.

time de•pos•it /'tīm diˌpäzit/ ▶ n. a deposit in a bank account that cannot be withdrawn before a set date or for which notice of withdrawal is required.

tomb•stone /'tōomˌstōn/ ▶ n. (also **tomb•stone ad•ver•tise•ment** or **tomb•stone ad**) an advertisement listing the underwriters or firms associated with a new issue of securities.

ton-mile /'tən 'mīl/ ▶ n. one ton of freight carried one mile, as a unit of traffic.

ton•nage /'tənij/ ▶ n. shipping considered in terms of total carrying capacity: *the port's total tonnage.*

ORIGIN early 17th cent.: from *ton* + *-age.*

ton•tine /'tänˌtēn; ˌtän'tēn/ ▶ n. an annuity shared by subscribers to a loan or common fund, the shares increasing as subscribers die until the last survivor enjoys the whole income.

ORIGIN mid 18th cent.: from French, named after Lorenzo *Tonti* (1630–95), a Neapolitan banker who started such a program to raise government loans in France (*c.*1653).

too•nie /'tōōnē/ (also **twoo•nie**) ▶ n. Canadian informal the Canadian two-dollar coin.

ORIGIN after **loonie**.

top-heav•y /'täp ˌhevē/ ▶ adj. (of an organization) having a disproportionately large number of people in senior administrative positions.

trade /trād/ ▶ n. **1** the action of buying and selling goods and services: *a move to ban all **trade in** ivory | a significant increase in foreign trade | the meat trade.*

2 a skilled job, typically one requiring manual skills and special training: *the fundamentals of the construction trade* | *a carpenter by trade.*
■ **(the trade)** [treated as sing. or pl.] the people engaged in a particular area of business: *in the trade this sort of computer is called "a client-based system."*
▶v. [intrans.] buy and sell goods and services: *middlemen trading in luxury goods.*
■ [trans.] buy or sell (a particular item or product): *she has traded millions of dollars' worth of metals.* ■ (esp. of shares or currency) be bought and sold at a specified price: *the dollar was trading where it was in January.* ■ exchange (something) for something else, typically as a commercial transaction: *they trade mud-shark livers for fish oil* | *the hostages were traded for arms.*
ORIGIN late Middle English (as a noun): from Middle Low German, literally 'track,' of West Germanic origin; related to *tread.*

trade def•i•cit /ˈtrād ˌdefəsit/ ▶n. the amount by which the cost of a country's imports exceeds the value of its exports.

trade dis•count /ˈtrād ˌdiskownt/ ▶n. a discount on the retail price of something allowed or agreed between traders or to a retailer by a wholesaler.

trad•ed op•tion /ˈtrādid ˈopsʜən / ▶n. an option on a stock exchange or futures exchange which can itself be bought and sold.

trade•mark /ˈtrādˌmärk/ ▶n. a symbol, word, or words legally registered or established by use as representing a company or product.
▶v. [trans.] **(trademarked)** [usu. as adj.] provide with a trademark: *they are counterfeiting trademarked goods.*

trade name /ˈtrād ˌnām/ ▶n. **1** a name that has the status of a trademark.
2 a name by which something is known in a particular trade or profession.

trade sur•plus /ˈtrād ˈsərˌpləs/ ▶n. the amount by which the value of a country's exports exceeds the cost of its imports.

trade-up /ˈtrād ˌəp/ ▶n. a sale of an article in order to buy something similar but more expensive and of higher quality.

trade war /ˈtrād ˌwôr/ ▶n. a situation in which countries try to damage each other's trade, typically by the imposition of tariffs or quota restrictions.

trad•ing floor /'trādiNG ˌflôr / ▶ **n.** an area within an exchange or a bank or securities house where dealers trade in stocks or other securities.

trad•ing stamp /'trādiNG ˌstæmp / ▶ **n.** a stamp given by some stores to a customer according to the amount spent, and exchangeable in the appropriate number for various articles.

tranche /träNSH/ ▶ **n.** a portion of something, esp. money: *they released the first **tranche of** the loan.*

ORIGIN late 15th cent.: from Old French, literally 'slice.'

trans•fer pay•ment /'trænsfər ˌpāmənt/ ▶ **n.** a payment made or income received in which no goods or services are being paid for, such as a benefit payment or subsidy.

trans•na•tion•al /'træns'næSH(ə)nl; 'trænz-/ ▶ **n.** a large company operating internationally; a multinational.

trav•el•er's check /'træv(ə)lərz ˌCHek/ ▶ **n.** a check for a fixed amount that can be cashed or used in payment after endorsement with the holder's signature.

treas•ur•er /'treZHərər/ ▶ **n.** a person appointed to administer or manage the financial assets and liabilities of a society, company, local authority, or other body.

ORIGIN Middle English: from Old French *tresorier*, from *tresor*, influenced by late Latin *thesaurarius* .

treas•ur•y /'treZHərē/ ▶ **n.** (pl. **treas•ur•ies**) the funds or revenue of a government, corporation, or institution: *the country's pledge not to spend more than it has in its treasury.*

■ (**Treas•ur•y**) (in some countries) the government department responsible for budgeting for and controlling public expenditure, management of the national debt, and the overall management of the economy.

ORIGIN Middle English: from Old French *tresorie*, from *tresor* (see **TREASURER**).

Treas•ur•y bill /'treZHərē ˌbil/ ▶ **n.** a short-dated government security, yielding no interest but issued at a discount on its redemption price.

Treas•ur•y bond /'trezɥərē ˌbänd/ ▶ n. a government bond issued by the US Treasury.

Treas•ur•y Branch /'trezɥərē ˌbrænch/ ▶ n. Canadian (in Alberta) one of a network of savings banks operated by the government of Alberta.

tri•al bal•ance /'trīəl ˌbæləns/ ▶ n. a statement of all debits and credits in a double-entry account book, with any disagreement indicating an error.

tri•ple A /'tripəl 'ā/ (also **AAA**) ▶ n. the highest grading available from credit rating agencies.

trough /trôf/ ▶ n. a low level of economic activity.
ORIGIN Old English *trog*, of Germanic origin; related to Dutch *trog* and German *Trog*, also to *tree*.

trust /trəst/ ▶ n. **1** confidence placed in a person by making that person the nominal owner of property to be held or used for the benefit of one or more others.
■ an arrangement whereby property is held in such a way: *a trust was set up* | *the property is to be **held in trust** for his son.*
2 a body of trustees.
■ an organization or company managed by trustees: *a charitable trust* | [in names] *the National Trust for Historic Preservation.*
■ dated a large company that has or attempts to gain monopolistic control of a market.
ORIGIN Middle English: from Old Norse *traust*, from *traustr* 'strong'.

trust•bust•er /'trəs(t)ˌbəstər/ ▶ n. informal a person or agency employed to enforce antitrust legislation.

trust com•pa•ny /'trəst ˌkəmpənē/ ▶ n. a company formed to act as a trustee or to deal with trusts.

trust•ee /ˌtrə'stē/ ▶ n. an individual person or member of a board given control or powers of administration of property in trust with a legal obligation to administer it solely for the purposes specified.

trust fund /'trəst ˌfənd/ ▶ n. a fund consisting of assets belonging to a trust, held by the trustees for the beneficiaries.

turn•a•round /'tərnəˌrownd/ ▶ n. the process of completing or the time needed to complete a task, esp. one involving receiving something, processing it, and sending it out again: *a seven-day turnaround.*

■ the process of or time taken for unloading and reloading a ship, aircraft, or vehicle.

turn•key /'tərnˌkē/ ▸ **adj.** of or involving the provision of a complete product or service that is ready for immediate use: *turnkey systems for telecommunications customers.*

turn•o•ver /'tərnˌōvər/ ▸ **n. 1** the amount of money taken by a business in a particular period: *a turnover approaching $4 million.*

■ the volume of shares traded during a particular period, as a percentage of total shares listed.

2 the rate at which employees leave a workforce and are replaced.

■ the rate at which goods are sold and replaced in a shop.

UNDERSTANDING YOUR CREDIT SCORE

Fair Isaac Corporation is a little-known firm based in San Rafael, California, that has developed the most influential credit-rating system around. What they do is take your credit reports and, based on such factors as your payment history, how much you owe, and how long you've been borrowing, assign you a number. This number, known as your FICO score, can be used by a bank, other financial institution, or anyone else who is trying to decide whether to lend you money.

Your payment history, for example, accounts for 35 percent of your FICO score. This reflects such things as the length of time that one of your accounts was overdue and the amount that you owed. Another 30 percent of your score reflects the amount that you owe on specific accounts, the proportion of balances to total credit limits on your line of credit or your credit cards, and the proportion of installment loan amounts that you still owe.

FICO scores range from 300 (really bad credit) to 850 (ideal borrower). About 720 is average—that is, pretty solid. Lenders consider many factors when they decide whether or not to approve your loan, such as the amount of debt you can reasonably handle given your income, your employment history, and your credit history. Even though you have a low FICO score, they may still extend credit to you. Likewise, they may decline your application for credit even though your score is high. But while FICO is not the only factor involved and, in fact, not even the only credit-scoring system in use, it's the most widely used, playing a role in three out of every four U.S. credit applications.

Until recently, FICO scores were secret. Only lenders had access to them. But these days, Fair Isaac is a bit more forthcoming. If you go to *www.myFico.com*, you can purchase 30-day access to your FICO report for $12.95. Even more important, the firm offers information on how to improve your FICO score.

Most obvious, for example, Fair Isaac advises you to pay your bills on time.

It also advises you to keep balances low on credit cards and other revolving credit and to pay off debt rather than move it around.

Your FICO score gives lenders a snapshot of your risk at a particular point in time. Your score changes as new information is added to your bank and credit bureau files. Scores change gradually as you change the way you handle credit. If you've had credit problems in the past, their impact has less impact on your score as time passes. Lenders always look at your most recent score when you apply for credit, so it makes sense to take the time to improve your score.

It may strike you as funny that this firm can score us, then sell us our score, and then offer tips on how to improve our score. But there's no getting around it—FICO scores have an impact on your ability to get the mortgage and loan rates that you want. With a FICO score of 720 to 850, for example, you would qualify for a loan at a rate that's more than 3 percent lower than the rate charged to someone with a FICO score of 500 to 559. So it's worth it to check out your score and make sure it's as high as you can make it.

U

UI ▸ **abbr.** Canadian unemployment insurance.

UIC ▸ **abbr.** Canadian informal unemployment insurance : *has been living on UIC.*

un•au•dit•ed /ˌənˈôdiṯid/ ▸ **adj.** (of financial accounts) not having been officially examined.

un•brand•ed /ˌənˈbrændid/ ▸ **adj.** (of a product) not bearing a brand name: *unbranded computer systems.*

un•bun•dle /ˌənˈbəndl/ ▸ **v.** [trans.] **1** market or charge for (items or services) separately rather than as part of a package.
2 split (a company or conglomerate) into its constituent businesses, esp. before selling them off.

un•cap /ˌənˈkæp/ ▸ **v.** (**uncapped, uncap•ping**) [trans.] remove a limit or restriction on (a price, rate, or amount).

un•cashed /ˌənˈkæsHt/ ▸ **adj.** (of a check or money order) not yet cashed.

un•charged /ˌənˈcHärjd/ ▸ **adj.** not charged to a particular account: *an uncharged fixed cost.*

un•cleared /ˌənˈkli(ə)rd/ ▸ **adj.** (of a check) not having passed through a clearinghouse and been paid into the payee's account.

un•com•mer•cial /ˌənkəˈmərsHəl/ ▸ **adj.** not making, intended to make, or allowing a profit.

un•com•pet•i•tive /ˌənkəmˈpetitiv/ ▸ **adj.** (with reference to business or commerce) not competitive: *that would destroy jobs and make industry uncompetitive.*

un•der•cap•i•tal•ize /ˌəndərˈkæpiṯlˌīz/ ▸ **v.** [trans.] provide (a company) with insufficient capital to achieve desired results.

un•der•charge /ˌəndər'CHärj/ ▸ v. [trans.] charge (someone) a price or amount that is too low.

un•der•con•sump•tion /ˌəndərkən'səm(p)SHən/ ▸ n. purchase of goods and services at a level lower than that of their supply.

un•der•cut /ˌəndər'kət/ ▸ v. (**un•der•cut•ting**; past and past part. **un• der•cut**) [trans.] offer goods or services at a lower price than (a competitor): *these industries have been undercut by more efficient foreign producers.*

un•der•de•vel•oped /ˌəndərdi'veləpt/ ▸ adj. (of a country or region) not advanced economically.

un•der•ground e•con•o•my /'əndər,grownd i'känəmē/ ▸ n. the part of a country's economic activity that is unrecorded and untaxed by its government.

un•der•in•sured /ˌəndərin'SHo͞ord/ ▸ adj. (of a person) having inadequate insurance coverage.

un•der•per•form /ˌəndərpər'fôrm/ ▸ v. [trans.] increase in value less than: *the shares have underperformed the market.*

un•der•price /ˌəndər'prīs/ ▸ v. [trans.] sell or offer something at a lower price than (the competition): *smaller banks may try to underprice the new giant in town.*

▪ sell or offer (something) at too low a price: *we try not to underprice our books, while making sure they are still a good buy.*

un•der•sell /ˌəndər'sel/ ▸ v. (past and past part. **un•der•sold**) [trans.] sell something at a lower price than (a competitor): *we can equal or undersell mail order.*

un•der•spend /ˌəndər'spend/ ▸ v. (past and past part. **un•der•spent**) [trans.] spend less than (a specified or allocated amount): *schools have underspent their training budgets.*

un•der•val•ue /ˌəndər'vælyo͞o/ ▸ v. (**un•der•val•ues, un•der•val• ued, un•der•val•u•ing**) [trans.] underestimate the financial value of (something): *the company's assets were undervalued in its balance sheet.*

un•der•weight /'əndər,wāt; ˌəndər'wāt/ (also **un•der•weight•ed**) ▸ adj. having less investment in a particular area than is considered desirable or appropriate: *the company is still underweight in Japan | underweighted in technology.*

un•der•write /'əndə(r)ˌrīt; ˌəndə(r)'rīt/ ▸ v. (past **un•der•wrote**; past part. **un•der•writ•ten**) [trans.] **1** sign and accept liability under (an insurance policy), thus guaranteeing payment in case loss or damage occurs.

■ accept (a liability or risk) in this way.

2 (of a bank or other financial institution) engage to buy all the unsold shares in (an issue of new securities).

■ undertake to finance or otherwise support or guarantee (something): *they were willing to underwrite the construction of a ship.*

DERIVATIVES **un•der•writ•er** n.

un•earned in•come /'ənˌərnd 'inˌkəm/ ▸ n. income from investments rather than from work.

un•earned in•cre•ment /'ənˌərnd 'inkrəmənt/ ▸ n. an increase in the value of land or property without labor or expenditure on the part of the owner.

un•ec•o•nom•ic /ˌənekə'nämik; -ēkə-/ ▸ adj. unprofitable: *costs for seven huge, uneconomic reactors.*

■ constituting an inefficient use of money or other resources: *it may be uneconomic to repair some goods.*

un•ec•o•nom•i•cal /ˌənekə'nämikəl; -ēkə-/ ▸ adj. wasteful of money or other resources; not economical: *the old buses eventually become uneconomical to run.*

un•em•ploy•a•ble /ˌənim'ploiəbəl/ ▸ adj. (of a person) not able or likely to get paid employment, esp. because of a lack of skills or qualifications.

▸ n. an unemployable person.

un•em•ployed /ˌənim'ploid/ ▸ adj. (of a person) without a paid job but available to work: *I was unemployed for three years* | [as plural n.] (**the unemployed**) *a training program for the long-term unemployed.*

un•em•ploy•ment /ˌənim'ploimənt/ ▸ n. the state of being unemployed.

■ the number or proportion of unemployed people: *a time of high unemployment.* ■ short for UNEMPLOYMENT BENEFIT. ■ Canadian informal see **unemployment insurance**: *some people work while on unemployment.*

un•em•ploy•ment ben•e•fit /ˌənem'ploimənt ˌbenəfit/ (also **un•em•ploy•ment com•pen•sa•tion**) ▸ n. a payment made by a government or a labor union to an unemployed person.

un•em•ploy•ment in•sur•ance /ˌənem'ploimənt inˌsHŌŌrəns/ (abbr.: **UI**) ▸ n. Canadian see **employment insurance**.

USAGE: The term **unemployment insurance** is no longer in official use in Canada, though it is common in unofficial use.

un•en•cum•bered /ˌunen'kəmbərd/ ▸ adj. free of debt or other financial liability.

un•freeze /ˌən'frēz/ ▸ v. (past **un•froze**; past part. **un•fro•zen**) [trans.] remove restrictions on the use or transfer of (an asset).

un•fund•ed /ˌən'fəndid/ ▸ adj. not funded, in particular:
■ not receiving public funds: *a new education bill remained unfunded.* ■ (of a debt) repayable on demand rather than having been converted into a more or less permanent debt at fixed interest.

un•hedged /ˌən'hejd/ ▸ adj. (of an investment or investor) not protected against loss by balancing or compensating contracts or transactions: *the bank collapsed due to unhedged trading.*

un•in•cor•po•rat•ed /ˌənin'kôrpəˌrāt̲id/ ▸ adj. (of a company or other organization) not formed into a legal corporation: *an unincorporated business.*

un•in•sur•a•ble /ˌənin'sHŌŌrəbəl/ ▸ adj. not eligible for insurance coverage: *some risky activities are uninsurable at any price.*

un•in•sured /ˌənin'sHŌŌrd/ ▸ adj. not covered by insurance: *an uninsured driver.*

un•is•sued /ˌən'isHŌŌd/ ▸ adj. (esp. of shares of stock) not yet issued: *his rights to acquire any unissued shares were eliminated.*

un•liq•ui•dat•ed /ˌən'likwiˌdāt̲id/ ▸ adj. (of a debt) not cleared or paid off.

un•list•ed /ˌən'listid/ ▸ adj. denoting or relating to a company whose shares are not listed on a stock exchange.

un•mar•ket•a•ble /ˌən'märkitəbəl/ ▸ adj. not marketable: *a quantity of unmarketable surplus produce.*

un•mer•chant•a•ble /ˌən'mərcHəntəbəl/ ▸ adj. not suitable for purchase or sale: *sufficiently serious defects can render even a secondhand car unmerchantable.*

un•peg /ˌən'peg/ ▸ v. (**un•pegged, un•peg•ging**) [trans.] cease to maintain a fixed relationship between (a currency) and another currency.

un•priced /ˌən'prīst/ ▸ adj. having no marked or stated price.

un•quot•ed /ˌən'kwōtid/ ▸ adj. not quoted or listed on a stock exchange: *an unquoted company.*

un•se•cured /ˌənsi'kyo͝ord/ ▸ adj. (of a loan) made without an asset given as security.

■ (of a creditor) having made such a loan.

un•taxed /ˌən'tækst/ ▸ adj. not subject to taxation.

■ (of an item, income, etc.) not having had the required tax paid on it.

up•front informal /'əp'frənt/ ▸ adv. (usu. **up front**) (of a payment) in advance: *the salesmen are paid commission up front.*

▸ adj. (of a payment) made in advance.

up•mar•ket /ˌəp'märkit; 'əpˌmär-/ (also **up-mar•ket**) ▸ adj. & adv. toward or relating to the more expensive or affluent sector of the market; upscale.

up•set price /'əpˌset ˌprīs/ ▸ n. the lowest acceptable selling price for a property in an auction; a reserve price.

up•side /'əpˌsīd/ ▸ n. [in sing.] an upward movement of stock prices.

u•til•i•ty /yo͞o'tilitē/ ▸ n. (pl. **u•til•i•ties**) an organization supplying a community with electricity, gas, water, or sewage; a public utility.

■ stocks and bonds in public utilities.

ORIGIN late Middle English: from Old French *utilite*, from Latin *utilitas*, from *utilis* 'useful.'

V

val•or•ize /'vælə,rīz/ ▸ v. [trans.] raise or fix the price or value of (a commodity or currency) by artificial means, esp. by government action.

ORIGIN 1920s: back-formation from *valorization* (from French *valorisation*, from *valeur* 'value').

val•u•a•tion /ˌvælyōō'āsHən/ ▸ n. the monetary worth of something, esp. as estimated by an appraiser.

val•ue /'vælyōō/ ▸ v. (**val•ues, val•ued, val•u•ing**) [trans.] (often **be valued**) estimate the monetary worth of (something).

ORIGIN Middle English: from Old French, feminine past participle of *valoir* 'be worth,' from Latin *valere* .

val•ue add•ed /'vælyōō 'ædid/ ▸ n. the amount by which the value of an article is increased at each stage of its production, exclusive of initial costs.

▸ adj. (**val•ue-add•ed**) (of goods) having features added to a basic line or model for which the buyer is prepared to pay extra.

■ (of a company) offering specialized or extended services in a commercial area.

val•ue-add•ed tax /'vælyōō 'ædid ,taks/ (abbr.: **VAT**) ▸ n. a tax on the amount by which the value of an article has been increased at each stage of its production or distribution.

val•ue a•nal•y•sis /'vælyōō ə,næləsis/ ▸ n. the systematic and critical assessment by an organization of every feature of a product to ensure that its cost is no greater than is necessary to carry out its functions.

val•ue stock /'vælyōō ,stäk/ ▸ n. shares of a company with solid fundamentals that are priced below those of its peers, based on analysis of price/earnings ratio, yield, and other factors. Compare with GROWTH STOCK.

va•lu•ta /vəˈlōōtə/ ▶ n. the value of one currency with respect to its exchange rate with another.

■ foreign currency.

ORIGIN late 19th cent.: from Italian, literally 'value.'

VAR ▶ abbr. value-added reseller, a company that adds extra features to products it has bought before selling them on.

■ value at risk, a method of quantifying the risk of holding a financial asset.

var•i•a•ble cost /ˈve(ə)rēəbəl ˈkôst/ ▶ n. a cost that varies with the level of output.

var•i•a•ble-rate mort•gage /ˈve(ə)rēəbəl ˈrāt ˌmôrgij/ ▶ n. another term for ADJUSTABLE-RATE MORTGAGE.

var•i•ance /ˈve(ə)rēəns/ ▶ n. (in accounting) the difference between expected and actual costs, profits, output, etc., in a statistical analysis.

ORIGIN Middle English: via Old French from Latin *variantia* 'difference,' from the verb *variare*, from *varius* 'diverse.'

VAT /væt/ ▶ abbr. value-added tax.

ve•loc•i•ty /vəˈläsitē/ ▶ n. (pl. ve•loc•i•ties) (also ve•loc•i•ty of cir•cu•la•tion) the rate at which money changes hands within an economy.

ORIGIN late Middle English: from French *vélocité* or Latin *velocitas*, from *velox*, *veloc-* 'swift.'

ven•dor /ˈvendər; -ˌdôr/ (also vend•er) ▶ n. a person or company offering something for sale, esp. a trader in the street.

■ a person or company whose principal product lines are office supplies and equipment.

ORIGIN late 16th cent.: from Anglo-Norman French *vendour*, ult. from Latin *vendere*, from *venum* 'something for sale' + a variant of *dare* 'give.'

ven•dor plac•ing /ˈvendər ˌplāsiNG/ ▶ n. a type of placing used as a method of financing a takeover in which the purchasing company issues its own shares as payment to the company being bought, with the prearranged agreement that these shares are then placed with investors in exchange for cash.

ven•ture /'venCHər/ ▸ **n.** a business enterprise involving considerable risk.

ORIGIN late Middle English: shortening of *adventure*.

ven•ture cap•i•tal /'venCHər ˌkæpiṯl/ ▸ **n.** capital invested in a project in which there is a substantial element of risk, typically a new or expanding business. Also called **RISK CAPITAL**.

ver•ti•cal /'vərṯikəl/ ▸ **adj.** involving all the stages from the production to the sale of a class of goods.

ORIGIN mid 16th cent.: from French, or from late Latin *verticalis*, from *vertex*, from *vertere* 'turn.'

ver•ti•cal in•te•gra•tion /'vərṯikəl inti'grāsHən/ ▸ **n.** the combination in one company of two or more stages of production normally operated by separate companies.

ver•ti•cal mar•ket /'vərṯikəl 'märkit/ ▸ **n.** a market comprising all the potential purchasers in a particular occupation or industry.

vi•at•i•cal set•tle•ment /vī'æṯikəl 'seṯlmənt/ ▸ **n.** an arrangement whereby a person with a terminal illness sells their life insurance policy to a third party for less than its mature value, in order to benefit from the proceeds while alive.

ORIGIN 1990s: *viatical* from Latin *viaticus* 'relating to a journey or departing' + *-al*.

vic•to•ry bond /'vikt(ə)rē ˌbänd/ ▸ **n.** a bond issued by a government during or immediately after a major war.

vis•i•ble /'vizəbəl/ ▸ **adj.** of or relating to imports or exports of tangible commodities: *the visible trade gap*.

ORIGIN Middle English: from Old French, or from Latin *visibilis*, from *videre* 'to see.'

vouch•er /'vowCHər/ ▸ **n.** a small printed piece of paper that entitles the holder to a discount or that may be exchanged for goods or services.

■ a receipt.

ORIGIN early 17th cent.: from *vouch*, from Old French *vocher* 'summon,' from Latin *vocare* 'call.'

TOP TEN PRINCIPLES FOR HIRING A FINANCIAL ADVISOR

Enlisting the help of a financial advisor is not a sign of laziness or weakness or ignorance. On the contrary, it's the smart thing to do.

But how do you find one—someone you can trust, who's professional, experienced, and knows the business, who will take time to get to know you and will always put your best interests first?

Here are ten golden rules for finding such a person:

Get a referral. You likely know someone with a great financial advisor. You just have to ask. Start with your accountant or your attorney. Ideally, ask them for at least three names. Another great source is to ask the wealthiest people you know. The wealthiest people tend to have the best advisors. Here are some questions to ask when you seek a referral:

- Why do you like your advisor?

- How long have you worked together?

- What specifically have they done for you?

- How often do you meet?

- How do you pay them?

- Have you had any problems or complaints?

- Will you be compensated for this referral? (Ask this one of your accountant, attorney, or other professional.)

If you can't get a referral, do your own research. If you know absolutely no one who can give you a referral, check the following Web sites for an advisor in your locale:

The Financial Planning Association
www.fpanet.org
Lists certified financial planners (CFPs) by zip code

National Association of Personal Financial Advisors
www.napfa.org
Lists financial planners, by zip code, who operate on a fee-only basis.

Certified Financial Planner
www.cfp-board.org
Refers you to a CFP in your area and provide a Financial
   Planning Resource Kit.

Alternatively, use the phone book to find a top-level, nationally recognized brokerage firm in your community such as A.G. Edwards, Charles Schwab, Edward Jones, Fidelity, Merrill Lynch, Morgan Stanley, PaineWebber, or Salomon Smith Barney. Ask for the manager and describe to him or her the type of advisor you're looking for.

Ask yourself five questions, based on my FinishRich Questionnaire™.

- Why do you want to hire a financial advisor, i.e., what do you want to achieve?

- What type of client are you: a delegator, collaborator, or instigator?

- What are you willing to pay per year for advice, and how do you want to pay for it—by commission or fee?

- What is your risk tolerance?

- Are you really committed to your financial goals?

Go to your first meeting prepared. My FinishRich Inventory Planner can help you prepare yourself. You can get more information about this useful financial tool at *www.finishrich.com.* Look on the Site Map under "Starting Out" and click on "Getting Organized".

A good financial advisor should be able to explain his or her investment philosophy. A real professional should have a brochure or other written document that shows you exactly what his or her process is and how you can expect it to work. He or she will have a unique method that should involve:

- interviewing you

- asking questions

- organizing your financial information

- designing a financial plan

- creating an investment policy statement that covers how your money will be managed, your goals, and your risk tolerance

- explaining his or her fees, in writing

- transferring your assets to the firm

- managing your money

- servicing your account

- providing written performance records of your account

- keeping you informed of required changes to your plan

Have your financial advisor explain the risk associated with investing. A good financial advisor creates your risk profile by asking you a series of questions aimed at determining how much risk you are comfortable with. It's worth repeating this process every few years as circumstances change. A financial advisor who doesn't discuss the concept of risk with you is probably not a good candidate to help you manage your financial affairs.

Decide how you want to pay your advisor. In the past, advisors were all paid by commission, earning a small fee every time they bought or sold an investment for you. Now they can be paid by commission, by a combination of commission and fee, a flat fee (usually between 1 and 2.5 percent of assets under management), or by the hour.

Check out a prospective advisor's background. Just because an advisor is well-spoken and friendly doesn't mean he is who he says he is. Always double-check a prospective advisor's credentials for accuracy at one of these Web sites:

National Association of Securities Dealers
www.nasdr.com
The best place to start. Lists everything you'll ever need to know about an advisor.

Certified Financial Planner Board of Standards
www.cfp-board.org
Allows you to check the status of a registered CFP.

North American Securities Administrators Association
www.nasaa.org
Devoted to investor protection and a good source of information on fraud.

National Association of Insurance Commissioners
www.naic.org
Find information on more than 2.5 million insurance agents and brokers.

Keep in regular contact with your financial advisor. You should meet your advisor at least once every six months, or more frequently if you think it's necessary.

Never delegate control of your money. When you hire a financial advisor, you don't give him the keys to your financial car and say, "Drive me wherever you want." You have to provide the direction. Your advisor is simply a guide. It's your money, and you are the decision maker.

W

wage /wāj/ ▸ n. (usu. **wages**) a fixed regular payment, typically paid on a daily or weekly basis, made by an employer to an employee, esp. to a manual or unskilled worker. Compare with SALARY.
ORIGIN Middle English: from Anglo-Norman French and Old Northern French, of Germanic origin.

wage dif•fer•en•tial /'wāj difə‚renCHəl/ ▸ n. the difference in earnings between workers with different skills in the same industry or between workers with similar skills in different industries or localities.

wage drift /'wāj ‚drift/ ▸ n. the tendency for the average level of wages actually paid to rise above wage rates through increases in overtime and other factors.

Wal•ras' law /'vælräz ‚lô / a law stating that the total value of goods and money supplied equals that of goods and money demanded.
ORIGIN 1940s: named after M. E. Léon *Walras* (1834–1910), French economist.

ware•house /'we(ə)r‚hows/ ▸ n. a large building where raw materials or manufactured goods may be stored before their export or distribution for sale.
■ a large wholesale or retail store: *a discount warehouse.*
▸ v. [trans.] store (goods) in a warehouse.
■ place (imported goods) in a bonded warehouse pending the payment of import duty.

ware•house club /'we(ə)r‚hows ‚kləb/ ▸ n. an organization that operates from a large store and sells goods in bulk at discounted prices to business and private customers who must first become club members.

ware•hous•ing /'we(ə)r‚howziNG/ ▸ n. the practice or process of storing goods in a warehouse.

war•rant /'wôrənt/ ▸ n. a document that entitles the holder to receive goods, money, or services: *we'll issue you with a travel warrant.*
■ a negotiable security allowing the holder to buy shares at a specified price at or before some future date.
ORIGIN Middle English: from variants of Old French *guarant*, of Germanic origin.

war•ran•ty /'wôrəntē/ ▸ n. (pl. **war•ran•ties**) a written guarantee, issued to the purchaser of an article by its manufacturer, promising to repair or replace it if necessary within a specified period of time.
ORIGIN Middle English: from Anglo-Norman French *warantie*, variant of *garantie* (see GUARANTY).

wa•ter /'wôṯər/ ▸ n. capital stock that represents a book value greater than the true assets of a company.
▸ v. [trans.] increase (a company's debt, or nominal capital) by the issue of new shares without a corresponding addition to assets.
ORIGIN Old English *wæter* (noun), *wæterian* (verb), of Germanic origin; related to Dutch *water*, German *Wasser*, from an Indo-European root shared by Latin *unda* 'wave' and Greek *hudōr* 'water.'

weak /wēk/ ▸ adj. not in a secure financial position: *people have no faith in weak banks.*
■ (of prices or a market) having a downward tendency.
ORIGIN Old English *wāc* 'pliant,' 'of little worth,' 'not steadfast,' reinforced in Middle English by Old Norse *veikr*, from a Germanic base meaning 'yield, give way.'

weight•ing /'wāṯiNG/ ▸ n. an allocated proportion of something, esp. an investment: *the company continues to recommend a 35% weighting in bonds.*

wel•come tax /'welkəm ‚tæks/ ▸ n. Canadian a municipal tax levied on all house purchases in the Province of Quebec.
ORIGIN translation of French *taxe de bienvenue.*

when-is•sued /'(h)wen 'isho͞od/ ▸ adj. of or relating to trading in securities that have not yet been issued.

whip•saw /'(h)wip‚sô/ ▸ v. (past part. **whip•sawn** or **whip•sawed**) [trans.] (usu. **be whipsawed**) informal subject to a double loss, as when buying a security before the price falls and selling before the price rises.

white goods /'(h)wīt ˌgo͝odz/ ▸ **plural n.** large electrical goods used domestically such as refrigerators and washing machines, typically white in color.

white knight /'(h)wīt 'nīt/ ▸ **n.** a person or company making an acceptable counteroffer for a company facing a hostile takeover bid.

white sale /'(h)wīt ˌsāl/ ▸ **n.** a store's sale of household linens.

whole-life /'hōl 'līf/ ▸ **adj.** relating to or denoting a life insurance policy that pays a specified amount only on the death of the person insured.

whole•sale /'hōlˌsāl/ ▸ **n.** the selling of goods in large quantities to be retailed by others.

▸ **adv.** being sold in such a way: *bottles from this region sell wholesale at about $72 a case.*

▸ **v.** [trans.] sell (goods) in large quantities at low prices to be retailed by others.

ORIGIN late Middle English: originally as *by whole sale* 'in large quantities.'

whol•ly-owned /'hōlē 'ōnd/ ▸ **adj.** denoting a company all of whose shares are owned by another company.

wind•fall prof•its tax /'windˌfôl ˌpräfits ˌtæks/ (also **wind•fall tax**) ▸ **n.** a tax levied on an unforeseen or unexpectedly large profit, esp. one regarded to be excessive or unfairly obtained.

wind•ing up /'wīndiNG 'əp/ ▸ **n.** [in sing.] the process of arranging and closing someone's business affairs: *the winding up of a deceased person's affairs.* ▪ the process of closing down a company or a financial institution: *the return of capital on a winding up* | [as adj.] *a winding-up order was issued against BCCI.*

wire fraud /'wīr ˌfrôd/ ▸ **n.** financial fraud involving the use of telecommunications or information technology.

with•hold•ing tax /wiTH'hōldiNG ˌtæks/ ▸ **n.** the amount of an employee's pay withheld by the employer and sent directly to the government as partial payment of income tax.

work•ers' co•op•er•a•tive /'wərkərz kō'äp(ə)rətiv/ ▸ **n.** a business or industry owned and managed by those who work for it.

work•group /'wərk,gro͞op/ ▸ n. a group within a workforce that normally works together.

work•ing cap•i•tal /'wərkiNG 'kæpi̱t̲l/ ▸ n. the capital of a business that is used in its day-to-day trading operations, calculated as the current assets minus the current liabilities.

World Bank /'wərld 'bæNGk/ an international banking organization established to control the distribution of economic aid between member nations and to make loans to them in times of financial crisis.

World Trade Or•gan•i•za•tion /'wərld 'trād ôrgəni,zāsHən/ (abbr.: **WTO**) an international body founded in 1995 to promote international trade and economic development by reducing tariffs and other restrictions.

write /rīt/ ▸ v. (past **wrote**; past part. **writ•ten**) [trans.] underwrite (an insurance policy).

▸**write something off** cancel the record of a bad debt; acknowledge the loss of or failure to recover an asset: *he urged the banks to write off debt owed by poorer countries.*

write something down reduce the value of an asset, for accounting purposes.

ORIGIN Old English *wrītan* 'score, form (letters) by carving, write,' of Germanic origin; related to German *reissen* 'sketch, drag.'

write-back /'rīt ,bæk/ ▸ n. the process of restoring to profit a provision for bad or doubtful debts previously made against profits and no longer required.

write-down /'rīt ,down/ ▸ n. a reduction in the estimated or nominal value of an asset, for accounting purposes.

write-off /'rīt ,ôf/ ▸ n. a cancellation from an account of a bad debt or worthless asset.

writ•er /'rītər/ ▸ n. a broker who makes an option available for purchase or sells options.

ORIGIN Old English *wrītere* (see **WRITE**).

write-up /'rīt ,əp/ ▸ n. an increase in the estimated or nominal value of an asset, for accounting purposes.

WTO ▸ abbr. World Trade Organization.

XYZ

xd ▸**abbr.** ex dividend.

year end /'yi(ə)r 'end/ (also **year's end**) ▸**n.** the end of the fiscal year.

yield /yēld/ ▸**v.** [trans.] (of a financial or commercial process or transaction) generate (a specified financial return): *such investments yield direct cash returns.*

▸**n.** the amount of money brought in, e.g., interest from an investment or revenue from a tax; return: *an annual dividend yield of 20 percent.*

ORIGIN Old English *g(i)eldan* 'pay, repay,' of Germanic origin.

yield curve /'yēld ˌkərv/ ▸**n.** a curve on a graph in which the yield of fixed-interest securities is plotted against the length of time they have to run to maturity.

yield gap /'yēld ˌgæp/ ▸**n.** the difference between the return on government-issued securities and that on ordinary shares.

zai•ba•tsu /zī'bät͵sōo; -'bæt-/ ▸**n.** (pl. same) a large Japanese business conglomerate.

ORIGIN Japanese, from *zai* 'wealth' + *batsu* 'clique.'

ze•ro-based /'zi(ə)rō 'bāst/ ▸**adj.** (of a budget or budgeting) having each item costed anew, rather than in relation to its size or status in the previous budget.

ze•ro-cou•pon bond /'zi(ə)rō 'k(y)ōōpän ˌbänd/ ▸**n.** a bond that is issued at a deep discount to its face value but pays no interest.

COMMON FINANCIAL
EQUATIONS

Ratio, etc.	How determined	Definition and use
accounts receivable days	(accounts receivable ÷ sales) × 365	average length of time between credit sales and payment receipts
accounts receivable turnover	net credit sales ÷ average accounts receivable	a short-term solvency ratio that measures how efficiently a company grants credit to produce revenue
acid test ratio	(current assets - inventories) ÷ current liabilities	a short-term solvency ratio that gives an indication of a company's liquidity and its ability to meet obligations. Also called **quick ratio** or **current ratio**.
asset/equity ratio	total assets ÷ stockholder equity	a ratio used to compare the revenue-producing abilities of companies within the same industry
asset turnover	net sales ÷ total assets	a ratio that measures the efficiency of a company's use of its assets. It is typically inversely related to the profit margin.
Average rate of return (ARR)	Average net earnings ÷ average investment	a percentage figure used to compare different investment vehicles over the long term
bid-to-cover ratio	bids received ÷ bids accepted	a rough measure of the success of a treasury security auction
bond ratio	par value of bonds ÷ (this figure + all other equity)	a figure that represents the percent-age of a company's capitalization in bonds
book-to-bill	orders taken ÷ orders filled (within the same period, e.g. one month)	a measure of supply and demand in a market or for a company's products, used especially in evaluating high-technology companies. Figures >1 indicate an expanding market.
cash flow coverage	EBITDA ÷ interest expense	a measure of a company's ability to service debt payments from operating cash flow
cash flow leverage	Total liabilities ÷ EBITDA	a measure of a company's ability to repay debt obligations from operating cash flow
debt/asset ratio	total liabilities ÷ total assets	a ratio used on companies within the same industry to compare their ability to manage their long-term debt
debt/equity ratio	long-term debt ÷ stockholder equity	a ratio that compares the assets of a company that are held by creditors to those held by owners. High ratios indicate aggressive use of debt to manage growth.

Ratio, etc.	How determined	Definition and use
debt-service coverage ratio	net operating income ÷ total debt service (in the same period, e.g. one year)	a ratio used to determine a company's or property's ability to remain viable.
earnings yield	yearly earnings per share ÷ share market price	a figure that essentially gives the percentage of earnings that one dollar of equity buys. It is the inverse of the price-earnings ratio.
EBITDA	revenues - expenses (excluding tax, interest, depreciation and amortization)	earnings before interest, tax, depreciation, and amortization
fixed-charge coverage ratio	(net earnings + interest paid + lease expense) ÷ (interest paid + lease expense)	a measure of a company's ability to meet its fixed-charge obligations
inventory days	(inventory ÷ cost of goods sold) × 365	a measure of the value of inventory on hand, sometimes used as an indication of a company's ability to respond to market changes
inventory turnover	annual sales ÷ average inventory	a measure of the speed at which inventory is produced and sold. Higher figures normally indicate strong sales and good turnover.
loan-to-value (LTV) ratio	value of loan ÷ market value of property	a general indication of the risk involved in a mortgage. Banks usually require a ratio of at least 75%.
loss ratio	claims paid ÷ premiums collected (in a similar period, e.g. one year)	a factor in the profitability and efficiency of an insurance company or insurance market.
management expense ratio (MRE)	total of all fees ÷ total value of portfolio	a percentage figure that expresses the amount of a mutual fund's value that is consumed by the expenses of managing it
member short sale ratio	total number of shares sold short ÷ total short sales	a tool used to anticipate bullish or bearish trends on the New York Stock Exchange
Macaulay duration	weighted average term to maturity ÷ bond price	an indicator of the volatility of a bond's price to a change in its yield
market to book ratio	share market price ÷ book value per share	a figure used in estimating the cost of capital of an enterprise
net operating margin	net operating income ÷ net sales	a performance indicator used on companies within the same industry or historically of the same company
operating cycle	accounts receivable days + inventory days	the time that elapses from when a product is added to inventory to receipt of the income from its sale
operating profit margin	operating profit ÷ net sales	a tool for measuring effective pricing strategy and operating efficiency
payout ratio	total dividend ÷ total earnings	a measure of how much profit a company is returning to stockholders in dividends, often used to mark historical trends
price-earnings (P/E) ratio	current share price ÷ earnings per share in the past 12 months	an often-quoted figure that is usually an indication of growth expectations. Useful only for comparisons within the same industry, or historically for the same company (also called **multiple**).

Ratio, etc.	How determined	Definition and use
price-to-book ratio	current share price ÷ last quarter's book value per share	a tool used for speculating on the accuracy of the valuation of a company's stock. A low ratio could mean that the company is under-valued, or that there is something fundamentally wrong with it.
price-to-sales ratio	current share price ÷ revenue per share in the year to date	a tool for comparing a stock's valuation relative to its own history, to its industry peers, or to the market generally.
profit margin	net income ÷ revenue (in the same period)	a percentage that expresses profitability, most often used in comparisons within the same industry.
prospective earnings growth (PEG) ratio	P/E ratio ÷ projected earnings growth rate	an indicator of a stock's potential value that is favored by some over the P/E ratio because it takes growth into account. Projected earnings growth rate is determined from proprietary sources.
Q ratio	market asset value ÷ asset replacement value	a figure used as an indication of the success of a company's investment strategy (also called **Tobin's Q ratio** after its inventor James Tobin)
receivables turnover ratio	total operating revenues ÷ average receivables	a figure that indicates efficiency in managing accounts receivable
retention rate	1 - payout ratio	the percentage of earnings retained by a company, which may be a factor in its investment and growth strategy
return on assets (ROA)	net income ÷ total assets	a percentage figure that indicates how profitable a company is relative to its assets
return on equity (ROE)	net income ÷ stockholder equity	a comparative indicator of profitability within the same industry, expressed as a percentage.
return on investment (ROI)	total income ÷ total capital	the percentage of income derived from the amount invested, used as a measure of a company's performance
return on net assets (RONA)	net income ÷ (fixed assets + net working capital)	a percentage figure used as a measure of the profitability of a company
return on sales (ROS)	net profit ÷ net sales	a percentage figure widely used as an indicator of operational efficiency
risk-reward ratio	expected return on an investment ÷ standard deviation of an index	a figure that roughly indicates the amount of risk in an investment relative to comparable investments
relative strength	(current share price ÷ year-ago share price) ÷ (current S&P 500 ÷ year-ago S&P 500)	a measure of the strength of a stock relative to the market; values >1 show relative strength (does not take risk into account)
rule of 72	72 ÷ rate of interest	a figure that tells how many years it will take to double your money at a given rate of compound interest
Sharpe ratio	(ROI - T-bill rate) ÷ standard deviation of a portfolio	a measure of a portfolio's excess return relative to its total variability. It may indicate whether returns are due to wise investment or excess risk (see also **Treynor ratio**)

Ratio, etc.	How determined	Definition and use
times-interest-earned ratio	earnings before interest and tax ÷ interest payments	a measure of a company's debt-servicing ability
total debt-service (TDS) ratio	Total obligations ÷ gross income (calculated for the same period)	the percentage of gross income required to cover all payments for housing and all other debts such as car payments; used typically to calculate creditworthiness of a household borrower
Treynor ratio	excess return ÷ portfolio standard deviation	a measure of the return on an investment in excess of what could have been earned on a riskless investment (also called **reward-to-volatility ratio**)
working capital ratio	(current assets - current liabilities) ÷ total sales	a percentage figure used for comparing operating efficiency within the same industry.

INTEREST RATE
CALCULATOR TABLE

To Use this Table:
On the left hand side of the table, find the number of monthly payments required for the loan. Then move across the page to the column with the appropriate interest rate. This will give you the monthly payment required for each $1000 of the loan.

Example 1:
You want to take out a $10,000 car loan. The payments are over a period of 4 years (or 48 months) at an interest rate of 8%. Starting at the '48' row on the left-hand side and going across to the 8% column, the table shows a payment of $24.41 per month for every $1000 borrowed. For a $10,000 loan, multiply this amount by 10. $24.41 x 10 = $244.10. $244.10 is the approximate monthly payment.

Example 2:
You want to apply for a $150,000 mortgage. The payments are over a period of 15 years (or 180 months) at an interest rate of 5.5%. Starting at the '180' row on the left hand side and going across to the 5.5% column, the table shows a payment of $8.17 per month for every $1000 borrowed. For a $150,000 loan, multiply $8.17 by 150. $8.17 x 150 = $1225.50. $1225.50 is the approximate monthly payment.

Payments on a $1,000 loan

Number of Months	INTEREST RATE PER YEAR					
	4.0%	4.5%	5.0%	5.5%	6.0%	6.5%
6	$168.62	$168.86	$169.11	$169.35	$169.60	$169.84
12	$85.15	$85.38	$85.61	$85.84	$86.07	$86.30
18	$57.33	$57.56	$57.78	$58.01	$58.23	$58.46
24	$43.42	$43.65	$43.87	$44.10	$44.32	$44.55
30	$35.08	$35.31	$35.53	$35.75	$35.98	$36.20
36	$29.52	$29.75	$29.97	$30.20	$30.42	$30.65
42	$25.55	$25.78	$26.00	$26.23	$26.46	$26.68
48	$22.58	$22.80	$23.03	$23.26	$23.49	$23.71
54	$20.27	$20.49	$20.72	$20.95	$21.18	$21.41
60	$18.42	$18.64	$18.87	$19.10	$19.33	$19.57
72	$15.65	$15.87	$16.10	$16.34	$16.57	$16.81
84	$13.67	$13.90	$14.13	$14.37	$14.61	$14.85
96	$12.19	$12.42	$12.66	$12.90	$13.14	$13.39
108	$11.04	$11.28	$11.52	$11.76	$12.01	$12.25
120	$10.12	$10.36	$10.61	$10.85	$11.10	$11.35
132	$9.38	$9.62	$9.86	$10.11	$10.37	$10.62
144	$8.76	$9.00	$9.25	$9.50	$9.76	$10.02
156	$8.23	$8.48	$8.73	$8.99	$9.25	$9.51
168	$7.78	$8.03	$8.29	$8.55	$8.81	$9.08
180	$7.40	$7.65	$7.91	$8.17	$8.44	$8.71
210	$6.63	$6.89	$7.15	$7.43	$7.70	$7.98
240	$6.06	$6.33	$6.60	$6.88	$7.16	$7.46
300	$5.28	$5.56	$5.85	$6.14	$6.44	$6.75
360	$4.77	$5.07	$5.37	$5.68	$6.00	$6.32

INTEREST RATE PER YEAR

7.0%	7.5%	8.0%	8.5%	9.0%	9.5%	10.0%	12.0%
$170.09	$170.33	$170.58	$170.82	$171.07	$171.32	$171.56	$172.55
$86.53	$86.76	$86.99	$87.22	$87.45	$87.68	$87.92	$88.85
$58.68	$58.91	$59.14	$59.37	$59.60	$59.83	$60.06	$60.98
$44.77	$45.00	$45.23	$45.46	$45.68	$45.91	$46.14	$47.07
$36.43	$36.66	$36.89	$37.12	$37.35	$37.58	$37.81	$38.75
$30.88	$31.11	$31.34	$31.57	$31.80	$32.03	$32.27	$33.21
$26.91	$27.14	$27.38	$27.61	$27.84	$28.08	$28.32	$29.28
$23.95	$24.18	$24.41	$24.65	$24.89	$25.12	$25.36	$26.33
$21.64	$21.88	$22.11	$22.35	$22.59	$22.83	$23.07	$24.06
$19.80	$20.04	$20.28	$20.52	$20.76	$21.00	$21.25	$22.24
$17.05	$17.29	$17.53	$17.78	$18.03	$18.27	$18.53	$19.55
$15.09	$15.34	$15.59	$15.84	$16.09	$16.34	$16.60	$17.65
$13.63	$13.88	$14.14	$14.39	$14.65	$14.91	$15.17	$16.25
$12.51	$12.76	$13.02	$13.28	$13.54	$13.81	$14.08	$15.18
$11.61	$11.87	$12.13	$12.40	$12.67	$12.94	$13.22	$14.35
$10.88	$11.15	$11.42	$11.69	$11.96	$12.24	$12.52	$13.68
$10.28	$10.55	$10.82	$11.10	$11.38	$11.66	$11.95	$13.13
$9.78	$10.05	$10.33	$10.61	$10.90	$11.19	$11.48	$12.69
$9.35	$9.63	$9.91	$10.20	$10.49	$10.78	$11.08	$12.31
$8.99	$9.27	$9.56	$9.85	$10.14	$10.44	$10.75	$12.00
$8.27	$8.56	$8.86	$9.16	$9.47	$9.78	$10.10	$11.41
$7.75	$8.06	$8.36	$8.68	$9.00	$9.32	$9.65	$11.01
$7.07	$7.39	$7.72	$8.05	$8.39	$8.74	$9.09	$10.53
$6.65	$6.99	$7.34	$7.69	$8.05	$8.41	$8.78	$10.29

Payments on a $1,000 loan

Number of Months	INTEREST RATE PER YEAR					
	14.0%	16.0%	18.0%	20.0%	22.0%	24.0%
6	$173.54	$174.53	$175.53	$176.52	$177.52	$178.53
12	$89.79	$90.73	$91.68	$92.63	$93.59	$94.56
18	$61.92	$62.86	$63.81	$64.76	$65.73	$66.70
24	$48.01	$48.96	$49.92	$50.90	$51.88	$52.87
30	$39.70	$40.66	$41.64	$42.63	$43.63	$44.65
36	$34.18	$35.16	$36.15	$37.16	$38.19	$39.23
42	$30.25	$31.25	$32.26	$33.30	$34.35	$35.42
48	$27.33	$28.34	$29.37	$30.43	$31.51	$32.60
54	$25.06	$26.10	$27.15	$28.23	$29.33	$30.45
60	$23.27	$24.32	$25.39	$26.49	$27.62	$28.77
72	$20.61	$21.69	$22.81	$23.95	$25.13	$26.33
84	$18.74	$19.86	$21.02	$22.21	$23.43	$24.68
96	$17.37	$18.53	$19.72	$20.95	$22.22	$23.51
108	$16.33	$17.53	$18.76	$20.03	$21.33	$22.67
120	$15.53	$16.75	$18.02	$19.33	$20.67	$22.05
132	$14.89	$16.14	$17.44	$18.79	$20.17	$21.58
144	$14.37	$15.66	$16.99	$18.37	$19.78	$21.23
156	$13.95	$15.27	$16.63	$18.04	$19.48	$20.95
168	$13.60	$14.95	$16.34	$17.77	$19.24	$20.74
180	$13.32	$14.69	$16.10	$17.56	$19.06	$20.58
210	$12.79	$14.21	$15.69	$17.20	$18.75	$20.32
240	$12.44	$13.91	$15.43	$16.99	$18.57	$20.17
300	$12.04	$13.59	$15.17	$16.78	$18.41	$20.05
360	$11.85	$13.45	$15.07	$16.71	$18.36	$20.02

FURTHER READING

A short list, by no means comprehensive, of interesting and useful books about money, investing, and budgeting.

Other Books by David Bach

Bach, David. *The Automatic Millionaire: The No-Budget, No-Discipline Commonsense Way to Live and Finish Rich.* Broadway Books, 2003.

Bach, David. *Smart Couples Finish Rich: 9 Steps to Creating a Rich Future for You and Your Partner.* Broadway Books, 2002.

Bach, David. *Smart Women Finish Rich: 9 Steps to Achieving Financial Security and Funding Your Dreams.* Broadway Books, 2002.

Bach, David and Kristine Puopolo. *The Finish Rich Workbook: Creating a Personalized Plan for a Richer Future.* Broadway Books, 2003.

Personal Finance and Investing

Abentrod, Susan. *10 Minute Guide to Beating Debt.* Howell Book House, 1996.

Bachrach, Bill. *Values-Based Financial Planning.* Aim High Publishing, 2000.

Bamford, Janet. *The Consumer Reports Money Book: How to Get It, Save It, and Spend It Wisely.* Consumer Reports Books, 2000.

Barra, Dianna. *Quick and Easy Budget Book: A Practical Workbook for Balancing Your Household Budget.* Idea Designs, 2002.

Benz, Christine. *Morningstar's Guide to Mutual Funds: 5-Star Strategies for Success.* John Wiley and Sons, 2002.

Bernstein, William J. *The Four Pillars of Investing: Lessons for Building a Winning Portfolio.* McGraw-Hill, 2002.

Bilker, Scott. *Credit Card & Debt Management: A Step-By-Step How-To Guide for Organizing Debt & Saving Money on Interest Payments.* Press On Pub, 1996.

Bogle, John C. *Common Sense on Mutual Funds.* John Wiley and Sons, 2002.

Brennan, Jack and Marta McCave. *Straight Talk on Investing: What You Need to Know.* John Wiley and Sons, 2002.

Bryan, Mark. *The Money Drunk: 90 Days to Financial Freedom.* Ballantine Books, 1992.

Clason, George S. *The Richest Man in Babylon.* New American Library, 1988.

Daskaloff, Alexander. *Credit Card Debt: Reduce Your Financial Burden In Three Easy Steps.* Avon, 1999.

Dent, Harry S. *The Roaring 2000s: How to Achieve Personal and Financial Success in the Greatest Boom in History.* Simon & Schuster, 1998.

Dominguez, Joe and Vicki Robin. *Your Money or Your Life: Transforming Your Relationship With Money and Achieving Financial Independence.* Penguin, 1999.

Edelman, Ric. *Ordinary People, Extraordinary Wealth: The 8 Secrets of How 5,000 Ordinary Americans Became Successful Investors—and How You Can Too.* HarperBusiness, 2000.

Edelman, Ric and Cal Thomas. *The Truth About Money: Because Money Doesn't Come With Instructions.* Georgetown University Press, 1996.

Fisher, Philip A. *Common Stocks and Uncommon Profits and Other Writings.* John Wiley and Sons, 1996.

Furhman, John. *The Credit Diet: How to Shed Unwanted Debt and Achieve Fiscal Fitness.* John Wiley and Sons, 2002.

Gabriel, Gwendolyn D. *Become Totally Debt-Free in Five Years or Less.* Brown Bag Press, 2000.

Gerlach, Douglas. *The Armchair Millionaire.* Fireside, 2002.

Glink, Ilyce R. *50 Simple Things You Can Do to Improve Your Personal Finances.* Crown, 2001.

Glink, Ilyce R. *100 Questions You Should Ask About Your Personal Finances: And the Answers You Need to Help You Save, Invest, and Grow Your Money.* Times Books, 1998.

Graham, Benjamin. *The Intelligent Investor.* HarperCollins, 1985.

Howard, Clark. *Get Clark Smart: The Ultimate Guide to Getting Rich from America's Money-Saving Expert.* Hyperion Press, 2002.

Hupalo, Peter I. *Becoming an Investor.* HCM Publishing, 2002.

Kiyosaki, Robert and Sharon Lechter. *Rich Dad Poor Dad.* Warner Books, 1999.

Lawrence, Judy. *The Budget Kit: The Common Cents Money Management Workbook (2nd Edition).* Dearborn, 1997.

Lynch, Peter and John Rothchild. *Beating the Street: How to Use What You Already Know to Make Money in the Market.* Fireside, 1993.

Lynch, Peter and John Rothchild. *Learn to Earn: A Beginner's Guide to the Basics of Investing and Business.* Fireside, 1996.

Lynch, Peter and John Rothchild. *One Up on Wall Street.* Penguin, 1990.

Malkiel, Burton Gordon. *A Random Walk Down Wall Street: Including a Life-Cycle Guide to Personal Investing.* W. W. Norton and Company, 1996.

Morris, Kenneth M. *The Wall Street Journal Guide to Understanding Money & Investing.* Prentice Hall, 1994.

Morris, Virginia B. *Creating Retirement Income.* McGraw-Hill, 1999.

Mundis, Jerrold. *How to Get Out of Debt, Stay Out of Debt & Live Prosperously.* Bantam Doubleday Dell, 2003.

Orman, Suze. *The Courage to be Rich: Creating a Life of Material and Spiritual Abundance.* Penguin Putnam, 2001.

Orman, Suze. *9 Steps to Financial Freedom: Practical and Spiritual Steps So You Can Stop Worrying.* Three Rivers Press, 2000.

Orman, Suze. *The Road to Wealth.* Riverhead Books, 2003.

Sander, Peter and Jennifer Basye Sander. *The Pocket Idiot's Guide to Living on a Budget.* Alpha Books, 1999.

Siegal, Alan. *The Wall Street Journal Guide to Understanding Personal Finance.* Fireside, 1993.

Siegal, Alan. *The Wall Street Journal Guide to Planning Your Financial Future: The Easy-To-Read Guide to Planning for Retirement.* Fireside, 1998.

Stanley, Thomas J. and William S. Danko. *The Millionaire Next Door: The Surprising Secrets of America's Wealthy.* Longstreet Press, 1996.

Strauss, Steven D. *The Complete Idiot's Guide to Beating Debt.* Alpha Books, 1999.

Swedroe, Larry E. *Rational Investing in Irrational Times: How to Avoid the Costly Mistakes Even Smart People Make Today.* Truman Talley Books, 2002.

Swedroe, Larry E. *The Successful Investor Today: 14 Simple Truths You Must Know When You Invest.* St. Martin's Press, 2003.

Tobias, Andrew. *The Only Investment Guide You'll Ever Need.* Harcourt, 1996.

Tyson, Eric. *Investing for Dummies.* Hungry Minds, 2002.

Tyson, Eric. *Personal Finance for Dummies.* Hungry Minds, 2003.

Tyson, Eric and James C. Collins. *Mutual Funds for Dummies.* Hungry Minds, 1998.

Personal Financing and Investing—Especially for Women

Judith, Dr Briles. *10 Smart Money Moves For Women: How To Conquer Your Financial Fears.* McGraw-Hill, 1999.

Morris, Virginia. *A Woman's Guide to Investing.* McGraw-Hill, 1999.

Morris, Virginia B. and Karen W. Lichtenberg. *A Woman's Guide to Personal Finance.* Lightbulb Press, 2001.

Stanny, Barbara. *Prince Charming Isn't Coming: How Women Get Smart About Money.* Penguin, 1999.

Stanny, Barbara. *Secrets of Six-Figure Women: Surprising*

Strategies to Up Your Earnings and Change Your Life.
HarperCollins, 2002.

Personal Growth

Allen, David. *Getting Things Done: The Art of Stress-Free Productivity.* Viking Press, 2001.

Altier, William J. *The Thinking Manager's Toolbox: Effective Processes for Problem Solving and Decision Making.* Oxford University Press, 1999.

Bossidy, Larry et al. *Execution: The Discipline of Getting Things Done.* Random House, 2002.

Buckingham, Marcus, and Donald O. Clifton. *Now, Discover Your Strengths.* Free Press, 2001.

Carnegie, Dale et al. *How to Win Friends and Influence People.* Pocket Books, 1994.

Scott, Susan. *Fierce Conversations: Achieving Success at Work & in Life, One Conversation at a Time.* Viking Press, 2002.

General Background and History

Bernstein, Peter L. *Against the Gods: The Remarkable Story of Risk.* John Wiley and Sons, 1998.

Klein, Maury. *Rainbow's End: The Crash of 1929.* New York: Oxford University Press, 2003.

Lefèvre, Edwin. *Reminiscences of a Stock Operator.* John Wiley and Sons, 1994.

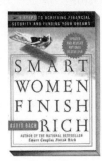

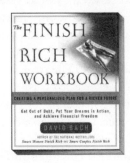